NEITHER HERE

NOR THERE

Neither Here Nor There

Travels in Europe

Bill Bryson

WILLIAM MORROW AND COMPANY, INC.

NEW YORK

It is the policy of William Morrow and Company, Inc., and its imprints and affiliates, recognizing the importance of preserving what has been written, to print the books we publish on acid-free paper, and we exert our best efforts to that end.

Library of Congress Cataloging-in-Publication Data

Bryson, Bill.
    Neither here nor there : travels in Europe / Bill Bryson.
       p.   cm.
    ISBN 0-688-10311-1
1. Europe—Description and travel—1971-   2. Bryson, Bill—
Journeys—Europe.
I. Title.
D923.B79   1991
914.04/55 Dc20   91-9745
                                                        CIP

Printed in the United States of America

First Edition

1 2 3 4 5 6 7 8 9 10

BOOK DESIGN BY BARBARA BACHMAN

TO CYNTHIA

CONTENTS

William James describes a man who got the experience from laughing-gas; whenever he was under its influence, he knew the secret of the universe, but when he came to, he had forgotten it. At last, with immense effort, he wrote down the secret before the vision had faded. When completely recovered, he rushed to see what he had written. It was "A smell of petroleum prevails throughout."

—BERTRAND RUSSELL, A HISTORY OF WESTERN PHILOSOPHY

~~~~~~~~~~~~~~~~~~~~~~~~~~~~~~~~~~~~

TO THE NORTH

~~~~~~~~~~~~~~~~~~~~~~~~~~~~~~~~~~~~

IN WINTER, Hammerfest is a thirty-hour ride by bus from Oslo, though why anyone would want to go there in winter is a question worth considering. It is on the edge of the world, the northernmost town in Europe, as far from London as London is from Tunis, a place of dark and brutal winters, where the sun sinks into the Arctic Ocean in November and does not rise again for ten weeks.

I wanted to see the Northern Lights. Also, I had long harbored a half-formed urge to experience what life was like in such a remote and forbidding place. Sitting at home in England with a glass of whiskey and a book of maps, this had seemed a capital idea. But now as I picked my way through the gray late December slush of Oslo, I was beginning to have my doubts.

Things had not started well. I had overslept at the hotel, missing breakfast, and had to leap into my clothes. I couldn't find a cab and had to drag my ludicrously overweight bag eight blocks through slush to the central bus station. I had had huge difficulty persuading the staff at the Kreditkassen Bank on Karl Johansgate to cash sufficient travelers' checks to pay the extortionate 1,200-kroner bus fare—they simply could not be made to grasp that the William McGuire Bryson on my passport and the Bill Bryson on my travelers' checks were both me—and now here I was arriving at the station two minutes before departure, breathless and steaming from the endless uphill exertion that is my life, and the girl at the ticket counter was telling me that she had no record of my reservation.

"This isn't happening," I said. "I'm still at home in England enjoying Christmas. Pass me a drop more port, will you, darling?" Actually, I said: "There must be some mistake. Please look again."

The girl studied the passenger manifest. "No, Mr. Bryson, your name is not here."

But *I* could see it, even upside down. "There it is, second from the bottom."

"No," the girl decided, "that says Bernt Bjørnson. That's a Norwegian name."

"It doesn't say Bernt Bjørnson. It says Bill Bryson. Look at the loop of the *y,* the two *l*'s. Miss, please."

But she wouldn't have it.

"If I miss this bus when does the next one go?"

"Next week at the same time."

Oh, splendid.

"Miss, believe me, it says Bill Bryson."

"No, it doesn't."

"Miss, look, I've come from England. I'm carrying some medicine that could save a child's life." She didn't buy this. "I want to see the manager."

"He's in Stavanger."

"Listen, I made a reservation by telephone. If I don't get on this bus I am going to write a letter to your manager that will cast a shadow over your career prospects for the rest of this century." This clearly did not alarm her. Then it occurred to me. "If this Bernt Bjørnson doesn't show up, can I have his seat?"

"Sure."

Why don't I think of these things in the first place and save myself the anguish? "Thank you," I said and lugged my bag outside.

THE BUS was a large double-decker, like an American Greyhound, but only the front half of the upstairs had seats and windows. The rest was solid aluminum covered with a worryingly psychedelic painting of an intergalactic landscape, like the cover of a pulp science fiction novel, with the words "Express 2000" emblazoned across the tail of a comet. For one giddy moment I thought the windowless back end might contain a kind of dormitory and that at bedtime we would be escorted back there by a stewardess who would invite us to choose a couchette. I was prepared to pay any amount of money for this option. But I was mistaken. The back end, and all the space below us, was for freight. "Express 2000" was really just a long-distance truck with passengers.

We left at exactly noon. I quickly realized that everything about the bus was designed for discomfort. I was sitting beside the heater, so that while chill drafts teased by upper extremities, my left leg grew so hot that I could hear the hairs on it crackle. The seats were designed by a dwarf seeking revenge on full-sized people; there was no other explanation. The young man in front of me had put his seat so far back that his head was all but in my lap. He had the sort of face that makes you realize God does have a sense of humor and he was reading a comic book called *Tommy og Tigern*. My own seat was raked at a peculiar angle that induced immediate and lasting neck-ache. It had a lever on its side, which I supposed might bring it back to a more comfortable position, but I knew from long experience that if I touched it even tentatively the seat would fly back and crush both the kneecaps of the sweet little old lady sitting behind me, so I left it alone. The woman beside me, who was obviously a veteran of these polar campaigns, unloaded quantities of magazines, tissues, throat lozenges, ointments, unguents, and fruit pastilles into the seat pocket in front of her, then settled beneath a blanket and slept more or less continuously through the whole trip.

We bounced through a snowy half-light, out through the sprawl-ing suburbs of Oslo and into the countryside. The scattered villages and farmhouses looked trim and prosperous in the endless dusk. Every house had Christmas lights burning cheerily in the windows. I quickly settled into that not unpleasant state of mindlessness that tends to overcome me on long journeys, my head lolling on my shoulders in the manner of someone who has lost all control of his neck muscles and doesn't really mind.

My trip had begun. I was about to see Europe again.

THE FIRST time I came to Europe was in 1972, skinny, shy, alone. In those days the only cheap flights were from New York to Luxembourg, with a refueling stop en route at Keflavík Airport at Reykjavík. The airplanes were engagingly past their prime—oxygen masks would sometimes drop unbidden from their overhead storage compartments and dangle there until a stewardess with a hammer and a mouthful of nails came along to put things right, and the door of the lavatory tended to swing open if you didn't hold it shut with a foot, which brought a certain dimension of challenge to anything else you planned to do in there—and they were achingly slow. It took a week and a half to reach Keflavík, a small gray airport in the middle of a flat gray nowhere, and another week and a half to bounce on through the skies to Luxembourg.

Everyone on the plane was a hippie, except the crew and two herring factory executives in first class. It was rather like being on a Greyhound bus on the way to a folksingers' convention. People were forever pulling out guitars and mandolins and bottles of Thunderbird wine and forging relationships with their seatmates that were clearly going to lead to lots of energetic sex on a succession of Mediterranean beaches.

In the long, exciting weeks preceding the flight I had sustained myself, I confess, with a series of bedroom ceiling fantasies that generally involved finding myself seated next to a panting young beauty, being sent by her father against her wishes to the Lausanne Institute for Nymphomaniacal Disorders, who would turn to me somewhere over the mid-Atlantic and say, "Forgive me, but would it be all right if I sat on your face for a while?" In the event, my seatmate turned out to be an acned string bean with Buddy Holly glasses and a lineup of ballpoint pens clipped into a protective plastic case in his shirt pocket. The plastic case said: "Gruber's Tru-Valu Hardware, Flagellation, Oklahoma. If We Don't Got It, You Don't Need It," or something like that. He had boils on his neck that looked like bullet wounds that had never quite healed, and he smelled oppressively of Vicks VapoRub.

He spent most of the flight reading Holy Scripture, moving both sets of fingertips across each line of text as he read and voicing the words just loud enough for me to hear them as a fervent whisper in my right ear. I feared the worst. I don't know why religious zealots have this compulsion to try to convert everyone who passes before them—I don't go around trying to make them into St. Louis Cardinals fans, for crying out loud—and yet they never fail to try.

Nowadays, when accosted I explain to them that anyone wearing white socks with Hush Puppies and a badge saying HI! I'M GUS! probably couldn't talk me into getting out of a burning car, much less into making a lifelong commitment to a deity, and I ask them to send someone more intelligent and with a better dress sense next time. But back then I was too meek to do anything but listen politely and utter noncommittal "hmmmms" to their suggestions that Jesus could turn my life around. Somewhere over the Atlantic, as I was sitting taking stock of my two hundred cubic centimeters of personal space, as one does on a long plane flight, I spied a coin under the seat in front of me, and with protracted difficulty leaned forward and snagged it. When I sat up, I saw my seatmate was at last looking at me with that ominous glow.

"Have you found Jesus?" he asked suddenly.

"Uh, no, it's a quarter," I answered and quickly settled down and pretended for the next six hours to be asleep, ignoring his whispered entreaties to let Christ build a bunkhouse in my heart.

In fact, I was secretly watching out the window for Europe. I still remember that first sight. The plane dropped out of the clouds, and there below me was this sudden magical tableau of small green fields and steepled villages spread across an undulating landscape, like a shaken-out quilt just settling back onto a bed. I had flown a lot in America and had never seen much of anything from an airplane window but endless golden fields on farms the size of Belgium and meandering rivers and pencil lines of black highway. It always looked vast and mostly empty. You felt that if you squinted hard enough you could see all the way to Los Angeles, even when you were over Kansas. But here the landscape had the ordered perfection of a model-railway layout. It was all so green and minutely cultivated, so compact, so tidy, so fetching, so . . . so European. I was smitten. I still am.

I had brought with me a yellow backpack so enormous that when I went through customs I half expected to be asked, "Anything to declare? Cigarettes? Alcohol? Dead horse?" and spent the day teetering beneath it through the ancient streets of Luxembourg city in a kind of vivid daze—an unfamiliar mixture of excitement and exhaustion and intense optical stimulation. Everything seemed so vivid and acutely focused and new. I felt like someone stepping out of doors for the first time. It was all so different: the language, the money, the cars, the license plates on the cars, the bread, the food, the newspapers, the parks, the people. I had never seen a zebra crossing before, never seen a tram, never seen an unsliced loaf of bread (never even considered it an option), never seen anyone wearing a beret who expected to be taken seriously, never seen people go to a different shop for each item of dinner or provide their own shopping bags, never seen feathered pheasants and unskinned rabbits hanging in a butcher's window or a pig's head smiling on a platter, never seen a packet of Gitanes or the Michelin man. And the people—why, they were Luxembourgers. I don't know why this amazed me so, but it did. I kept thinking: "That man over there, he's a Luxembourger. And so is that girl. They don't know anything about the New York Yankees, they don't know the theme tune to the Mickey Mouse Club, they are from another world." It was just wonderful.

In the afternoon I bumped into my acned seatmate on the Pont Adolphe, high above the gorge that cuts through the city. He was trudging back toward the center beneath an outsized backpack of his own. I greeted him as a friend—after all, of the three hundred million people in Europe he was the only one I knew—but he had none of my fevered excitement.

"Have you got a room?" he asked gloomily.

"No."

"Well, I can't find one anywhere. I've been looking all over. Every place is full."

"Really?" I said, worry stealing over me like a shadow. This was potentially serious. I had never been in a position where I had to arrange for my own bed for the night—I had assumed that I would present myself at a small hotel when it suited me and that everything would be all right after that.

"Fucking city, fucking Luxembourg," my friend said, with unexpected forthrightness, and trudged off.

I presented myself at a series of semisqualid hotels around the central station, but they were all full. I wandered farther afield, trying other hotels along the way, but without success, and in a not very long time—for Luxembourg city is as compact as it is charming—found myself on a highway out of town. Not sure how to deal with this unfolding crisis, I decided on an impulse to hitchhike into Belgium. It was a bigger country; things might be better there. I stood for an hour and forty minutes beside the highway with my thumb out, watching with little stabs of despair as cars shot past and the sun tracked its way to the horizon. I was about to abandon this plan as well—and do what? I didn't know—when a battered Citroën 2CV pulled over. I lugged my rucksack over to find a young couple arguing in the front seat. For a moment I thought they weren't stopping for me at all, that the man was just pulling over to slap the woman around, as I knew Europeans were wont to do from watching Jean-Paul Belmondo movies on public television, but then the woman got out, fixed me with a fiery look and allowed me to clamber into the back, where I sat with my knees around my ears amid stacks of shoe boxes.

The driver was very friendly. He spoke good English and shouted at me over the lawn-mower roar of the engine that he worked as a traveling shoe salesman and his wife as a clerk in a Luxembourg bank and that they lived just over the border in Arlon. He kept turning around to rearrange things on the backseat to give me more space, throwing shoe boxes at the back window ledge, which I would have preferred him not to do because more often than not they clonked me on the head, and at the same time he was driving with one hand at seventy miles an hour in heavy traffic.

Every few seconds his wife would shriek as the back of a truck loomed up and filled the windshield and he would attend to the road for perhaps two and a half seconds before returning his attention to my comfort. She constantly berated him for his driving, but he acted as if this were some engaging quirk of hers, and kept throwing me mugging, conspiratorial, deeply Gallic looks, as if her squeaky bitching were a private joke between the two of us.

I have seldom been more certain that I was about to die. The man drove as if we were in an arcade game. The highway was a three-lane affair—something else I had never seen before—with one lane going east, one lane going west, and a shared middle lane for overtaking from either direction. My new friend did not appear to grasp the system. He would zip into the middle lane and seem genuinely astonished to find a forty-ton truck bearing down on us like something out of a Road Runner cartoon. He would veer out of the way at the last possible instant and then hang out the window shouting abuse at the passing driver, before being shrieked back to the next crisis by me and his wife. I later learned that Luxembourg has the highest highway fatality rate in Europe.

It took half an hour to reach Arlon, a dreary industrial town. Everything about it looked gray and dusty, even the people. The man insisted that I come to their apartment for dinner. Both the wife and I protested—I politely, she with undisguised loathing—but he dismissed our demurrals as yet more engaging quirks of ours, and before I knew it I was being bundled up a dark staircase and shown into the tiniest and barest of flats. They had just two rooms—a cupboard-sized kitchen and an everything-else room containing a table, two chairs, a bed, and a portable record player with just two albums, one by Gene Pitney and the other by an English colliery brass band. He asked me which I would like to hear. I told him to choose.

He put on Gene Pitney, vanished into the kitchen, where his wife pelted him with whispers, and reappeared looking sheepish and bearing two tumblers and two large brown bottles of beer. "Now this will be very nice," he promised and poured me a glass of what turned out to be very warm lager. "Oom," I said, trying to sound appreciative. I wiped some froth from my lip and wondered if I could survive a dive out an upstairs window. We sat drinking our beer and smiling at each other. I tried to think what the beer put me in mind of and finally decided it was a very large urine sample, possibly from a circus animal. "Good, yes?" asked the Belgian.

"Oom," I said again, but didn't lift it to my lips.

I had never been away from home before. I was on a strange continent where they didn't speak my language. I had just traveled four thousand miles in a chest freezer with wings, I had not slept for thirty hours, or washed for twenty-nine, and here I was in a tiny, spartan apartment in an unknown town in Belgium about to eat dinner with two very strange people.

Madame Strange appeared with three plates, each bearing two fried eggs and nothing else, which she placed in front of us with a certain ringing vehemence. She and I sat at the table. Her husband perched on the edge of the bed. "Beer and eggs," I said. "Interesting combination."

Dinner lasted four seconds. "Oom," I said, wiping the yolk from my mouth and patting my stomach. "That was really excellent. Thank you very much. Well, I must be going." Madame Strange fixed me with a look that went well beyond hate, but Monsieur Strange leaped to his feet and held me affectionately by the shoulders. "No, no, you must listen to the other side of the album and have some more beer." He adjusted the record and we listened in silence and with small sips of beer.

Afterward, he took me in his car to the center of town to a small hotel that may once have been grand but was now full of bare light bulbs and run by a man in an undershirt. The man led me on a long trek up flights of stairs and down hallways before abandoning me at a large bare-floored room that contained within its shadowy vastness a chair with a thin towel on its back, a chipped sink, an absurdly grand armoire, and an enormous oak bed that had the warp and whiff of 150 years of urgent sex ground into it.

I dropped my pack and tumbled onto the bed, still in my shoes, and realized that the light switch to the twenty-watt bulb hovering somewhere in the murk overhead was on the other side of the room, but I was too weary to get up and turn it off, too weary to do anything but wonder briefly whether my religious zealot acquaintance was still roomless in Luxembourg and now shivering miserably in a doorway or on a park bench, wearing an extra sweater and stuffing his jeans with pages from the *Luxembourger Zeitung* to keep out the cold.

"Hope so," I said and snuggled down for an eleven-hour sleep.

I   S P E N T a few days tramping through the wooded hills of the Ardennes. The backpack took some getting used to. Each morning when I donned it I would stagger around for a minute in the manner of someone who has been hit on the head with a mallet, but it made me feel incredibly fit. It was like taking a trunk on holiday. I don't know that I have ever felt so content or alive as in those three or four days in the south of Belgium. I was twenty years old and at large in a perfect world. The weather was kind and the countryside green and fetching and dotted with small farms, where geese and chickens loitered along roadsides that seldom saw a passing car.

Every hour or two I would wander into some drowsy village where two old men in berets would be sitting outside a café with glasses of Bols and would silently watch me approach and pass, responding to my cheery "Bonjour!" with the tiniest of nods; and in the evenings, when I had found a room in a small hotel and gone to the local café to read a book and drink beer, I would get those same tiny nods again from a dozen people, which I in my enthusiasm took as a sign of respect and acceptance. I believe I may even have failed to notice them edging away when, emboldened by seven or eight glasses of Jupiler pils or the memorably named Donkle Beer, I would lean toward one of them and say in a quiet but friendly voice, "Je m'appelle Guillaume. J'habite Des Moines."

AND SO the summer went. I wandered for four months across the continent, through Britain and Ireland, through Scandinavia, Germany, Switzerland, Austria, and Italy, lost in a private astonishment. It was as happy a summer as I have ever spent. I enjoyed it so much that I came home, tipped the contents of my backpack into an incinerator, and returned the next summer with a high school acquaintance named Stephen Katz, which I quickly realized was a serious mistake.

Katz was the sort of person who would lie in a darkened hotel room while you were trying to sleep and talk for hours in graphic, sometimes luridly perverted, detail about what he would like to do to various high school nymphets, given his druthers and some of theirs, or announce his farts by saying, "Here comes a good one. You ready?" and then grade them for volume, duration, and odorosity, as he called it. The best thing that could be said about traveling abroad with Katz was that it spared the rest of America from having to spend the summer with him.

He soon became background noise, a person across the table who greeted each new plate of food with "What is *this* shit?," a hyperactive stranger who talked about boners all the time and unaccountably accompanied me wherever I went, and after a while I more or less tuned him out and spent a summer that was almost as enjoyable, and in a sense as solitary, as the one before.

Since that time, I had spent almost the whole of my adulthood, fifteen of the last seventeen years, living in England, on the fringe of this glorious continent, and seen almost none of it. A four-day visit to Copenhagen, three trips to Brussels, a brief swing through the Netherlands—this was all I had to show for my fifteen years as an adopted European. It was time to put things right.

I decided at the outset to start at the North Cape, the northernmost point of the European mainland, and to make my way south to Istanbul, taking in along the way as many of the places Katz and I had visited as I could manage. My intention had been to begin the trip in the spring, but just before Christmas I made a phone call to the University of Tromsø, the northernmost university in the world and hotbed of Northern Lights research, to find out when the best time would be to see this celestial lightshow. The phone line was so bad that I could barely hear the kindly professor I spoke to—he appeared to be talking to me from the midst of a roaring blizzard; I imagined a door banging open and swirling snow blowing into his frail and lonely hut somewhere out in the wilds—but I did catch enough to gather that the only reliable time to come was now, in the depths of winter, before the sun rose again in late January. This was a very good year for Northern Lights, as it happened—something to do with intense solar activity—but you needed a clear sky to see them, and in northern Norway this could never be guaranteed.

"You should plan to come for at least a month," he shouted at me.

"A month?" I said with genuine alarm.

"At least."

A month. A month in the coldest, darkest, bleakest, remotest place in Europe. Everyone I told this to thought it was most amusing. And now here I was heading north on a bouncing bus, inescapably committed.

N O T   L O N G after leaving Oslo I became aware with a sense of unease that no one on the bus was smoking. I could see no NO

SMOKING signs, but I wasn't going to be the first person to light up and then have everyone clucking at me in Norwegian. I was pretty certain that the man in the seat across the aisle was a smoker—he looked suitably out of sorts—and even more sure that the young man ahead of me must be. I have yet to meet a grown-up reader of comic books who does not also have an affection for tobacco and tattoos. I consulted the "Express 2000" leaflet that came with each seat and read with horror the words "tilsammen 2,000km nonstop i 30 timer."

Now I don't know Norwegian from alphabet soup, but even I could translate that. Two thousand kilometers! Nonstop! Thirty hours without a cigarette! Suddenly all the discomfort came flooding back. My neck ached, my left leg sizzled like bacon in a skillet, the young man ahead of me had his head closer to my crotch than any man ever had before, I had less space to call my own than if I'd climbed into my suitcase and mailed myself to Hammerfest, and now I was going to go thirty hours without an infusion of nicotine. This was just too much.

Fortunately, it wasn't quite as desperate as that. At the Swedish border, some two hours after leaving Oslo, the bus stopped at a customs post in the woods, and while the driver went into the hut to sort out the paperwork most of the passengers, including me and the two I'd forecast, clattered down the steps and stood stamping their feet in the cold snow and smoking cigarettes by the fistful. Who could tell when we would get this chance again? Actually, after I returned to the bus and earned the undying enmity of the lady beside me by stepping on her foot for the second time in five minutes, I discovered from further careful study of the "Express 2000" leaflet that three rest stops appeared to be built into the itinerary.

The first of these came in the evening at a roadside cafeteria in Skellefteå, Sweden. It was a strange place. On the wall at the start of the food line was an outsized menu. Beside each item listed was a red button, which when pushed alerted the people in the kitchen to start preparing that dish. Having done this, you slid your empty tray along to the check-out, pausing to select a drink, and then waited with the cashier for twenty minutes until your food was brought out. Rather defeats the purpose of a cafeteria, don't you think? As I was the last in the line and the line was going nowhere, I went outside and smoked many cigarettes in the bitter cold and then returned. The line was only fractionally depleted, but I took a tray and regarded the menu. I had no idea what any of the foods were, and as I have a dread of ever inadvertently ordering liver, which I so much detest that I am going to have to leave you here for a minute and go throw up in the wastebasket from just thinking about it, I elected to choose nothing (though I thought hard about pressing *all* the buttons just to see what would happen).

Instead, I selected a bottle of Pepsi and some little pastries, but when I arrived at the check-out, the cashier told me that my Norwegian money was no good, that I needed Swedish money. This surprised me. I had always thought the Nordic peoples were all pals and freely exchanged their money, as they do between Belgium and Luxembourg. Under the cashier's heartless gaze, I replaced the cakes and Pepsi and took instead a free glass of iced water and went to a table. Fumbling in my jacket pocket, I discovered a Dan-Air cookie left over from the flight from England and dined on that.

When we returned to the bus, sated on our lamb cutlets and vegetables and/or cookie and iced water, the driver extinguished the interior lights and we had no choice but to try to sleep. It was endlessly uncomfortable. I finally discovered, after trying every possibility, that the best position was to lie down on the seat more or less upside down with my legs dangling above me. In this manner, I fell into a deep, and surprisingly restful, sleep. Ten minutes later, Norwegian coins began slipping one by one from my pocket and dropping on to the floor behind me, where (one supposes) they were furtively scooped up by the little old lady sitting there.

And so the night passed.

WE WERE awoken early for another rest stop, this one in Where The Fuck, Finland. Actually, it was called Muonio and it was the most desolate place I had ever seen: a filling station and lean-to café in the middle of a tundra. The good news was that the café accepted Norwegian currency; the bad news was that it had nothing that anyone outside a famine zone would want to eat. The driver and his mate were given heaped and steaming platters of eggs, potatoes, and ham, but there appeared to be nothing like that on offer for the rest of us. I took a bottle of mineral water and a slice of crispbread with a piece of last year's cheese on it, for which I was charged an astonishing twenty-five kroner, and retired to a corner booth. Afterward, while the driver and his mate lingered over coffees and suppressed contented burps, the other passengers and I milled around in the shop part of the complex, looking at fan belts and snow shovels, and stood in the perishing cold out by the bus and smoked more fistfuls of cigarettes.

We hit the road again at seven-thirty. Only another whole day of this, I thought cheerfully. The landscape was inexpressibly bleak, just mile after tedious mile of snowy waste and scraggly birch forest. Reindeer grazed along the roadside and often on the road itself, coming out to lick the salt scattered on the ice. We passed through a couple of Lapp villages, looking frigid and lifeless. There were no Christmas lights in the windows here. In the distance, the sun just peeked over the low hills, lingered uncertainly, and then sank back. It was the last I would see of it for three weeks.

The bus rolled on.

Just after five o'clock we crossed a long, lonely toll bridge onto the island of Kvaløya, home of Hammerfest. We were now as far north as you can get in the world by public transport. Hammerfest is almost unimaginably remote—1,000 miles north of the Shetlands, 800 miles beyond the Faroes, 200 miles north of the northernmost tip of Iceland, 150 miles north even of my lonely professor friend at the northernmost university in the world at Tromsø. I was closer now to the North Pole than to London. The thought of it roused me and I pressed my nose to the cold glass.

We approached Hammerfest from above, on a winding coast road, and when at last it pivoted into view it looked simply wonderful—a fairyland of golden lights stretching up into the hills and around an expansive bay. I had pictured it in my mind as a village—a few houses around a small harbor, a church perhaps, a general store, a bar if I was lucky—but this was a little city. A golden little city. Things were looking up.

2.

~~~~~~~~~~~~~~~~~~~~~~~~~~~~~~~~~~~~

HAMMERFEST

~~~~~~~~~~~~~~~~~~~~~~~~~~~~~~~~~~~~

I TOOK a room in the Håja Hotel near the quay, a pleasant hotel and a pleasant room: small but comfortable, with a telephone, a small color television, and its own bathroom. I was highly pleased and full of those little pulses of excitement that come with finding yourself in a new place. I dumped my things, briefly investigated the amenities, and went out to look at Hammerfest.

It seemed an agreeable enough town in a thank-you-God-for-not-making-me-live-here sort of way. The hotel was in a dark neighborhood of shipping offices and warehouses. There were also a couple of banks, a very large police station, and a post office with a row of telephone kiosks in front. In each of these, I noticed as I passed, the telephone books had been set alight by some desperate thrill-seeker and now hung charred from their chains.

I walked up to the main street, Strandgatan, which ran for about three hundred yards along the harbor, lined on the inland side by an assortment of businesses—a bakery, a bookstore, a movie house (closed), a café called Kokken's—and on the harbor side by the town hall, a few more shops, and the dark hulking mass of a Birds Eye-Findus fish-processing plant. Christmas lights were strung cheerily at intervals across the street, but all the shops were shut and there wasn't a sign of life anywhere, apart from an occasional cab speeding past as if on an urgent mission.

It was cold out, but nothing like as cold as I had expected. This pleased me because I had very nearly bought a ridiculous Russian-style fur hat—the kind with ear flaps—for four hundred kroner in Oslo. Much as I hate to stand out in a crowd, I have this terrible occasional compulsion to make myself a source of merriment for the world, and I had come close to scaling new heights with a Russian hat. Now, clearly, that would be unnecessary.

Beyond the main street, the road curved around the bay, leading out to a narrow headland, and after a half mile or so it presented a fetching view back to the town, sheltering in a cleft of black mountains, as if in the palm of a giant hand. The bay itself was black and impenetrable; only the *whooshing* sound of water hinted at what was out there. But the town itself was wonderfully bright and snug-looking, a haven of warmth and light in the endless Arctic night.

Satisfied with this initial reconnaissance, I trudged back to the hotel, where I had a light but astonishingly expensive dinner and climbed gratefully into bed.

In the night I was awakened by a storm. I crept to the window and peered cautiously out. Snow was blowing wildly, like a plague of white insects, and the wind howled. Lightning lit the sky. I had never seen lightning in a snowstorm. Murmuring, "Oh, sweet Jesus, where am I?" I climbed back into bed and buried myself deep in the covers. I don't know what time I awoke, but I dozed and tossed for perhaps an hour in the dark until it occurred to me that it never was going to get light. I got up and looked out the window. The storm was still raging. In the police station parking lot below, two squad cars marked "Politi" were buried in drifts almost to their rooftops.

After breakfast, I ventured out into the gale. The streets were still deserted, snow piled in the doorways. The wind was playing havoc with the town. Street lights flickered and swayed, throwing spastic shadows across the snow. The Christmas decorations rattled. A cardboard box sailed across the road ahead of me and was wafted high out over the harbor. It was bitterly cold. On the exposed road out to the headland I began to wish again that I had bought the Russian hat. The wind was unrelenting: It drove before it tiny particles of ice that seared my cheeks and made me gasp. I had a scarf with me, which I tied around my face bandit-style, and trudged on, leaning heavily into the wind.

Ahead of me out of the swirling snow appeared a figure. He was wearing a Russian hat, I was interested to note. As he drew nearer, I pulled my scarf down to make some cheering greeting—"Bit fresh out, what?" or something—but he passed by without even looking at me. A hundred yards farther on, I passed two more people, a man and his wife tramping stolidly into town, and they, too, passed as if I were invisible. Strange people, I thought.

The headland proved unrewarding, just a jumble of warehouses and small ship-repair yards, loomed over by groaning cranes. I was about to turn back when I noticed a sign pointing the way to something called the Meridianstøtten and decided to investigate. This took me down a lane on the seaward side of the headland. Here, wholly exposed to the pounding sea, the wind was even more ferocious. Twice it all but picked me up and carried me forward several yards. Only the toetips of my boots maintained contact with the ground. I discovered that by holding out my arms I could sail along on the flats of my feet, propelled entirely by the wind. It was the most wonderful fun. Irish windsurfing, I dubbed it. I had a great time until an unexpected burst whipped my feet from under me. I cracked my head on the ice so hard that I saw stars and suddenly recalled where I had put the coal shed key the summer before. The pain of it, and the thought that another gust might heft me into the sea like the cardboard box I had seen earlier, made me abandon the sport and I proceeded to the Meridianstøtten with prudence.

The Meridianstøtten was an obelisk on a small elevation in the middle of a graveyard of warehouses. I later learned that it was a memorial erected to celebrate the completion in 1840, on this very spot, of the first scientific measurement of the earth's circumference. (Hammerfest's other historical distinction is that it was the first town in Europe to have electric street lights.) I clambered up to the obelisk with difficulty, but the snow was blowing so thickly that I couldn't read the inscription, and I returned to town thinking I would come back again another day. I never did.

IN THE evening I dined in the hotel's restaurant and bar, and afterward sat nursing Mack beers at fifty øre a sip, thinking that surely things would liven up in a minute. It was New Year's Eve, after all. But the bar was like a funeral parlor with a beverage service. A pair of mild-looking men in reindeer sweaters sat with beers staring silently into space. After a time I realized there was another

customer, sitting alone in a dark corner. Only the glow of his cigarette revealed him in the gloom. When the waiter came to take my
plate away, I asked him what there was to do for fun in Hammerfest.
He thought for a moment and said: "Have you tried setting fire to
the telephone directories by the post office?"

Actually, he didn't say that, because just as he was about to speak,
the lone figure in the corner addressed some slurred remark to him,
which I gathered was something along the lines of "Hey, you dismal, slope-headed slab of reindeer shit, what does it take to get some
service around here?" The waiter dropped my plate back onto the
table with a suddenness that made the silverware jump and went
straight to the man and began furiously dragging him by his arm and
shoulder from his seat and then pushing him with enormous difficulty to the door, where he finally heaved him out into the snow.
When the waiter returned, looking flushed and disconcerted, I said
brightly: "I hope you don't show all your customers out like that!"
but he was in no mood for pleasantries and retired sulkily to the bar,
so I was unable to determine just what there was to do in Hammerfest to pass the time, other than set telephone books alight, insult the
waiter, and weep.

At 11:30, with the bar still dead, I went out to see if there was any
life anywhere. The wind had died, but there was hardly anyone
about. Every window in every house blazed with light, but there
was no sign of revelry within. Then just before midnight, as I was
about to return to the hotel, an odd thing happened. Every person
came out of every house and began to set off fireworks—big
industrial-sized fireworks that shrieked across the sky and exploded
with a sharp bang and filled the night with color and sparks. For half
an hour, from all around the peninsula, fireworks popped and glit-
tered over the harbor and drifted spent into the sea. And then, precisely thirty minutes after it all began, everyone went back inside and
Hammerfest slept again.

THE DAYS passed. At least three times a day I went for long
walks and searched the sky, and in the evenings I went out every
hour to see if anything was happening yet, but it never was. Some-

times I arose in the night to look out the window, but I never saw anything. Once or twice a day it would snow—fat, fluffy snow-flakes, like the ones you used to see in a Perry Como Christmas special—but the rest of the time the sky was clear. Everyone told me it was perfect Northern Lights weather. "You should have been here just before Christmas—ah, fabulous," they would say and then as-sure me that tonight would almost certainly be the night. "About eleven o'clock you go out. Then you'll see." But it didn't happen.

When I wasn't walking or searching the sky, I sat in the bar of the hotel drinking beer or lay on my bed reading. I tried once or twice to watch television in my room. There is only one network in Nor-way and it is stupefyingly bad. It's not just that the programs are dull, though in this respect they could win awards, but that the whole thing is so wondrously unpolished. Films finish and you get thirty seconds of scratchy white circles like you used to get when your home movies ran out and your dad didn't get to the projector fast enough, and then suddenly the lights come up on the day's host, looking faintly startled, as if he had been just about to do something he wouldn't want a nation to see. The host, always a handsome young man or woman with a lively sweater and sculpted hair, fills the long gaps between programs by showing endless trailers for the rest of the evening's highlights: a documentary on mineral extraction in Narvik, a Napoleonic costume drama in which the main charac-ters wear moustaches that are patently not their own and strut around as if they have had a fence post inserted rectally (but are trying not to let it affect their performance), and a jazz session with somebody truly hopeless and unheard-of—the Sigi Wurtmuller Rhythm Ca-dettes or something. The best that can be said for Norwegian tele-vision is that it gives you the sensation of a coma without the worry and inconvenience.

I began to feel as if a doctor had told me to go away for a complete rest ("someplace really boring, where there's nothing at all to do"). Never had I slept so long and so well. Never had I had this kind of leisure to just potter about. Suddenly I had time to do all kinds of things: unlace my boots and redo them over and over until the laces were *precisely* the same length, rearrange the contents of my wallet, deal with nose hairs, make long lists of all the things I would do if I had anything to do. Sometimes I sat on the edge of the bed with my hands on my knees and just gazed about me. Often I talked to myself. Mostly I went for long, cold walks, bleakly watching the unillumined sky, then stopped for coffee at Kokken's Café, with its steamy windows and luscious warmth.

It occurred to me that this was just like being retired. I even began taking a small notebook with me on my walks and keeping a pointless diary of my daily movements, just as my dad had done when he retired. He used to walk every day to the lunch counter at our neighborhood supermarket and if you passed by you would see him writing in his notebook. After he died, we found a closet full of these notebooks. Every one of them was filled with entries like this: "January 4. Walked to supermarket. Had two cups of decaf. Weather mild." Suddenly I understood what he was up to.

LITTLE by little I began to meet people. They began to recognize me in Kokken's and the post office and the bank, and to treat me to cautious nods of acknowledgment. I became a fixture of the bar of the hotel, where I was clearly regarded as a harmless eccentric, the man from England who came and stayed and stayed.

One day, lacking anything at all to do, I went and saw the mayor. I told him I was a journalist, but really I just wanted someone to talk to. He had an undertaker's face and wore blue jeans and a blue work shirt, which made him look unsettlingly like a prisoner on day release, but he was a kind man. He told me at length about the problems of the local economy, and as we parted he said: "You must come to my house one evening. I have a sixteen-year-old daughter."

Gosh, that's jolly gracious of you, I thought, but I'm a happily married man.

"She would like to practice her English."

Ah. I'd have gone, but the invitation never came. Afterward, I went to Kokken's and wrote in my diary: "Interviewed mayor. Weather cold."

ONE SUNDAY afternoon in the hotel, I overheard a man about my age talking to the proprietor in Norwegian but to his own children in Home Counties English. His name was Ian Tonkin. He was an Englishman who had married a Hammerfest girl and now taught English at the local high school. He and his lovely wife, Peggy, invited me to their home for dinner, fed me lavishly on reindeer (delicious) and cloudberries (mysterious but also delicious), and were kindness itself, expressing great sympathy for my unluckiness with the Northern Lights. "You should have seen it just before Christmas—ah, fabulous," they said.

Peggy told me a sad story. In 1944, the retreating Germans, in an attempt to deprive the advancing Russian Army of shelter, burned down the town. The residents were evacuated by ship to live out the rest of the war billeted with strangers. As the evacuation flotilla left the harbor, they could see their houses going up in flames. Peggy's father took the house keys from his pocket and dropped them overboard, saying with a sigh: "Well, we shan't be needing those anymore." After the war the people returned to Hammerfest to find nothing standing but the chapel. With their bare hands and almost nothing else, they built their town again, one house at a time. It may not have been much, it may have been on the edge of nowhere, but Hammerfest was theirs and they loved it and I don't think I have ever admired any group of people quite so much.

From Peggy and Ian and others I met I learned all about the town—about the parlous state of the fishing industry on which everyone in the town depended in one way or another, about the previous year's exciting murder trial, about accusations of incompetence concerning snow removal. I began to find it engrossing. Hammerfest grew to feel like home. It seemed entirely natural to be there, and my real life in England began to feel oddly distant and dreamlike.

O N M Y sixteenth day in Hammerfest, it happened. I was returning from the headland after my morning walk and in an empty piece of sky above the town there appeared a translucent cloud of many colors—pinks and greens and blues and pale purples. It glimmered and seemed to swirl. Slowly it stretched across the sky. It had an oddly oily quality about it, like the rainbows you sometimes see in a pool of petrol. I stood transfixed.

I knew from my reading that the Northern Lights are immensely high up in the atmosphere, something like two hundred miles up, but this show seemed to be suspended just above the town. There are two kinds of Northern Lights—the curtains of shimmering gossamer that everyone has seen in pictures, and the rather rarer gas clouds that I was gazing at now. They are never the same twice. Sometimes they shoot wraithlike across the sky, like smoke in a wind tunnel, moving at enormous speed, and sometimes they hang like luminous drapes or glittering spears of light, and very occasionally—perhaps once or twice in a lifetime—they creep out from every point on the horizon and flow together overhead in a spectacular, silent explosion of light and color.

In the depthless blackness of the countryside, where you may be a hundred miles from the nearest artificial light, they are capable of the most weird and unsettling optical illusions. They can seem to come out of the sky and fly at you at enormous speeds, as if trying to kill you. Apparently, it's terrifying. To this day, many Lapps earnestly believe that if you show the lights a white handkerchief or a sheet of white paper, they will come and take you away.

This display was relatively small stuff, and it lasted for only a few minutes, but it was the most beautiful thing I had ever seen and it would do me until something better came along.

In the evening, something did—a display of lights that went on for hours. They were of only one color, that eerie luminous green you see on radar screens, but the activity was frantic. Narrow swirls of light would sweep across the great dome of sky, then hang there like vapor trails. Sometimes they flashed across the sky like falling stars and sometimes they spun languorously, reminding me of the lazy way smoke used to rise from my father's pipe when he was reading. Sometimes the lights would flicker brightly in the west, then vanish in an instant and reappear a moment later behind me, as if teasing me. I was constantly turning and twisting to see it all. You have no idea how immense the sky is until you try to monitor it all. The eerie thing was how silent it was. Such activity seemed to demand at the very least an occasional low boom or a series of staticlike crackles, but there was none. All this immense energy was spent without a sound.

I was very cold—inside my heavy boots I wore three pairs of

socks, but still my toes felt like ice cubes and I began to worry seriously about frostbite—but I stayed and watched for perhaps two hours, unable to pull myself away.

The next day I went to the tourist office to report my good news to Hans, the tourism director who had become something of a friend, and to reserve a seat on the following week's bus. There was no longer any need to hang around. Hans looked surprised and said: "Didn't you know? There's no bus next week. It's going to Alta for its annual maintenance."

I was crushed. Two more weeks in Hammerfest. What on earth was I going to do with myself for two more weeks?

"But you're in luck," Hans added. "You can go today."

I couldn't take this in. "What?"

"The bus should have arrived yesterday but it didn't get through because of heavy snows around Kautokeino. It arrived this morning. Didn't you see it out there? They're going back again today."

"Today? Really? When?"

He looked at his watch with the casualness of someone who has lived for years in the middle of nowhere and will be living there for years more yet. "Oh, in about ten minutes, I should think."

Ten minutes! I have seldom moved so quickly. I ran to the bus, begged them not to leave without me, though without any confidence that this plea was understood, ran to the hotel, threw everything in my suitcase, paid the bill, made my thanks, and arrived at the bus, trailing oddments of clothes behind me, just as it was about to pull out.

The funny thing is that as we were leaving Hammerfest, just for an instant I had a sudden urge not to go. It was a nice town. I liked the people. They had been kind to me. In other circumstances, I might just have settled down and stayed. But then, I realized, such thinking was crazy. It was time to return to Oslo and the real world. Besides, I had a hat to buy.

3

OSLO

I REMEMBER on my first trip to Europe going alone to a movie in Copenhagen. In Denmark you are given a ticket for an assigned seat. I went into the theater and discovered that my ticket directed me to sit beside the only other people in the place, a young couple locked in the sort of passionate embrace associated with dockside reunions at the end of long wars. I could no more have sat beside them than I could have asked to join in—it would have come to much the same thing—so I took a place a few discreet seats away.

People came in the theater, consulted their tickets, and filled the seats around us. By the time the film started, there were about thirty of us sitting together in a tight pack in the middle of a vast and otherwise empty auditorium. Two minutes into the movie, a woman laden with shopping made her way with difficulty down my row, stopped beside my seat, and told me in a stern voice, full of glottals and indignation, that I was in her place. This caused much play of flashlights among the usherettes and fretful reexamining of tickets by everyone in the vicinity until word got around that I was an American tourist and therefore unable to follow simple seating instructions and was escorted in some shame back to my assigned place.

So we sat together and watched the movie, thirty people crowded together like refugees in an overloaded lifeboat, rubbing shoulders and sharing small noises, and it occurred to me then that there are certain things that some nations do better than everyone else and certain things that they do far worse, and I began to wonder why that should be.

Sometimes a nation's little contrivances are so singular and clever that we associate them with that country alone—double-decker buses in Britain, windmills in Holland (what an inspired addition to a flat landscape; think how they would transform Nebraska), sidewalk cafés in Paris. And yet there are some things that most countries do without difficulty that others cannot get a grasp of at all.

The French, for instance, cannot get the hang of standing in line. They try and try, but it is beyond them. Wherever you go in Paris, you see orderly lines waiting at bus stops, but as soon as the bus pulls up, the line instantly disintegrates into something like a fire drill at a lunatic asylum as everyone scrambles to be the first aboard, quite unaware that this defeats the whole purpose of lining up.

The British, on the other hand, do not understand certain fundamentals of eating, as evidenced by their instinct to consume hamburgers with a knife and fork. To my continuing amazement, many of them also turn their fork upside down and balance the food on the back of it. I've lived in England for a decade and a half and I still have to quell an impulse to go up to strangers in pubs and restaurants and say, "Excuse me, can I give you a tip that'll help stop those peas bouncing all over the table?"

Germans are flummoxed by humor, the Swiss have no concept of fun, the Spanish think there is nothing at all ridiculous about eating dinner at midnight, and the Italians should never, ever have been let in on the invention of the motorcar.

One of the small marvels of my first trip to Europe was the discovery that the world could be so full of variety, that there were so many different ways of doing essentially identical things, like eating and drinking and buying movie tickets. It fascinated me that Europeans could at once be so alike—that they could be so universally bookish and cerebral, and drive small cars, and live in little houses in ancient towns, and love soccer, and be relatively unmaterialistic and law-abiding, and have chilly hotel rooms and cozy and inviting places to eat and drink—and yet be so endlessly, unpredictably different from each other as well. I loved the idea that you could never be sure of anything in Europe.

I still enjoy that sense of never knowing quite what's going on. In my hotel in Oslo, where I spent four days after returning from Hammerfest, the chambermaid each morning left me a packet of something called Bio Tex Blå, a "minipakke for ferie, hybel og weekend," according to the instructions. I spent many happy hours sniffing it and experimenting with it, uncertain whether it was for washing out clothes or gargling or cleaning the toilet bowl. In the end I decided it was for washing out clothes—it worked a treat—but for all I know for the rest of the week everywhere I went in Oslo, people were saying to each other, "You know, that man smelled like toilet bowl cleaner."

When I told friends in London that I was going to travel around Europe and write a book about it, they said, "Oh, you must speak a lot of languages."

"Why, no," I would reply with a certain pride, "only English," and they would look at me as if I were foolish or crazy. But that's the glory of foreign travel, as far as I am concerned. I don't *want* to know what people are talking about. I can't think of anything that excites a greater sense of childlike wonder than to be in a country where you are ignorant of almost everything. Suddenly you are five years old again. You can't read anything, you have only the most rudimentary sense of how things work, you can't even reliably cross a street without endangering your life. Your whole existence becomes a series of interesting guesses.

I get great pleasure from watching foreign TV and trying to imagine what on earth is going on. On my first evening in Oslo, I watched a science program in which two men in a studio stood at a lab table discussing a variety of sleek, rodentlike animals that were crawling over the surface and occasionally up the host's jacket. "And you have sex with all these creatures, do you?" the host was saying.

"Certainly," replied the guest. "You have to be careful with the porcupines, of course, and the lemmings can get very neurotic and hurl themselves off cliffs if they feel you don't love them as you once did, but basically these animals make very affectionate companions, and the sex is simply out of this world."

"Well, I think that's wonderful. Next week we'll be looking at how you can make hallucinogenic drugs with simple household chemicals from your own medicine cabinet, but now it's time for the screen to go blank for a minute and then for the lights to come up suddenly on the host of the day looking as if he was *just* about to pick his nose. See you next week."

AFTER HAMMERFEST, Oslo was simply wonderful. It was still cold and dusted with grayish snow, but it seemed positively tropical after Hammerfest, and I abandoned all thought of buying a furry hat. I went to the museums and took a daylong walk out around the Bygdøy Peninsula, where the city's finest houses crouch on the wooded hillsides, with fetching views across the icy water of the harbor to the downtown. But mostly I hung around the city center, wandering back and forth between the train station and the royal palace, gazing in the store windows along Karl Johansgate, the long and handsome main pedestrian street, cheered by the bright lights, mingling with the happy, healthy, relentlessly youthful Norwegians, very pleased to be alive and out of Hammerfest and in a world of daylight. When I grew cold, I sat in cafés and bars and eavesdropped on conversations that I could not understand or brought out my *Thomas Cook European Timetable* and studied it with a kind of humble reverence, planning the rest of my trip.

The *Thomas Cook European Timetable* is possibly the finest book ever produced. It is impossible to leaf through its five hundred pages of densely printed timetables without wanting to dump a double armload of clothes into an old Gladstone and just take off. Every page whispers romance: "Montreux—Zweisimmen—Spiez—Interlaken," "Beograd—Trieste—Venezia—Verona—Milano," "Goteborg—Laxå (Hallsberg)—Stockholm," "Ventimiglia—Marseille—Lyon—Paris." Who could recite these names without experiencing a tug of excitement, without seeing in his mind's eye a steamy platform full of expectant travelers and piles of luggage standing beside a sleek, quarter-mile-long train with a list of exotic locations slotted into every carriage? Who could read the names "Moskva—Warszawa—Berlin—Basel—Genève" and not feel a melancholy envy for all those lucky people who get to make a grand journey across a storied continent? Who could glance at such an itinerary and not want to climb aboard? Well, Sunny Von Bülow for a start. But as for me, I could spend hours just poring over the tables, each one a magical thicket of times, numbers, distances, mysterious little pictograms showing crossed knives and forks, wine glasses, daggers, miners' pickaxes (whatever could

they be for?), ferryboats and buses, and bewilderingly abstruse foot-
notes:

873–4—To/from Storlien—see Table 473.
977—Lapplandspillen—see Table 472. Stops to set down only.
On (7) cars run in train 421.
k—Reservation advisable.
t—Passengers may not join or alight at these stations.
x—Via Vasteras on (4), (5), (6), (7).

What does it all mean? I have no idea. You could study the Thomas Cook book for years and never truly understand its deeper
complexities. And yet these are matters that could affect one's life.
Every year there must be scores of people who end up hundreds of
miles from their destination because they failed to notice the footnote
that said: "Nonstop to Arctic Circle after Karlskrona—see Table
721a/b. Hot water bottle advisable. Hard tack only after Murmansk.
Return journey via Anchorage and Mexicali. Boy, oh boy, have you
fucked up this time, pal."
Hammerfest had been a kind of overextended limbering-up exercise, but now I was going to get down to some serious traveling—
and by that I mean the moving-about kind of traveling. I had an itch
to roam. I wanted to wander through Europe, to see movie posters
for films that would never come to England, gaze wonderingly at
billboards and shop notices full of exotic umlauts and cedillas and No
Parking-sign *o*'s, hear pop songs that could not by even the most
charitable stretch of the imagination be a hit in any country but their
own, encounter people whose lives would never again intersect with
mine, be hopelessly unfamiliar with everything, from the workings
of a phone box to the identity of a foodstuff.
I wanted to be puzzled and charmed, to experience the endless,
beguiling variety of a continent where you can board a train and an
hour later be somewhere where the inhabitants speak a different
language, eat different foods, work different hours, live lives that are
at once so different and yet so oddly similar. I wanted to be a tourist.
But first it was time to go home.

4.

~~~~~~~~~~~~~~~~~~~~~~~~~~~~~~~~~~~~

PARIS

~~~~~~~~~~~~~~~~~~~~~~~~~~~~~~~~~~~~

I **RETURNED** to England and waited for winter to go. I spent an absurd amount of time shopping for things for the trip—a travel clock, a Swiss army knife, a bright green and yellow rucksack, which my wife assured me would be just the thing if I decided to do any gay camping—and spent a day crawling around the attic searching mutteringly for my beloved Kümmerly and Frey maps. I bought nearly the whole European set in 1972, and it was one of the few intelligent investments of my younger years. What am I saying? It was *the* intelligent investment of my younger years.

Printed in Switzerland, with all the obsessive precision, and expense, that that implies, each Kümmerly and Frey map covered one or two countries within its smart blue and yellow folders. Unfolded, the maps were vast and crisp and beautifully printed on quality paper. Best of all, the explanatory notes were in German and French only, which gave them an exotic ring that appealed to me in 1972 and appeals to me still. There is just something inherently more earnest and worldly about a traveler who carries maps with titles like "Jugoslawien 1:1 Mio" and "Schwarzwald 1:250 000." It tells the world: "Don't mess with me. I'm a guy who knows his maps."

With a stack of K&Fs and the latest *Thomas Cook European Timetable,* I spent long, absorbed evenings trying to draw up an itinerary that was both comprehensive and achievable, and failed repeatedly on both counts. Europe isn't easy to systematize. You can't go from coast to coast. There are few topographical features that suggest a natural beginning and end, and those that do—the Alps, the Rhine, the Danube—were either physically beyond me or had been written about a thousand times. And besides, it's just too big, too packed with things to see. There isn't anyplace that's not worth going to.

In the end, I decided on a fairly random approach. I would return to Oslo to pick up the trail where I had left off and go wherever fancy took me. Then a week or so before I was due to fly out, I suddenly had the cold realization that Oslo was the last place I wanted to be. It was still winter in Oslo. I had been there only two months before. A voice that seemed not to be my own said: "Hell, Bill, go to Paris." So I did.

THE GIRL at my travel agency in Yorkshire, whose grasp of the geography of the world south of Leeds is a trifle hazy (I once asked her to book me an airplane ticket to Brussels and she phoned back ten minutes later to say, "Would that be the Brussels in Belgium, Mr. Bryson?"), had booked me into a hotel in the 742nd *arrondissement,* a charmless neighborhood somewhere on the outskirts of Calais. The hotel was opposite a spanking new sports complex, which had been built to look vaguely like a hill: It had short, cropped grass growing up its sides. Quite what the idea of this was I couldn't say because the walls sloped so sharply that you couldn't walk on the grass or sit on it, so it had no function. Its only real purpose was to enable the architect to say, "Look at this, everybody. I've designed a building with grass growing on it. Am I something?" This, as we shall see again, is the great failing of Paris architects.

The hotel was one of those sterile, modern places that always put me in mind of a hospital, but at least it didn't have the curious timer switches that used to be a feature of hotel hallways in France. These were a revelation to me when I first arrived from America. All the light switches in the hallways were timed to go off after ten or fifteen seconds, presumably as an economy measure. This wasn't so bad if your room was next to the elevator, but if it was very far down the hall, and hotel hallways in Paris tend to wander around like an old man with Alzheimer's, you would generally proceed the last furlong in total blackness, feeling your way along the walls with flattened palms, and invariably colliding scrotally with the corner of a nineteenth-century oak table put there, evidently, for that purpose. Occasionally, your groping fingers would alight on something soft and hairy, which you would recognize after a moment as another person, and if he or she spoke English, you could exchange tips.

You soon learned to have your key out and to sprint like hell for your room. The trouble was that when eventually you reemerged, it was to total blackness once more and to a complete and—mark this—*intentional* absence of light switches, and there was nothing to do but stumble straight-armed through the darkness, like Boris Karloff in *The Mummy,* and hope that you weren't about to blunder into a stairwell. And from this I learned one very important lesson: The French do not like us.

On my first trip to Paris, I kept wondering: "Why does everyone hate me so much?" Fresh off the train, I went to the tourist booth at the Gare du Nord, where a severe young woman in a blue uniform looked at me as if I were infectious. "What do *you* want?" she said, or at least seemed to say.

"I'd like a room, please," I replied, instantly meek.

"Fill this out." She pushed a long form at me. "Not here. Over there." She indicated with a flick of her head a counter for filling out forms, then turned to the next person in line and said: "What do *you* want?" I was amazed—I came from a place where *everyone* was friendly, where even funeral home directors told you to have a nice day as you left to bury your grandmother—but I soon learned that everyone in Paris was like that. You would go into a bakery and be greeted by some vast sluglike creature with a look that told you you would never be friends. In halting French you would ask for a small loaf of bread. The woman would give you a long, cold stare and then put a dead beaver on the counter.

"No, no," you would say, hands aflutter, "not a dead beaver. A loaf of *bread.*"

The sluglike creature would stare at you in patent disbelief, then turn to the other customers and address them in French at much too high a speed for you to follow, but the drift of which clearly was that this person here, this *American tourist,* had come in and asked for a dead beaver and she had given him a dead beaver and now he was saying that he didn't want a dead beaver at all, he wanted a loaf of bread. The other customers would look at you as if you had just tried to fart in their handbags, and you would have no choice but to slink away and console yourself with the thought that in another four days you would be in Brussels and probably able to eat again.

The other thing I have never understood about the French is why they are so ungrateful. I've always felt that since it was us that liberated them—because let's face it, the French Army couldn't beat a girls' hockey team—they ought to give all Allied visitors to the country a book of coupons good for free drinks in Pigalle and a ride to the top of the Eiffel Tower. But they never thank you. I have had Belgians and Dutch people hug me around the knees and let me drag them down the street in gratitude to me for liberating their country, even after I have pointed out to them that I wasn't even sperm in 1945, but this is not an experience that is ever likely to happen to anyone in France.

IN THE evening I strolled the eighteen miles to the Île de la Cité and Notre-Dame, through the sort of neighborhoods where swarthy men in striped Breton shirts lean on lampposts cleaning their teeth with switchblades and spit between your legs as you pass. But it was a lovely March evening, with just the faintest tang of spring in the air, and once I stumbled onto the Seine, at the Pont de Sully, I was met with perfection. There facing me was the Île St.-Louis, glowing softly and floating on the river like a vision, a medieval hamlet magically preserved in the midst of a modern city. I crossed the bridge and wandered up and down its half dozen shuttered streets, half expecting to find chickens wandering in the road and peasants pushing carts loaded with plague victims, but what I found instead were tiny, swish restaurants and appealing apartments in old buildings.

Hardly anyone was about—a few dawdling customers in the restaurants, a pair of teenaged lovers tonguing each other's uvulas in a doorway, a woman in a fur coat encouraging a poodle to leave *un doodoo* on the pavement. The windows of upstairs apartments were pools of warm light and from the street gave tantalizing glimpses of walls lined with books and windowsills overflowing with pot plants and decorative antiques. It must be wonderful to live on such streets on such an island and to gaze out on such a river. The very luckiest live at the western end, where the streets are busier but the windows overlook Notre-Dame. I cannot imagine tiring of that view, though I suppose in August, when the streets are clogged with tour buses and a million tourists in Bermuda shorts that SHOUT, the sense of favored ecstasy may flag.

Even now the streets around the cathedral teemed. It was eight o'clock, but the souvenir shops were still open and doing a brisk trade. I made an unhurried circuit of Notre-Dame and draped myself over a railing by the Seine and watched the *bateaux-mouches* slide by, trimmed with neon, like floating jukeboxes. It was hopelessly romantic.

I dined modestly in a half-empty restaurant on a side street and afterward, accompanied by small burps, wandered across the river to Shakespeare & Co., a wonderfully gloomy English-language bookstore full of cobwebs and musty smells and old forgotten novels by writers like Warwick Deeping. Plump chairs and sagging sofas were scattered about the rooms and on each a young person in intellectual-looking glasses was curled up reading one of the proprietor's books, evidently from cover to cover (I saw one owlish young man turn down the corner of a page and replace the book on its shelf before scowling at me and departing into the night). The bookstore had an engagingly clubby atmosphere, but how it stays in business I have no idea. Not only was the guy at the till conspicuously underemployed—only at the most considerable of intervals did he have to stir from his own book to transact a small sale—but the store's location, on the banks of the Seine in the very shadow of Notre-Dame, must surely push its rent into the stratosphere.

Anywhere else in the world Shakespeare & Co. would be a souvenir emporium, selling die-cast models of the cathedral, Quasimodo ashtrays, slide strips, postcards, and Ooh-La-La T-shirts, or else one of those high-speed cafés where the waiters dash around frantically, leave you waiting forty minutes before taking your order, and then make it clear that you have twenty-five seconds to drink your coffee, eat your rum baba and clear off, and don't even *think* about asking for a glass of water if you don't want spit in it. How it has managed to escape this dismal fate is a miracle, but it left me in the right admiring frame of mind, as I wandered back to my hotel through the dark streets, to think that Paris was a very fine place indeed.

*   *   *

IN THE morning I got up early and went for a long walk through the sleeping streets. I love to watch cities wake up and Paris wakes up more abruptly, more startlingly, than any place I know. One minute you have the city to yourself. It's just you and a guy delivering crates of bread, and a couple of droning street-cleaning machines. (It might be worth noting here that Paris spends a hundred dollars a year per head on street cleaning compared with thirty dollars per head in London, which explains why Paris gleams and London is a toilet.) Then all at once it's frantic: cars and buses swishing past in sudden abundance, cafés and kiosks opening, people flying out of the Métro stations like flocks of startled birds, movement everywhere, thousands and thousands of pairs of hurrying legs.

By eight-thirty Paris is a terrible place for walking. There's too much traffic. A blue haze of uncombusted diesel hangs over every boulevard. I know Baron Haussmann made Paris a grand place to look at, but the man had no concept of traffic flow. At the Arc de Triomphe alone, thirteen roads come together. Can you imagine? I mean to say, here you have a city with the world's most pathologically aggressive drivers—drivers who in other circumstances would be given injections of Valium from syringes the sizes of bicycle pumps and confined to their beds with leather straps—and you give them an open space where they can all try to go in any of thirteen directions at once. Is that asking for trouble or what?

It is interesting to note that the French have had this reputation for bad driving since long before the invention of the internal combustion engine. Even in the eighteenth century, British travelers to Paris were remarking on what lunatic drivers the French were, on "the astonishing speed with which the carriages and people moved through the streets. . . . It was not an uncommon sight to see a child run over and probably killed." I quote from Christopher Hibbert's *Grand Tour,* a book whose great virtue is in pointing out that the peoples of Europe have for at least three hundred years been living up to their stereotypes. As long ago as the sixteenth century, travelers were describing the Italians as voluble, unreliable, and hopelessly corrupt; the Germans as gluttonous; the Swiss as irritatingly officious and tidy; the French as, well, insufferably French.

You also constantly keep coming up against these monumental squares and open spaces that are all but impossible to cross on foot. My wife and I, still mere children, went to Paris on our honeymoon and foolishly tried to cross the Place de la Concorde without first leaving our names at the embassy. Somehow she managed to get to the obelisk in the center, but I was stranded in the midst of a Circus Maximus of killer automobiles, waving weakly to my dear spouse of two days and whimpering softly, while hundreds and hundreds of little buff-colored Renaults were bearing down on me with their drivers all wearing expressions like Jack Nicholson in *Batman*.

It still happens. At the Place de la Bastille, a vast open space dominated on its northeastern side by the glossy new Paris Opera House, I spent three quarters of an hour trying to get from the Rue de Lyon to the Rue de St. Antoine. The problem is that the pedestrian crossing lights have been designed with the clear purpose of leaving the foreign visitor confused, humiliated, and, if all goes according to plan, dead.

This is what happens: You arrive at a square to find all the traffic stopped, but the pedestrian light is red and you know that if you venture so much as a foot off the curb all the cars will surge forward and turn you into a gooey crepe. So you wait. After a minute, a blind person comes along and crosses the great cobbled plain without hesitating. Then a ninety-year-old lady in a motorized wheelchair trundles past and wobbles across the cobbles to the other side of the square a quarter of a mile away.

You are uncomfortably aware that all the drivers within fifty yards are sitting with moistened lips watching you expectantly, so you pretend that you don't really want to cross the street at all, that actually you've come over here to look at this interesting *fin de siècle* lamppost. After another minute, 150 preschool children are herded across by their teachers, and then the blind man returns from the other direction with two bags of shopping. Finally, the pedestrian light turns green, and you step off the curb and all the cars come charging at you. And I don't care how paranoid and irrational this sounds; I know for a fact that the people of Paris want me dead.

Eventually, I gave up trying to cross streets in any kind of methodical way and instead just followed whatever route looked least threatening. So it was with some difficulty and not a little surprise that I managed to pick my way by early afternoon to the Louvre, where I found a long, immobile line curled around the entrance courtyard like an abandoned garden hose.

I hovered, undecided whether to join the line, come back later in the faint hope that it would have shrunk, or act like a Frenchman and just jump it. The French were remarkably shameless about this. Every few minutes one would approach the front of the line, pretend to look at his wristwatch, then duck under the barrier and disappear through the door with the people at the front. No one protested, which surprised me. In New York, from where many of these people came, judging by their accents and the bullet holes in their trench coats, the line jumpers would have been seized by the crowd and had their limbs torn from their sockets. Even in London the miscreants would have received a vicious rebuke: "I say, kindly take your place at the back of the line, there's a good fellow"—but here there was not a peep of protest.

I couldn't bring myself to jump the line, but equally I couldn't stand among so much motionless humanity while others were flouting the rule of order and getting away with it. So I passed on, and was rather relieved. The last time I went to the Louvre, in 1972 with Katz, it was swarming with visitors and impossible to see anything. The "Mona Lisa" was like a postage stamp viewed through a crowd of heads from another building, and clearly things had not improved since then.

Besides, there was only one painting I especially wanted to see and that was a remarkable eighteenth-century work, evidently unnoticed by any visitor but me for two hundred years among the Louvre's endless corridors. I almost walked past it myself, but something nicked the edge of my gaze and made me turn. It was a painting of two aristocratic ladies, young and not terribly attractive, standing side by side and wearing nothing at all but their jewels and sly smiles. And here's the thing: One of them had her finger plugged casually— one might almost say absentmindedly—into the other's fundament. I can say with some certainty that this was an activity quite unknown in Iowa, even among the wealthy and well traveled, so I went straight off to find Katz, who had cried in dismay fifteen minutes after entering the Louvre, "There's nothing but pictures and shit in this place," and departed moodily for the coffee shop, saying he would wait there for me for thirty minutes and no more. I found him sitting with a Coke, complaining bitterly that he had had to pay two francs for it *and* give a handful of centimes to an old crone for the privilege of peeing in the men's room ("And she watched me the whole time").

"Never mind about that," I said. "You've got to come and see this painting."

"What for?"

"It's very special."

"Why?"

"It just is, believe me. You'll be thanking me in a minute."

"What's so special about it?"

I told him. He refused to believe it. No such picture had ever been painted, and if it had been painted, it wouldn't be hanging in a public gallery. But he came. And the problem was, I couldn't for the life of me find it again. Katz was convinced it was just a cruel joke, designed to waste his time and deprive him of the last two ounces of his Coke, and he spent the rest of the day in a tetchy frame of mind.

Katz was in a tetchy frame of mind throughout most of our stay in Paris. He was convinced everything was out to get him. On the morning of our second day, we were strolling down the Champs-Elysées when a bird shit on his head. "Did you know," I asked a block or two later, "that a bird's shit on your head?"

Instinctively, Katz put a hand to his head, looked at it in horror, and with only a mumbled "Wait here," walked with ramrod stiffness in the direction of our hotel. When he reappeared twenty minutes later, he smelled overpoweringly of Brut aftershave and his hair was plastered down like a third-rate Spanish gigolo's, but he appeared to have regained his composure. "I'm ready now," he announced.

Almost immediately another bird shit on his head. Only this time it *really* shit. I don't want to get too graphic, in case you're snacking or anything, but if you can imagine a pot of yogurt upended onto his scalp, I think you'll get the picture. It was running down the sides of his head and everything. "Gosh, Steve, that was one sick bird," I observed helpfully.

Katz was literally speechless. Without a word he turned and

walked stiffly back to the hotel, ignoring the turning heads of pass-ersby. He was gone for nearly an hour. When at last he returned, he was wearing a poncho with the hood up. "Just don't say a word," he warned me and strode past. He never really warmed to Paris after that.

WITH THE Louvre packed, I went to the new—new to me, at any rate—Musée d'Orsay, on the Left Bank opposite the Tuileries. When I had last passed it, sixteen years earlier, it had been a derelict hulk, the shell of the old Gare d'Orsay, but some person of vision had decided to restore the old station as a museum, and it is simply wonderful, both as a building and as a collection of pictures. I spent two happy hours there, and afterward checked out the situation at the Louvre—still hopelessly crowded—and went instead to the Pom-pidou Center, which I was determined to try to like, but I couldn't. Everything about it seemed wrong. For one thing, it was a bit weath-ered and faded, like a child's toy that has been left out over winter, which surprised me because it is only a dozen years old and the government had just spent $75 million refurbishing it, but I guess that's what you get when you build with plastic. And it seemed much too overbearing a structure for its cramped neighborhood. It would be an altogether different building in a park.

But what I really dislike about buildings like the Pompidou Cen-ter, and Paris is choking on them, is that they are just showing off. Here's Richard Rogers saying to the world: "Look, I put all the pipes on the *outside*. Am I cute enough to kiss or *what*?" I could excuse that if some consideration were given to function. But no one seems to have thought what the Pompidou Center should do—be a gathering place, a haven—because inside it is just crowded and confusing. The center has none of the sense of space and light and majestic calm of the Musée d'Orsay. It's like a department store on the first day of a big sale. There's hardly any place to sit and no focal point—no big clock or anything—at which to meet someone. It has no heart.

Outside things are no better. The main plaza on the Rue St.-Martin is in the shade during the best part of the day and it is built on a slope, so it's dark and the rain never dries and again there's no place to sit. If they had made the slope into a kind of amphitheater, people could sit on the steps, but now if you sit down you feel as if you are going to slide to the bottom.

I have nothing against novelty in buildings—I am quite taken with the glass pyramid at the Louvre and those buildings at La Défense that have the huge holes in the middle—but I just hate the way architects, city planners, and everyone else responsible for urban life seem to have lost sight of what cities are for. They are for people. That is obvious enough, but for half a century we have been building cities that are designed for almost anything else: for cars, for businesses, for developers, for people with money and bold visions who refuse to see cities from ground level, as places in which people must live and function and get around. Why should I have to walk through a damp tunnel and negotiate two sets of stairs to get across a busy street? Why should cars be given priority over me? How can we be so rich and so stupid at the same time? It is the curse of our century— too much money, too little sense—and the Pompidou Center seems to be a kind of celebration of that in plastic.

ONE EVENING I walked over to the Place de la République and had a nostalgic dinner at a bistro called Le Thermomètre. My wife and I spent our honeymoon in the Hôtel Moderne across the way (now a Holiday Inn, alas, alas) and dined nightly at the Thermomètre because it was cheap and we had next to no money. I had spent the whole of my savings, some eighteen pounds, on a suit for the wedding—a remarkable piece of apparel with lapels that had been modeled on the tail fins of a 1957 Coupe de Ville and bell-bottom pants so copiously flared that when I walked, you didn't see my legs move—and had to borrow twelve pounds spending money from my father-in-law in order, as I pointed out, to keep his daughter from starving during her first week of married life.

I expected the Thermomètre to be full of happy memories, but I couldn't remember anything about it at all except that it had the fiercest toilet attendant in Paris, a woman who looked like a Russian wrestler (a male Russian wrestler) and who sat at a table in the basement with a pink dish full of small coins and craned her head to watch you to make sure you didn't dribble on the tiles or pocket any of the urinal cakes. It is hard enough to pee when you are aware that someone's eyes are on you, but when you fear that at any moment you will be felled by a rabbit chop to the kidneys for taking too much time, you seize up altogether. You couldn't have cleared my system with Drāno. So eventually I would zip up and return unrelieved to the table, and spend the night back at the hotel doing a series of Niagara Falls impressions. This time around, I'm pleased to say, the toilet attendant was no longer there; there actually was none at all. But just the same, I didn't take any urinal cakes.

It took me two or three days to notice it, but the people of Paris had become polite over the last twenty years. They didn't exactly rush up and embrace you and thank you for winning the war for them, but they had certainly become more patient and accommodating. The cab drivers were still complete jerks, but everyone else—shopkeepers, waiters, the police—seemed almost friendly. I even saw a waiter smile once. And somebody held open a door for me instead of letting it bang in my face.

It began to unsettle me. Then on my last night, as I was strolling near the Seine, a well-dressed family of two adults and two teenaged children swept past me on the narrow sidewalk and, without breaking stride or interrupting their animated conversation, flicked me into the gutter. I could have hugged them.

They still haven't got the hang of lining up in Paris. I had forgotten about this until the morning of my departure when I trudged through a gray rain to the Gare de Lyon to get a cab to the Gare du Nord and a train to Brussels. Because of the rain, there were no cabs, so I stood and waited. For five minutes I was the only person there, but gradually other people came along and took places behind me.

When at last a cab arrived and pulled up directly in front of me, I was astonished to discover that seventeen grown men and women believed they had a perfect right to try to get in ahead of me. A middle-aged man in a cashmere coat who was obviously wealthy and well-educated actually laid hands on me. I maintained possession by making a series of aggrieved Gallic honking noises—"Mais, non! Mais, non!"—and using my bulk to block the door. I leaped in, resisting the chance to catch the pushy man's tie in the door and let him trot along with us to the Gare du Nord, and told the driver to get me the hell out of there. He looked at me as if I were a large, imperfectly formed turd, and with a disgusted sigh engaged first gear. I was glad to see some things never change.

5

BRUSSELS

I GOT off at the wrong station in Brussels, which is easy enough to do if you are a little bit stupid and you have been dozing and you awake with a start to see a platform sign outside the window that says BRUXELLES. I leaped up in a mild panic and hastened to the exit, knocking passengers on the head with my rucksack as I passed, like a boy with a stick on a picket fence, and sprang Peter Pan–like onto the platform just as the train threw a steamy *whoosh!* at my legs and pulled out.

It didn't seem odd to me that I was the only passenger to alight at the station, or that the station itself was eerily still, until I stepped outside into that gritty drizzle that hangs perpetually over Brussels, and realized I was in a part of the city I had never seen before; one of those anonymous neighborhoods where the buildings are gray and every end wall has a three-story advertisement painted on it and the shops sell things like swimming pool pumps and signs that say NO PARKING—GARAGE IN CONSTANT USE. I had wanted Bruxelles Centrale and would have settled for the Gare du Nord or the Gare du Midi or even the obscure Gare Josaphat, but this was none of these, and I had no idea where I was. I set my face in a dogged expression and trudged toward what I thought might be the downtown—a hint of tall buildings on a distant, drizzly horizon.

I had been to Brussels a couple of times before and thought I knew the city reasonably well, so I kept telling myself that any minute I would start to recognize things, and sometimes even said, "Say, that looks kind of familiar," and would trudge a quarter of a mile to what I thought might be the back of the Palais de Justice, but which proved to be a dog food factory. I walked and walked down long

streets that never changed character or even acquired any, just endless blocks of gray sameness, which Brussels seems to possess in
greater abundance than almost anywhere else in Europe.

I hate asking directions. I am always afraid that the person I approach will step back and say, "You want to go *where*? The center of
Brussels? Boy, are you lost. This is *Lille,* you dumb shit." So I
trudged on. Just when I reached the point where I was beginning to
think seriously about phoning my wife in England and asking her to
come and find me ("And listen, honey, bring some candy bars and
the Sunday papers"), I turned a corner and there to my considerable
surprise was the Manneken-Pis, the chubby little statue of a naked
boy having a pee, the inexpressibly kitschy symbol of the city, and
suddenly I knew where I was and all my little problems melted. I
celebrated by buying a Manneken-Pis cake plate and a family-sized
Toblerone at one of the 350 souvenir shops that line the street, and
felt better still.

Fifteen minutes later, I was in a room at the Hôtel Adolphe Sax,
lying on the bed with my shoes on (disintegrating into a hermitic
slobbiness is one of the incidental pleasures of solitary travel), breaking my teeth on the Toblerone, and watching some daytime television offering on BBC-1—a panel discussion involving people who
were impotent or from Wolverhampton or suffering some other
personal catastrophe, the precise nature of which eludes me now—
and in half an hour was feeling sufficiently refreshed to venture out
into Brussels.

I always stay in the Adolphe Sax because it gets BBC-1 on the TV
and because the elevators are so interesting, a consideration that I was
reminded of now as I stood in the corridor beside an illuminated
DOWN button, passing the time, as one does, by humming the "Waiting for an Elevator Song" ("Doo dee doo dee doo dee doo doo"),
looking speculatively at my neck in the mirror, and wondering idly
why hotel hallway carpet is always *so* ugly.

Generally speaking, they don't understand elevators in Europe.
Even in the newer buildings, the elevators are almost always pain-
fully slow, and often they lack certain features that are elsewhere
considered essential, like an inside door, so that if you absentmindedly lean forward, you are likely to end up with one arm twenty-

seven feet longer than the other. But even by these standards the elevators at the Adolphe Sax are exceptional.

You get on, intending to go downstairs for breakfast, but find that the elevator descends without instructions, past the lobby, past the underground garage and basement, and down to an unmarked sub-basement, where the doors open briefly to reveal a hall full of steam and toiling coolies. As you fiddle uselessly with the buttons (which are obviously not connected to anything), the doors clang shut and, with a sudden burst of vigor, the elevator shoots upward to the eleventh floor at a speed that makes your face feel as if it were melting, pauses for a tantalizing half second, drops ten feet, pauses again, and then free-falls to the lobby. You emerge, blood trickling from your ears, and walk with as much dignity as you can muster into the dining room.

So you can perhaps conceive my relief at finding now that the elevator conveyed me without incident to my destination, apart from an unscheduled stop at the second floor and a brief, but not unpleasant, return trip to the fourth.

BRUSSELS, IT must be said, is not the greatest of cities for venturing through. After Paris, it was a relief just to cross a street without feeling as if I had a bull's-eye painted on my butt, but once I'd done a couple of circuits of the Grand' Place and looked politely in the windows of one or two of the many thousands of shops selling chocolates or lace (they appear to sell nothing else in Brussels), I began to find myself glancing at my watch and wondering if 9:47 in the morning was too early to start drinking.

I settled instead for another circuit of the Grand' Place. It is fetching, no doubt about it. It is the centerpiece of the city, a nicely proportioned cobbled square surrounded by grand and ornate buildings: the truly monumental Hôtel de Ville and opposite it the only slightly less grand Maison du Roi (which despite its name has never been a royal palace—don't say you never learned anything from me), all of them linked by narrow, ornately decorated guildhalls. The ground floors of these guildhalls almost all contain dark, cozy cafés, full of wooden furniture and crackling fires, where you can sit over a coffee or beer and gaze out on this most beguiling of backdrops. Many people seem to spend whole days doing little else. I opted for De Gulden Boot, even though on a previous visit I had been shamelessly shortchanged there by a waiter who mistook me for a common tourist just because I was wearing a Manneken-Pis tracksuit, and I had to put on my severest "Don't fuck with me, Gaston" look in order to get my full complement of change. But I don't bear grudges, except against Richard Nixon, and didn't hesitate to go in there now. It's the nicest café on the square and I believe that a little elegance with a cup of coffee is worth paying for. But watch your change, ladies.

I spent two and a half days seeing the sights—the grand and splendid Musée d'Art Ancien, the Musée d'Art Moderne, the two historical museums in the ponderously named Parc du Cinquantenaire (the museums were a bit ponderous, too), the Musée Horta, and even the gloomy and practically forgotten Institut des Sciences Naturelles—and in between times I just shuffled around among the endless office complexes in a pleasantly vacant state of mind.

Brussels is a seriously ugly place, full of wet litter, boulevards like freeways, and muddy building sites. It is a city of gray offices and faceless office workers, the briefcase capital of Europe. It has fewer parks than any city I can think of, and almost no other features to commend it—no castle on a hill, no mountainous cathedral, no street of singularly elegant shops, no backdrop of snowy peaks, no fairy-lighted seafront. It doesn't even have a river. How can a city not at least have a river? They did once have some city walls, but all that remains of them is a crumbly fragment stuck next door to a bowling alley on the Rue des Alexiens. The best thing that can be said for Brussels is that it is only three hours from Paris. If I were in charge of the EEC, and frankly you could do worse, my first move would be to transfer the capital to Dublin or Glasgow or possibly Naples, where the jobs would be appreciated and where the people still have some pride in their city, because in Brussels, alas, they simply don't.

It would be hard to think of a place that has shown less regard for its heritage. Example: Brussels was for thirty-five years the home of the father of Art Nouveau architecture, Victor Horta, who was so celebrated in his lifetime that they made him a baron—Horta was to

Brussels what Mackintosh was to Glasgow and Gaudí to Barcelona—but even so the sluggardly city authorities over the years allowed developers to demolish almost all his finest buildings: the Galeries Anspach department store, the Maison du Peuple, the Brugmann hospital, the Rogier house. Now there is remarkably little in Brussels worth looking at. You can walk for hours and not see a single sight to lift the heart.

I am assured that things are getting better. It used to be that when you emerged from the central station your first view of Brussels was downhill across the roofs of the old town, and in the very center of this potentially arresting setting, in the sort of open space into which other cities would have inserted a golden cathedral or baroque town hall, sat a parking lot and gas station. Now both of those have been torn down, and some new brick buildings—not brilliant architecturally, but certainly an improvement on the gas station—have been erected in their place. I was assured again and again by locals that the city government has at last recognized its slack attitude toward development and begun to insist on buildings of some architectural distinction, but the evidence of this so far is rather less than overwhelming.

The one corner of charm in the city is a warren of narrow, pedestrian-only streets behind the Grand' Place called, with a mildly pathetic dash of hyperbole, the Sacred Isle. Here the little lanes and passageways are packed with restaurants and crowds of people wandering around in the happy state of deciding where to eat, nosing among the iced barrows of lobsters, mussels, and crayfish that stand outside each establishment. From every doorway wafts a warm, rich draft of grilling aromas, and every window reveals crowds of people enjoying themselves at almost any hour of the day or night. It is remorselessly picturesque and appealing, and it has been like this since the Middle Ages, and yet even this lovable, clubby little neighborhood came within an ace of being bulldozed in the 1960s. Wherever you go in Europe, you find yourself wondering what sort of brain-wasting disease it was that affected developers and architects in the 1960s and 1970s, but nowhere is this sensation stronger than in Brussels.

Yet I like Brussels. I like it a lot. It's the friendliest big city in

Europe (which may or may not have something to do with the fact that a quarter of its residents come from abroad), it has a couple of good museums, the oldest shopping arcade in Europe, the small but pleasurable Galerie St. Hubert, lots of terrific bars, and the most wonderful restaurants. Eating out is the Belgian national sport, and Brussels alone has fifteen hundred restaurants, twenty-three of them carrying Michelin rosettes. You can eat incredibly well for less than almost anywhere else on the Continent. I dined in the Sacred Isle every night. The restaurants are invariably tiny—to reach a table at the back you have to all but climb over half a dozen diners—and the tables are squeezed so tightly together that you cannot cut your steak without poking your neighbor in the cheek with an elbow or dragging your sleeve through his sauce Béarnaise, but in an odd way that's part of the enjoyment. You find that you are in effect dining with the people next to you, sharing bread rolls and little pleasantries. This is a novel pleasure for the lone traveler, who usually gets put at the darkest table, next to the Gents', and spends his meal watching a procession of strangers adjusting their flies and giving their hands a shake as they pass.

After dinner each night I would go for a necessarily aimless stroll—there is nothing much to aim for—but, like most cities, Brussels is always better at night. I walked one evening up to the massive Palais de Justice, which broods on a small eminence overlooking the old town and looks like an American state capitol building that has been taking steroids. It is enormous—it covers 280,000 square feet and was the largest building built anywhere in the world in the nineteenth century—but the only truly memorable thing about it is its bulk. Another evening, I walked out to the headquarters of the EEC. In a city of buildings so ugly they take your breath away, the headquarters of the EEC at Rond-Point Schuman manages to stand out. It was only six o'clock, but there wasn't a soul about, not a single person working late, which made me think of the old joke: How many people work in the European Commission? Answer: About a third of them. You cannot look at all those long rows of windows without wondering what on earth goes on in there. I suppose there are whole wings devoted to making sure that post office lines are of a uniform length throughout the community and that a soft-drinks machine in France dispenses the same proportion of upside-down cups as one in Italy.

As an American, I find it interesting to watch the richest countries of Europe enthusiastically ceding their sovereignty to a body that appears to be out of control and answerable to no one. Did you know that because of its byzantine structure, the European Commission does not even know "how many staff members it has or what they all do"? (I quote from *The Economist*.) I find this worrying. For my part I decided to dislike the EEC when I discovered that they were taking away Britain's smart hardbacked navy blue passports and replacing them with flimsy red books that look like the identity papers of a Polish seaman. This is always the problem with large institutions. They have no style.

I don't know much about how the EEC works, but here is an interesting fact that I think gives some perspective to its achievements: In 1972, the European Conference on Post and Telecommunications called for a common international telephone code for Common Market nations—namely 00. Since then the various member states have been trying to reach agreement. So far, not one of them has adopted the code, but give them another eighteen years and things may start to happen.

~~~~~~

6

BELGIUM

~~~~~~

I SPENT a couple of pleasantly pointless days wandering around Belgium by train. As countries go, Belgium is a curiosity. It's not one nation, but two: northern, Dutch-speaking Flanders and southern, French-speaking Wallonia. The southern half possesses the most outstanding scenery, the prettiest villages, the best gastronomy and, withal, a Gallic knack for living well, while the north has the finest cities, the most outstanding museums and churches, the ports, the coastal resorts, the bulk of the population, and most of the money.

The Flemings can't stand the Walloons and the Walloons can't stand the Flemings, but when you talk to them a little you realize that what holds them together is an even deeper disdain for the French and the Dutch. I once walked around Antwerp for a day with a Dutch-speaking local, and on every corner he would indicate to me with sliding eyes some innocent-looking couple and mutter disgustedly under his breath: "Dutch." He was astonished that I couldn't tell the difference between a Dutch person and a Fleming.

When pressed on their objections, the Flemings become a trifle vague. The most common complaint I heard was that the Dutch drop in unannounced at mealtimes and never bring gifts. "Ah, like our own dear Scots," I would say.

I learned much of this in Antwerp, where I stopped for an afternoon to see the cathedral and stayed on into the evening, wandering among the many bars, which must be about the finest and most numerous in Europe: small, snug, smoky places, full of dark paneling and dim, yellowy light, and always crowded with bright, happy-looking people having a good time. It is an easy city in which to strike up conversations because the people are so open and their English is nearly always perfect. I talked for an hour to two young street sweepers who had stopped for a drink on their way home. Where else but northern Europe could an outsider talk to street sweepers in his own tongue?

It struck me again and again how much they know about us and how little we know about them. You could read English newspapers for months, and American newspapers forever, and never see a single article about Belgium, and yet interesting things happen there.

Consider the Gang of Nijvel. This was a terrorist group which, for a short period in the mid-1980s, roamed the country (to the extent that it is possible to roam in Belgium), and from time to time would burst into supermarkets or crowded restaurants and spray the area with gunfire, killing at random—women, children, anyone who happened to be in the way. Having left bodies everywhere, the gang would take a relatively small sum of money from the tills and disappear into the night. The strange thing is this: The gang never revealed its motives, never took hostages, never stole more than a few hundred pounds. The group didn't even have a name that anyone knew. The Gang of Nijvel label was pinned on it by the press because its getaway cars were Volkswagen GTIs stolen from somewhere in the Brussels suburb of Nijvel. After about six months, the attacks abruptly stopped and have never been resumed. The gunmen were never caught, their weapons were never found, the police haven't the faintest idea who they were or what they wanted. Now isn't that strange? Yet you probably have never read about it in your local newspaper. I think *that's* pretty strange, too.

I **WENT** to Bruges for a day. It's only thirty miles from Brussels and so beautiful, so deeply, endlessly gorgeous, that it is hard to believe it could be the same country. Everything about Bruges was perfect—its cobbled streets, bottle-green canals, steep-roofed medieval houses, market squares, slumbering parks, everything. No city has been better favored by decline. For two hundred years Bruges—I don't know why we persist in calling it that because the locals spell it Brugge and it is pronounced "Broogah"—was the most prosperous city in Europe, but the silting up of the river Zwyn and changing political circumstances made it literally a backwater, and for five hundred years, while other cities grew and were endlessly transformed, Bruges remained forgotten and untouched. When Wordsworth visited in the nineteenth century, he found grass growing in the streets. Antwerp, I've been told, was more beautiful still, even as late as the turn of this century, but developers moved in and pulled down everything they could get their hands on, which was pretty much everything. Bruges was saved by its obscurity.

It is a rare place. I walked for a day with my mouth open. I looked in at the Groeninge Museum and visited the famous Béguinage, its courtyard lawns swimming in daffodils, but mostly I just walked the streets, agog at such a concentration of perfection. Even the size of Bruges was perfect—big enough to be a city, to have bookstores and interesting restaurants, but compact enough to feel contained and friendly. You could walk every street within its encircling canal in a day or so. I did just that and never once saw a street I wouldn't want to live on, a bar I wouldn't like to get to know, a view I wouldn't wish to call my own. It was hard to accept that the place was real—that people came home to these houses every night and shopped in these shops and walked their dogs on these streets and went through life thinking that this is the way of the world. They must go into a deep, reverberating shock when they first see Brussels.

An insurance claims adjuster I got to talking to in a bar on St. Jakobstraat told me sadly that Bruges had become insufferable for eight months of the year because of the tourists, and related to me what he clearly thought were disturbing anecdotes about visitors peeking through his letter box and crushing his geraniums in the pursuit of snapshots. But I didn't listen to him, partly because he was the most boring person in the bar, possibly in Flanders, and partly because I just didn't care to hear it. I wanted my illusions intact.

For that reason I left early in the morning, before any tour buses could arrive. I went to Dinant, a riverside town on the banks of the stately Meuse, crouching this day beneath a steady rain. It was an attractive place, and I would doubtless have been highly pleased with it if I hadn't just come from Bruges and if the weather hadn't been so dreadful. I stood on the bridge across the river and watched raindrops the size of bullets beat circles in the water. My intention had been to hike through the southern Ardennes for a couple of days to see if I could recognize any of the little villages and roads I had walked around on my first trip, but I hadn't packed for this kind of weather—I was already soaked through and shivering as if I had forgotten to take my malaria tablets—and instead, after only an hour in Dinant, I walked back to the station, caught the first train to Namur, and traveled on to Spa. One of the virtues of Belgium is that its tininess allows you to be anywhere else within an hour or two. It takes a while to get used to the idea that the whole country is effectively a suburb of Brussels.

I had no particular reason to go to Spa, except that it always sounded like a nice place, and indeed it proved to be, set in a bowl of green hills, with a wooded park, the Parc de Sept Heures, a grand casino out of all proportion to the surrounding town, and a pair of big white hotels standing around a little island of green called the Place Verte. I liked it immediately. The rain had stopped and left the town with a clean, fresh feel, vaguely reminiscent of sheets lifted warm from a tumble dryer, and it had an eerily timeless air of convalescence about it. I half expected to see limbless soldiers in brown uniforms being pushed through the park in wheelchairs.

Spa is the original spa town, from which all the others take their name, and for two hundred years it was the haunt of Europe's royalty. Even up to the First World War it catered to aristocrats and grandees. It was from Spa that Kaiser Wilhelm abdicated, a milestone that marked its decline as much as his own. Today it didn't seem to cater to anyone much, at least not at this time of year. I went to the tourist information center in the park, and, after browsing politely at the displays, asked the man behind the counter where all the kings and queens were.

"Ah, they do not come anymore," he said with a sad smile. "Not so much since Peter the Great."

"Why not?"

He shrugged. "Fashions change. Now they want the sunshine, the sea. We still get the odd baron, but mostly it is wealthy Germans. There are many treatments available if you are interested." He waved a hand over a selection of brochures and went off to help a new caller.

The brochures were all for places with no-nonsense names like the Professor Henrijean Hydrology Institute and the Spa Therm Institution's Department of Radiology and Gastro-Enterology. Between them they offered an array of treatments that ran from immersion in "natural carbogazeous baths" and slathering in hot and gooey mud-packs to being connected to a freestanding electrical substation and briskly electrocuted, or so it appeared from the photograph. These treatments were guaranteed to do a number of things I didn't realize it was desirable to do—"dilate the dermal vessels," "further the repose of the thermoregulatory centers," and "ease periarticular contractures," to name but three.

I decided without hesitation that my thermoregulatory centers were reposed enough, if not actually deceased, and although I do have the occasional periarticular contracture and pitch forward into my spaghetti, I decided I could live with this after seeing what the muscular, white-coated ladies of the Spa institutes do to you if they detect so much as a twinge in your periarticulars or suspect any backsliding among the dermals. The photographs showed a frankly worried-looking female patient being variously covered in tar, blown around a shower stall with a high-pressure hose, forced to recline in bubbling copper vats, and otherwise subjected to a regimen that in other circumstances would bring ineluctably to mind the expression "war crimes." I looked at the list of the town's approved doctors to see if Josef Mengele appeared anywhere, but the only memorable name was a Dr. Pitz. Resisting the impulse to phone him up and say, "Well, are you?," I went instead to a small hotel recommended to me by the man in the tourist office.

I showered, dined, had a diverting stroll through the town, and repaired to a convivial little bar on the Rue Royale for an evening with Martin Gilbert's grave and monumental history of the Second World War. It is not a pub book, I can tell you now. You read a little and before long you find yourself staring vacantly around you and longing for a conversation.

But hardly anyone in Wallonia speaks English. I began to regret that I didn't understand French well enough to eavesdrop. I took three years of French in school, but learned next to nothing. The trouble was that the textbooks were so amazingly useless. They were always written by somebody clearly out of touch with the Franco-phile world—Professor Marvis Frisbee of the Highway 68 State Teachers College at Windsock, North Dakota, or something—and at no point did they intersect with the real world. They never told you any of the things you would need to know in France—how to engage a bidet, deal with a toilet matron, or kneecap a line-jumper. They were always tediously preoccupied with classroom activities: hanging up coats in the cloakroom, cleaning the blackboard, opening the window, shutting the window, setting out the day's lessons. Even in the seventh grade I could see that this sort of thing would be of limited utility in the years ahead. How often on a visit to France do you need to tell someone you want to clean a blackboard? How frequently do you wish to say: "It is winter. Soon it will be spring." In my experience, people know this already.

I AWOKE to find rain streaming down the windows. The streets were half flooded and the cars below *whooshed* as they passed. I went out to cash a traveler's check and window-shopped along the Place Verte, sheltering beneath awnings on which the rain drummed steadily and soothingly. Every shop was filled with the most tempting foodstuffs—La Raclette Fromagerie, with cheeses the size of automobile tires; the Boucherie Wagener, where strings of sausages hung in the window and thinly sliced smoked Ardennes ham lay neatly stacked; La Gâterie, in whose window was a delirium of marzipan fruits, hyperventilating cream cakes, and other frothy delights. How clever these continentals are with their shop windows. Even the windows of pharmacies are so tidy and clean and scrupulously arranged that you find yourself gazing longingly at corn plasters and incontinence pads.

When I reached the last shop, I stared emptily for a long moment at the Place Verte, not certain what to do with myself, and decided impulsively to push on to Durbuy in the hope that the weather would be better there. This was unlikely, considering that Durbuy was only fifteen miles away. Nonetheless, thanks to the bewildering peculiarities of the Belgian railway system, to get to Durbuy took most of the morning and required three separate (albeit short) journeys, and even then I couldn't quite get there, as Durbuy has no station. The closest I could get was Barvaux, which on the map is about half a millimeter to the left of Durbuy, but which in reality is four kilometers away, with a monumentally steep hill in between. Even from the station I could hear trucks straining to climb it. But at least the rain had stopped.

I thought I would take a cab, but there was none at the station, so I walked into the town—really a large village on the bend of a busy road—looking for a bus stop or a cab office, and went into a hotel on the main street and discovered from the dour patroness that Barvaux had neither cabs nor buses. In my best schoolboy French, I asked how then one gets to Barvaux when one is *sans auto*. I braced for the lady to put a dead beaver on the counter, but she just said, "À pied, monsieur," and gave me one of those impassive Gallic shrugs—the kind where the chin is dropped to belt level and the ears are pushed to the top of the head with the shoulders. You have to be Gallic to do it. It translates roughly as "Life is a bucket of shit, monsieur, I quite agree, and while I am prepared to acknowledge this fact, I shall offer you no sympathy because, monsieur, this is your bucket of shit."

Thanking her for playing such a small and passing role in my life, I walked to the edge of town and was confronted by a feature of landscape that was more wall than hill. The road was lined by the sort of unappealing houses that get built along any busy road and look as if they are being slowly shaken to pieces by heavy traffic. Each yard was enclosed with a chain link fence, behind each of which dozed a dog named Spike, who would leap to life and come flying down the front path as I approached and fling himself repeatedly at the gate, barking and baring his teeth and wanting to strip the flesh from my flanks in the worst way.

I don't know why it is, but something about me incites dogs to a frenzy. I would be a rich man if I had a nickel for every time a dog tried to get at the marrow in my ankle bone while the owner just stood there and said, "Well, I don't understand it, he's never done anything like this before. You must have said something to him." That always knocks me out. What would I say to the dog? "Hello, boy, like to open a vein in my leg?"

The only time a dog will not attack me with a view to putting me in a wheelchair is when I'm a guest at someone's house, sitting on a deep sofa with a drink filled to the brim. In this case the dog—it's always a large dog with a saliva problem—will decide he doesn't want to kill me but to have sex with me. "Come on, Bill, get your pants off. I'm *hot*," he seems to be saying. The owner says: "Is he bothering you?" I answer: "No, Jim, I adore it when a dog gets his teeth around my balls and frantically rubs the side of my head with his rear leg."

"I can put him out if he's bothering you," the owner adds. Hey, I want to reply, don't put him out, put him *down*.

It wouldn't bother me in the least if all the dogs in the world were placed in a large sack and taken to some distant island—Greenland springs attractively to mind—where they could romp around and sniff each other's anuses to their hearts' content and would never bother or terrorize me again. The only kind of dog I would excuse from this roundup is poodles. Poodles I would shoot.

To my mind, the only possible pet is a cow. Cows love you. They are harmless, they look nice, they don't need a box to crap in, they keep the grass down, and they are so trusting and stupid that you can't help but lose your heart to them. Where I live in Yorkshire, there's a herd of cows down the lane. You can stand by the wall at any hour of the day or night, and after a minute the cows will all waddle over and stand with you, much too stupid to know what to do next, but happy just to be with you. They will stand there all day, as far as I can tell, possibly till the end of time. They will listen to your problems and never ask a thing in return. They will be your friends forever. And when you get tired of them, you can kill them and eat them. Perfect.

D U R B U Y   L A Y at the foot of a startlingly steep road on the other side of the hill. It looked to be about a half a mile below me. It was the kind of hill that once you started down, you couldn't guarantee to stop. I walked with an increasing loss of control, my legs moving beneath me as if on stilts. By the last bend I was really just a passenger on a pair of alien stumps, which were frantically scissoring me toward a stone barn at the foot of the road. I could see myself going through it like a character in a cartoon, leaving a body-shaped hole, but instead I did a more interesting thing. I stepped heavily in a wobbly drain, spectacularly spraining my ankle—I'm sure I heard a crack as of splintering wood—did a series of graceless pirouettes, putting me in mind of the Frankenstein monster on roller skates, spun across the road, smacked face first into the barn wall, and, after teetering theatrically for a moment, fell backward.

I lay still in the tall grass, taking a minute to accommodate the idea that down at the bottom of my right leg there was an unusual measure of agony going on. At intervals I raised my chin to my chest and gazed down the length of my body to see if my right foot was facing backward or otherwise composed in a way that would account for the vividness of the pain, but it looked normal enough. From where I lay I could also see back up the hill, and I spent some time wondering, in a curiously abstracted way, how I was gong to get back up there with no buses or cabs to call on.

Eventually, I hauled myself upright, using the barn as support, and hobbled erratically to a café, where I fell into a chair near the door and ordered a Coca-Cola. I took off my boot and sock and examined my ankle, expecting—and indeed, in that perverse manner of the injured male, rather hoping—to find some splintered bone straining at the skin like a tent pole, making everyone who saw it queasy. But the ankle was just faintly bluish and tender and very slightly swollen, and I realized that once more in my life I had merely achieved acute pain and not the sort of grotesque injury that would lead to a mercy flight by helicopter and a fussing-over by young nurses in erotically starched uniforms. I sat glumly sipping my Coke for half an hour and discovered upon arising that the worst of the pain had subsided and I was able to walk after a fashion.

So I had a limping look round Durbuy. It was exceptionally pretty and pleasant, with narrow back streets and houses built of stone beneath slate roofs. At one end stood a chateau lifted wholesale from a fairy tale. Beneath it was a shallow, racing river, the Ourthe. All around were strangely overbearing green hills that for centuries had kept the outside world outside. I gathered from the size of the parking lots that this was a popular spot with day-trippers, but there was hardly anyone about now and most of the shops were shut. I spent a couple of hours in the town, mostly sitting on a bench by the river, absorbed by scenery and birdsong. It was impossible to imagine that this perpetually tranquil place had been the epicenter, more or less, of the Battle of the Bulge almost within my lifetime. I lugged out Gilbert's magisterial history of the Second World War and skimmed through the index. Durbuy and Barvaux didn't get a mention, but many of the other neighboring towns and villages did—Malmédy, where 72 captured American soldiers were taken into a field by an SS unit and machine-gunned rather than be kept as prisoners; Stavelot, where two days later the ever-busy subhumans of the SS killed 130 Belgian civilians, including 23 children; Bastogne, where American forces were besieged for a month and hundreds lost their lives; and many others. I simply couldn't take it in—that these terrible, savage things had happened here, in these hills and woods, to people as close to me in time as my father. And yet now it was as if it had never happened. Germans who had once slaughtered women and children in these villages returned as tourists, with cameras around their necks and wives on their arms, as if it had all been just a Hollywood movie. I have been told more than once that one of the more trying things about learning to live with the Germans after the war was having to watch them return with their wives and girlfriends to show off the places they had helped to ruin.

At about three o'clock, it occurred to me that I had better head back to Barvaux. It took me until just after six to reach the station because of the painful slowness of my walking and the frequent rests I took along the route, apart from Mad Dog Hill, as I dubbed it. The station was dark and untended when I arrived. No other passengers were about and the walls were without timetables. I sat on the platform on the opposite side from which I had arrived, not knowing when the next train might come along, not knowing indeed if there might be a next train. It was as lonely a station as you could imagine in such a small and crowded country as Belgium. The tracks stretched in a straight line for two or three miles in either direction. I was cold and tired and my ankle throbbed. More than that, I was hungry. I hadn't eaten all day.

In my lonely, enfeebled state, I began to think about my old hometown diner. It was called the Y Not Grill, which everyone assumed was short for Y Not Come In and Get Food Poisoning. It was a strange place. I was about to say it was an awful place, but in fact, like most things connected with one's adolescence, it was wonderful and awful at the same time. The food was terrible, the waitresses notoriously testy and stupid, and the cooks were escaped convicts of doubtful hygiene. They generally had one of those permanent, snuffly colds that mark a dissolute life-style, and invariably a droplet of moisture hung from the tips of their noses. You always knew, with a sense of stoic doom, that when the chef turned around and put your food before you, the drip would be gone from his nose and instead lay glistening on top of your hamburger bun, like a bead of morning dew.

The Y Not had a waitress named Shirley who was the most unpleasant person I have ever met. Whatever you ordered, she would look as if you just asked to borrow her car to take her daughter to Tijuana for a filthy weekend.

"You want *what?*" she would say.

"A guinea grinder and onion rings," you would repeat apologetically. "Please, Shirley. If it's not too much trouble. When you get a minute."

Shirley would stare at you for up to five minutes, as if memorizing your features for the police report, then scrawl the order on a pad and shout out to the cook in the curious dopey lingo they use in diners: "Two loose stools and a bucket of mud," or whatever.

In a Hollywood movie, Shirley would have been played by Marjorie Main. She would be gruff and bossy, but you would see in an instant that inside her ample bosom there beat a heart of pure gold. If you unexpectedly gave her a birthday present, she would blush and say, "Aw, ya shouldana oughtana done it, ya big palooka." If you gave the real Shirley a birthday present, she would just say: "What the fuck's this?" Shirley, alas, didn't have a heart of gold. I don't think she had a heart at all, or indeed any redeeming features. She couldn't even put her lipstick on straight.

Yet the Y Not had its virtues. For one thing, it was open all night, which meant that it was always there if you found you were having a grease crisis or just wanted to be among other people in the small hours. It was a haven, a little island of light in the darkness of downtown, very like the diner in Edward Hopper's painting "Nighthawks."

The Y Not is gone now, alas. The owner, it was said, ate some of his own food and died. However, even now I can see it: the steam on the windows, the huddled clusters of night workers, Shirley lifting a passed-out customer's head up by his hair to give the counter a wipe with a damp cloth, a lone man in a cowboy hat lost in daydreams with a cup of coffee and an unfiltered Camel. And I still think of it from time to time, especially in places like southern Belgium, when it's dark and chilly and an empty railway line stretches out to the horizon in two directions.

7

AACHEN AND

COLOGNE

I TOOK a train to Aachen. I hadn't been there before, but it was only a short journey from Liège, where I had spent the night, and I had always wanted to see Aachen Cathedral. This is an odd and pleasantly neglected corner of Europe. Aachen, Maastricht, and Liège are practically neighbors—only about twenty miles separate them—but they are in three countries, and three distinct languages are spoken (Dutch, French, and German); yet the people of the region employ a private dialect that enables them to understand each other better than they can understand their fellow countrymen.

I got a room in a small hotel across from the station, dumped my rucksack, and went straight out. After a lunch of burger and fries in a hamburger chain called Quick (short apparently for "Quick—a bucket"), I then set off to see the town. My eagerness surprised me a little, but I hadn't been to Germany in seventeen years and I wanted to see if it had changed. It had. It had grown even richer. It was rich enough in 1973, but now—golly. Even prosperous Flanders paled beside it. Here, almost every store looked rich and busy and was full of stylish and expensive goods like Mont Blanc pens and Audemars Piguet watches. Even the stores selling mundane items were riveting—J. von der Driesel, for instance, a purveyor of kitchenware and other household goods at the top of a hill near the old market square. This shop's windows displayed nothing more exciting than ironing boards, laundry baskets, and pots and pans, but every pan gleamed, every piece of plastic shone. A little farther on, I passed not one but two shops selling caskets, which seemed a bit chillingly

Germanic, but even they looked sleek and inviting, and I found myself staring in admiration at the quality of the linings and the shine on the handles.

I couldn't get used to the pervasive wealth. I still had the American habit of thinking of Europe as one place and Europeans as essentially one people. For all that you read that Denmark's per-capita gross domestic product is 40 percent higher than Britain's, the Danes don't look 40 percent richer than the British, they don't wear 40 percent shinier shoes or drive 40 percent bigger cars. But in Aachen people *did* look rich and different, and by a factor of much more than 40 percent. Everyone was dressed in clothes that looked as if they had been purchased that morning. Even the children's sneakers weren't scuffed. Every car had a showroom shine on it. Even the taxis were all Mercedes. It looked like Beverly Hills. And this was just an obscure little city on the edge of the country.

Not everything was perfect. Much of the architecture in the city center was blatantly undistinguished, especially the modern shopping precinct, and the bars and restaurants didn't have the snug and convivial air of those in Holland and Belgium. But then I found my way to the calm of the cathedral close and warmed to Aachen anew. I went first to the Schatzkammer, the treasure-house, which contained the finest assortment of reliquaries I ever expect to see, including the famous life-sized golden bust of Charlemagne, looking like a god; a carved sixteenth-century triptych of Pope Gregory's Mass, which I could look at almost forever; and assorted other baubles of extraordinary beauty and craftsmanship.

The whole collection is displayed in three small, plain, feebly lit rooms, but what a collection. Next door was the octagonal cathedral, modeled on the church of San Vitale at Ravenna, and all that remains of a palace complex mostly destroyed during the Second World War. The cathedral was small and dark but exquisite, with its domed roof, its striped bands of contrasting marble, and its stained glass, so rich that it seemed almost liquid. It must have been cramped even in Charlemagne's day—it couldn't seat more than a hundred or so—but every inch of it was superb. It was one of those buildings that you don't so much look at as bathe in. I would go to Aachen tomorrow to see it again.

Afterward I passed the closing hours of the afternoon with a gentle stroll around the town, still favoring my sore ankle. I looked at the large cobbled Marktplatz and tottered out to the preternaturally quiet residential streets around the Lousberg Park. It was curious to reflect that this pleasant backwater was once one of the great cities of Europe, the seat of the Holy Roman Empire, Charlemagne's capital. I didn't realize, until I turned again to Gilbert's history of the Second World War a day or so later, that Aachen was the first German city to fall to the Allies, after a seven-day street battle in 1944 that left almost the whole of it in ruins. You would never guess it now.

IN THE evening I went looking for a restaurant. This is often a problem in Germany. For one thing, there's a good chance that there will be three guys in *lederhosen* playing polka music, so you have to look carefully through the windows and question the proprietor closely to make sure that Willi and the Bavarian Boys won't suddenly bound onto a little stage at half-past eight, because there is nothing worse than being just about to tuck into your dinner, a good book propped in front of you, only to find yourself surrounded by ruddy-faced Germans waving beer steins and singing the "Horst Wessel Lied" for all they're worth. It should have been written into the armistice treaty that the Germans would be required to lay down their accordions along with their arms.

I went to six or eight places and studied the menus by the door, but they were all full of foods with ominous Germanic names— "Schweinensnout mit Spittle und Grit," or "Ramsintestines und Oder Grosser Stuff." I expect that if ordered they would turn out to be reasonably digestible, and possibly even delicious, but I can never get over this nagging fear that I will order at random and the waiter will turn up with a steaming plate of tripe and eyeballs. Once, in Bavaria, Katz and I recklessly ordered Kalbsbrann from an indecipherable menu, and a minute later the proprietor appeared at our table, looking hesitant and embarrassed, wringing his hands on a slaughterhouse apron.

"Excuse me so much, gentlemens," he said, "but are you knowing what Kalbsbrann *is?*"

We looked at each other and allowed that we did not.

"It is, how you say, what ze little cow thinks wiz," he said.

Katz swooned. I thanked the man profusely for his thoughtfulness in drawing this to our attention, though I daresay it was a self-interested desire not to have two young Americans projectile-vomiting across his dining room that brought him to our table, and asked him to provide us something that would pass for food in Iowa. It takes a special kind of vigilance to make your way across a continent where people voluntarily ingest tongues, kidneys, horsemeat, frogs' legs, intestines, sausages made of congealed blood, and the brains of little cows.

Eventually, after walking some distance, I found an Italian restaurant called Capriccio just around the corner from my hotel on Theaterstrasse. The food was Italian, but the employees were all German. My waitress spoke no English, and I had the most extraordinary difficulty getting myself understood. I asked for a beer and she looked at me askance. "Wass? Tier?"

"Nein, beer," I said, and her puzzlement grew.

"Fear? Steer? Queer? King Leer?"

"Nein, nein, *beer.*" I pointed at the menu.

"Ah, *beer,*" she said, with a private "tut," as if I had been intentionally misleading her. I felt abashed for not speaking German, but comforted myself with the thought that if I did understand the language I would know what the pompous man at the next table was boasting about to his wife (or possibly mistress) and then I would no doubt be as bored as she clearly was. She was smoking heavily from a packet of Lord's cigarettes and looking with undisguised interest at all the men in the room except, of course, me. Her companion didn't notice. He was too busy telling her how he had just sold a truckload of Hula Hoops and Leo Sayer albums to the East Germans, and basking in his cunning.

When he laughed, he looked uncannily like Arvis Dreck, my junior high school woodworking teacher, which was an unsettling coincidence, since Mr. Dreck was the very man who had taught me what little German I knew.

I had signed up for German only because it was taught by a walking wet dream named Miss Webster, who had the most magnificent breasts in creation and buttocks that adhered to her skirt like melons in cellophane. Whenever Miss Webster stretched to write on the blackboard, eighteen adolescent boys would breathe hard and let their hands slip below the table. But two weeks after the school year started, Miss Webster departed in mysterious circumstances—mysterious to us, anyway—and Mr. Dreck was drafted in to take over until a replacement could be appointed.

This was a catastrophe. Mr. Dreck knew slightly less than nothing about German. The closest he had come to Germany was a beerfest in Milwaukee. I'm sure he wasn't even remotely qualified to teach the language. He taught it to us from an open book, running a stubby finger over the lines and skipping anything that got too tricky. I don't suppose he needed a lot in the way of advanced degrees to teach junior high school woodworking, but it was clear that even there he was operating on the outer limits of his mental capabilities. I learned more German from watching *Hogan's Heroes.*

I hated Mr. Dreck as much as I have ever hated anyone. For two long years he made my life hell. I used to sit during his monotone lectures on hand tools, their use and care, genuinely trying to pay attention, but after a few minutes I would find my gaze drifting helplessly out the window to where a girls' gym class was romping around—thirty-six adolescent girls, all wearing little blue pleated skirts that didn't *quite* cover their pert little bottoms—and my imagination would break free, like a dog off its leash, and scamper playfully among them, sniffing and panting around all those long, tanned legs. After a minute or two, I would turn back to the class with a dreamy leer tugging at my lips to find that everyone in the class was watching me. Mr. Dreck had evidently just launched a question in my direction.

"Pardon, Mr. Dreck?"

"I said what kind of blade is this, Mr. Bryson?"

"That's a sharp blade, Mr. Dreck."

Mr. Dreck would emit one of those exasperated sighs that stupid people reserve for those rare and happy occasions when they chance upon someone more stupid than they, and would say in a wearied voice: "It's a fourteen-inch Hungarian dual nasal borer, Mr. Bryson." Then he would make me stand for the rest of the hour at the back of the room holding a piece of coarse sandpaper to the wall with my nose.

I had no gift for woodworking. Everyone else in the class was building things like cedar chests and oceangoing boats and getting to play with dangerous and noisy power tools, but I had to sit at the Basics Table with Tubby Tucker and a kid who was so stupid that I don't think we ever learned his name. We just called him "Drooler." The three of us weren't allowed anything more dangerous than sandpaper and Elmer's Glue, so we would sit week after week making little nothings out of offcuts, except for Drooler who would just eat the glue. Mr. Dreck never missed a chance to humiliate me. "And what is *this*?" he would say, seizing some mangled block of wood on which I had been laboring for the last twenty-seven weeks and holding it aloft for the class to titter at. "I've been teaching shop for sixteen years, Mr. Bryson, and I have to say that this is the worst beveled edge I've ever seen." He held up a birdhouse of mine once and it just collapsed in his hands. The class roared. Tubby Tucker laughed so hard that he almost choked. He laughed for twenty minutes, even when I whispered to him across the table that if he didn't stop it I would bevel his testicles.

THE WAITRESS brought my beer and I became uncomfortably aware that I had spent the last ten minutes adrift in a little universe of my own, very possibly chuckling quietly and murmuring to myself in the manner of people who live in bus stations. I looked around and was relieved to see that no one appeared to have noticed. The man at the next table was too busy boasting to his wife/mistress how he had sold 2,000 *Hullabaloo* videotapes and the last 68,000 copies of the American edition of *The Lost Continent* to the Romanians for loft insulation. His companion meanwhile was making love with her eyes to a man dining alone across the room, though the man was too busy struggling with three-foot-long strands of tangled spaghetti to notice that he was being used as a sex aid.

I took a big draft of my beer, warmed by my reminiscences, and quietly delighted at the thought that my schooldays were forever behind me, that never again for as long as I lived would I have to bevel an edge or elucidate the principles of the Volstead Act in not less than 250 words or give even a mouse-sized shit about which far-flung countries produce jute and what they do with it. It is a thought that never fails to cheer me.

IN THE morning I went to the station to catch a train to Cologne. I had half an hour to kill, so I wandered into the station café, a little one-woman operation. The woman running it saw me take a seat, but ignored me and busied herself tidying the shelves behind the counter. She was only a foot or so from me. I could have leaned over and used her buttocks as bongos, but it gradually dawned on me that if I wanted service I would have to present myself at the counter and make a formal request. It would never occur to her that I was a foreign visitor who didn't know the drill and to say to me in a pleasant voice: "Kaffee, mein Liebchen?" or even just signal that I should step to the counter. No, I was breaking the rule and for this I had to be ignored. This is the worst characteristic of the Germans. Well, actually a predilection for starting land wars in Europe is their worst characteristic, but this is right up there with it.

I once knew an English journalist living in Bonn who was phoned at work by his landlady one day and instructed to come home and take his washing down from the line and rehang it in a more systematic manner. He told her, in so many words, to go screw herself, but every time he put out washing after that, he would find later that it had all been taken down and rehung. The same man came in one weekend from cutting the grass to find an anonymous note on the doormat informing him that it was illegal to mow one's lawn in North Rhine-Westphalia between noon on Saturday and 9:00 A.M. on Monday, and that any further infractions would be reported to the lawn-mower police or whatever. Eventually, he was transferred to Bogotá, and he said it was the happiest day of his life.

COLOGNE IS a dismal place, which rather pleased me. It was comforting to see that the Germans could make a hash of a city as well as anyone else, and they certainly have done so with Cologne. You come out of the station and there, at the top of an open-air escalator, is the cathedral, the largest Gothic structure in the world. It is awesome and imposing, no question, but it stands in the midst of a vast, windswept, elevated concrete plaza that is heart-numbingly barren and forlorn. If you can imagine Salisbury Cathedral in the middle of a shopping-center parking lot, you may get the picture. I don't know what they were thinking of when they built it. Certainly it wasn't people.

I had been to Cologne briefly once before, the summer I traveled alone, but I could remember little of it except that it was dominated by the cathedral, a mountain of stone in the midst of a modern city, soot black and oddly satanic-looking, and that I stayed in a guesthouse somewhere on a back street in the permanent shadow of an iron bridge across the Rhine. I remembered the guesthouse much better than the city. In the hallway outside my room stood a table stacked high with German weekly magazines, all of which seemed to be concerned exclusively with sex and television, and since television in Germany seemed also to be concerned almost exclusively with sex, sex was something of a feature in these publications. There was nothing pornographic about them, you understand. They just covered sex the way British magazines cover gardening. I spent much of an afternoon and a whole evening traveling between my room and the table with armloads of these diverting periodicals for purposes of cultural study.

I was particularly fascinated by a regular feature in, I think, *Neue Revue,* which focused on a young couple each week—a truck mechanic from Duisburg named Rudi and his dishy librarian wife, Greta, that sort of thing. Each week it was a different couple, but they all looked as if they had been squeezed from the same tube of toothpaste. They were all young and good-looking and had superb bodies and dazzling smiles. Two or three of the photographs would show the couple going about their daily business—Rudi lying under a DAF truck with a monkey wrench and a big smile, Greta at the local supermarket beaming at the frozen chickens. Then the rest of the pictures treated us to the sight of Rudi and Greta without any clothes on, doing things around the house: standing together at the sink washing dishes, sharing a spoonful of soup from the stove, playing Scrabble buttocks-up on a furry rug.

There was never anything overtly sexual about the pictures. Rudi never got a hard-on—he was having much too good a time drying those dishes and tasting that soup! He and Greta looked as if every moment of their existence was bliss. They smiled straight at the camera, as happy as anything to have their neighbors and workmates and everyone else in the Federal Republic of Germany see them chopping vegetables and loading the washing machine in their birthday suits. And I thought then what curious people the Germans are.

That was about all I could remember of Cologne, and I began to fear, as I lingered on the precipice of the cathedral plaza looking down on the grim shopping streets below, that that was about all that was worth remembering. I stood at the base of the cathedral and gazed up at it for a long time, impressed by its sheer mass. It is over five hundred feet long and more than two hundred feet wide, with towers that soar almost as high as the Washington Monument. It can hold forty thousand people. You can understand why it took nine hundred years to build—and that was with German workers. In Britain they would still be digging the foundations.

I went inside and spent a half hour looking dutifully at the contents, but without feeling any of that sense of wonder and exhilaration that the vastly smaller cathedral at Aachen had stirred in me the day before, then wandered back outside, and went to the edge of the terrace overlooking the Rhine, broad and brown and full of long fleets of barges. This done, I wandered over to the main shopping street, Hohestrasse, a long, straight pedestrian artery which, I had read in *The Economist,* is one of the two most expensive streets in Europe on which to rent retail space (the other is Kaufingerstrasse in Munich). It's more expensive even than Bond Street in London or the Rue du Faubourg-St.-Honoré in Paris. Bernard Levin wrote glowingly of Hohestrasse in *To the End of the Rhine,* but to me it just looked liked any shopping street anywhere—a succession of featureless department stores, shoe stores, record stores, places selling cameras and video recorders. It was aswarm with Saturday shoppers, but they didn't look particularly discerning and nothing like as well dressed as the citizens of Aachen.

I stopped outside one of the many electronics shops and looked over the crowded window, idly wondering if the goods on offer would be German-made, but no, they were the same Japanese videos and cameras you see everywhere else, apart from the odd Grundig slide projector or some other relic of a simpler age. Having grown up in a world dominated by American goods, I used to get patriotically chagrined seeing Japanese products appearing everywhere, and I would read with sympathy magazines articles about how they were ruthlessly stealing our markets.

Then one time while I was flying on a Boeing 747, I plugged in a pair of earphones that offered the audio quality of a paper cup at the end of a length of string and watched a film that looked as if it were being projected onto a bath mat, and I had a shocking thought—namely, that this was as far as American consumer electronics had ever got. We got up to about 1972 and just stopped there. If the field had been left to RCA and Westinghouse and other American companies, we would now all be wheeling around personal stereos the size of suitcases and using video recorders that you would have to thread yourself. And since that moment I have been grateful to the Japanese for filling my life with convenient items like a wristwatch that can store telephone numbers, calculate my overdraft, and time my morning egg.

Now my only complaint is that we have to live with all the embarrassing product names the Japanese give us. No one ever seems to remark on this—on what a dumb, misguided name Walkman is, for instance. It doesn't walk, it's not a man. It sounds like something you'd give a blind person to keep him from bumping into walls ("You want to turn up the bleeper on your Walkman, Harry"). If it had been developed in America, it would have been given a name like the SoundBlaster or MuzixMaster or Dynam-O-Box or something with a little zip to it. But these things aren't developed in America any longer, alas, so we have to accept the sort of names that appeal to Japanese engineers—the Sony Handycam, the Panasonic Explorer, the Toyota Tercel. Personally, I would be embarrassed to buy a car that sounds like a new kind of polyester, but I imagine to the Japanese these names are as exciting and stellar as all get-out. I suppose that's what you have to expect from people who wear white shirts every day of their lives.

*　　*　　*

I RETURNED to the station, where I had left my bag in a locker, and couldn't decide what to do with myself. My intention had been to spend a couple of days in Cologne going to the museums—it has some excellent ones—but now I couldn't muster much enthusiasm for the idea. And then I saw something that gave me an instant urge to get out of there. It was a nonstop porno movie house, and quite a gross one at that, to judge from the candid glossy pictures on display by the ticket booth. The movie house was in the station, one of the services permitted to travelers by the thoughtful management of Deutsche Bundesbahn, the national railway company. I don't know precisely why, but I found this hugely repellent. I have no special objection to pornography, but in a train station? There was just something so seedy about the idea of a businessman stopping off at the end of the day to watch twenty minutes of heaving bonking before catching the 5:40 to his home and family in Bensberg, and there was something seedier still in the thought of a national railway endorsing it.

Just then the huge timetable board high above me went *chickata chickata,* announcing an express train to Amsterdam. "Hold that train!" I muttered, and scurried off to the ticket window.

~~~~~~

8

AMSTERDAM

~~~~~~

ARRIVING AT Amsterdam's central station is a strange experience. It's in the middle of town on a sunny plaza at the foot of the main street, the Damrak. You step out of the front door and there in front of you is—gosh!—every hippie that's left in Europe. I had no idea there were still so many of them, but there were scores, if not hundreds, lounging around in groups of six or eight, playing guitars, passing reefers, sunning themselves. They look much as you would expect people to look who have devoted a quarter of a century to lounging around in public places and smoking dope. A lot of them seemed to be missing teeth and hair, but they had compensated somewhat by acquiring large numbers of children and dogs. The children amused themselves by frolicking barefoot in the sun and the dogs by nipping at me as I passed.

I walked up the Damrak in a state of high anticipation. Amsterdam had been Katz's and my favorite European city by a factor too high to compute. It was beautiful, it was friendly, it had excellent bars and legal dope. If we had lingered another week, I could well be there yet, sitting on the station plaza with an acoustic guitar and some children named Sunbeam and Zippity Doo Dah. It was that close.

The Damrak was heaving with tourists, hippies, and Saturday shoppers, all moving at different speeds; the tourists shuffling as if their shoelaces were tied together, looking everywhere but where they were going, the hippies hunched and hurried, and the shoppers scurrying around among them like windup toys. It was impossible to walk with any kind of rhythm. I tried several of the hotels along the street, but they were all full, so I dodged behind the prisonlike royal palace at Dam Square and branched off into some side streets, where I had vague recollections of there being a number of small hotels. There were, but these too were full. At most of them it wasn't even necessary to inquire, because a sign in the window announced NO VACANCY in half a dozen languages.

Things had clearly changed since Katz and I had stepped off the train at the height of summer, asked our way to the Sailors' Quarter, and got a room in the first hotel we came to. It was a wonderful little place called the Anco, in a traditional Amsterdam house: narrow and gabled, with steep, dark staircases, and a restful view of the O. Z. Voorburgwal canal four floors below. It cost five dollars a night, with an omelet for breakfast thrown in (almost literally), though we did have to share a room with two slightly older guys.

Our first meeting was inauspicious. We opened the door to find them engaged in a session of naked bedtop wrestling—an occurrence that surprised the four of us equally.

"Pardon us, ladies!" Katz and I blurted and scuffled backward into the hallway, closing the door behind us and looking confounded. Nothing in twenty years of life in Iowa had quite prepared us for this. We gave them a minute to disengage and don bathrobes before we barged back in, but it was clear that they considered us boorish intruders, an opinion reinforced by our knack, developed over the next two days, of always returning to the room in the middle of one of their workouts. Either these guys never stopped or our timing was impeccable.

They spoke to us as little as was humanly possible. We couldn't place their accents, but we thought the smaller guy might be Australian since he seemed so at home down under. Their contempt for us became irredeemable in the middle of the second night when Katz stumbled heavily from his bed after a gala evening at the Club Paradiso and, with an enormous sigh of relief, urinated in the wastebasket.

"I thought it was the sink," he explained, a trifle lamely, the next morning. Our roommates moved out after breakfast and for the rest of the week we had the room to ourselves.

We quickly fell into a happy routine. We would arise each morning for breakfast, then return to the room, shut out every trace of daylight, and go back to bed for the day. At about four o'clock we would stir again, have a steaming shower in a cubicle down the hall, change into fresh clothes, press our hair flat against our heads, and descend to the bar of the Anco, where we would sit with Heinekens in the windowseat, watching the passing scene and remarking on what fine people the Dutch were to fill their largest city with pleasant canals and winsome whores and plentiful intoxicants.

The Anco had a young barman, with a Brillo-pad beard and a red jacket three sizes too snug for him, who had clearly taken one toke too many some years earlier and now looked as if he should carry a card with his name on it in case he needed to remember it in a hurry. He sold us small quantities of hash, and at six o'clock we would have a reefer, as a sort of appetizer, and then repair to an Indonesian restaurant next door. Then, as darkness fell over the city and the whores took up their positions on the street corners, and the evening air filled with the heady smells of cannabis and frîtes, we would wander out into the street and find ourselves being led gently into mayhem.

We went frequently to the Paradiso, a nightclub converted from an old church, where we tried without success to pick up girls. Katz had the world's worst opening line. Wearing an earnest, almost worried look, he would go up to a girl and say: "Excuse me, I know you don't know me, but could you help me move something six inches?"

"What?" the girl would reply.

"One and half fluid ounces of sperm," Katz would say with a sudden beam. It never worked, but then it was no less successful than my own approach, which involved asking the least attractive girl in the room if I could buy her a drink and being told to fuck off. So instead we spent the nights getting ourselves into a state of what we called ACD—advanced cognitive dysfunction. One night we fell in with some puzzled-looking black Africans whom Katz encouraged to foment rebellion in their homeland. He got so drunk that he gave them his watch (he seemed to think that punctual timekeeping would make all the difference in the revolution), a Bulova that had belonged to his grandfather and was worth a fortune, and for the rest of the summer whenever I forgot and asked him the time, he would reply sourly: "I don't know. I have a man in Zululand who looks after these things for me." At the end of the week we discovered we had spent exactly half our funds of seven hundred dollars each and concluded that it was time to move on.

*　　*　　*

THE DUTCH are very like the English. They are both rather slobby (and I mean that in the nicest possible way): in the way they park their cars, in the way they set out their litter bins, in the way they dump their bikes against the nearest tree or wall or railing. There is none of that fastidiousness you find in Germany or Switzerland, where the cars on some residential streets look as if they were lined up by somebody with a yardstick and a spirit level. In Amsterdam they just sort of abandon their cars at the canalside, often on the brink of plunging in.

They even talk much the same as the English. This has always puzzled me. I used to work with a Dutch fellow on *The Times,* and I once asked him whether the correct pronunciation of the artist's name was Van Go or Van Gok. And he said, a little sharply, "No, no, it's Vincent van—" and he made a sudden series of desperate hacking noises, as if a moth had lodged in his throat. After that, when things were slow around the desk, I would ask him how various random expressions were said in Dutch—International Monetary Fund, poached eggs, cunnilingus—and he would always respond with these same abrupt hacking noises. Passersby would sometimes slap him on the back or offer to get him a glass of water. I've tried it with other Dutch people—it's a good trick if you've got a Dutch person at a party and can't think what to do with him— always with the same result. Yet the odd thing is that when you hear the Dutch speaking to each other, they hardly hack at all. In fact, the language sounds like nothing so much as a peculiar version of English.

Katz and I often noticed this. We would be walking down the street when a stranger would step from the shadows and say: "Hello, sailors, care to grease my flanks?," and all he would want was a light for his cigarette. It was disconcerting. I found this again when I presented myself at a small hotel on the Prinsengracht and asked the kind-faced proprietor if he had a single room. "Oh, I don't believe so," he said, "but let me check with my wife." He thrust his head through a doorway of beaded curtains and called: "Marta, what stirs in your leggings? Are you most moist?"

From the back a voice bellowed: "No, but I tingle when I squirt."

"Are you of assorted odors?"

"Yes, of beans and sputum."

"And what of your pits—do they exude sweetness?"

"Truly."

"Shall I suckle them at eventide?"

"Most heartily!"

He returned to me wearing a sad look. "I'm sorry, I thought there might have been a cancellation, but unfortunately no."

"A smell of petroleum prevails throughout," I said by way of thanks, and departed.

THERE WERE no rooms to be had anywhere. In the end, despondent, I trudged back to the station plaza, to the office of the VVV, the state tourist bureau, where I assumed there would be a room-finding service. I went inside and up some stairs and found myself in a hall that brought to mind Ellis Island. There were eight straggly lines of weary tourists, with at least thirty people in each line. The VVV staff were sending people all over—to Haarlem, to Delft, to Rotterdam, to The Hague—because there was not a single hotel room left in Amsterdam at any price. This was only April. What on earth can it be like in July? They must send people to Iceland. A big handwritten sign on the wall said: NO TICKETS FOR THE VAN GOGH EXHIBITION. SOLD OUT. That was great, too. One of the reasons I had come was to see the exhibition.

I took a place in one of the lines. Progress was glacial. It was hot, I was sweaty, I was tired, I was hungry. My feet hurt. I wanted a bath. I wanted a large dinner and several beers. There wasn't a single part of me that was happy.

Almost every one of us in the room was an American. Upon reaching the front of the line, each new customer had to be interviewed regarding his or her requirements in terms of toilet facilities, breakfast arrangements, room amenities, accessibility by public transport, and price. This took ages because of all the permutations involved. Then almost invariably the customer had to turn to his or her mate—who had been standing there all along *seeming* to take it in but evidently not—and explain all the possibilities all over again.

This would prompt a lengthy discussion and a series of supplementary questions: Can we get there by bus instead of by train? Are there any vegetarian restaurants near the hotel? Does the hotel have no-smoking rooms? Will there be a cab at the station when we get there or do we have to call one, and if we have to call one can you give us the number? Is there a Laundromat in Delft? What time does the last train run? Do you think I should be taken outside and shot for having such an enormous butt and asking so many stupid questions?

Once they had arrived at an agreement in principle, the VVV person would make anything up to twenty phone calls to outlying hotels, with a look of infinite patience and low expectations—most hotels weren't even bothering to answer their phones by now—before announcing that nothing was available in that price range. So then they would have to discuss another more expensive or more distant set of options. It all took so long that you felt like applauding whenever anyone left the window and the line pushed forward six inches.

The one lucky thing was that the VVV girl at the head of my line was beautiful—not just extraordinarily good-looking, with the sort of bottom that made your palms sweat when she went to the filing cabinet, but intelligent, sweet-natured, patient, sympathetic, and with an exquisite, dusky Dutch accent that simply melts your heart. She dealt with every customer gracefully and expertly, and switched effortlessly between French, German, English, and Dutch—all with that delectable accent. I was infatuated. I freely admit it. Stuck in a line that was going nowhere, there was nothing I could do but stare dumbly and admire everything about her—the way she hooked her hair behind her ear, the way she wrinkled her nose when she looked in the phone book, the way she dialed the phone with the eraser end of her pencil. By the time I reached her window, it was all I could I do to keep from blurting: "Can we have sex a few times and then talk marriage?" But all I did was shyly ask for a hotel room somewhere in the Northern Hemisphere. She found me one in Haarlem.

HAARLEM WAS very pleasant. People ahead of me in the line had been falling into swoons when told they would have to leave Amsterdam to get a room, but I was rather pleased. Haar-

lem was only twenty minutes away by train. It was a handsome
little city with a splendid cathedral and cozy cathedral square, and
lots of good restaurants that were cheaper and emptier than those
in Amsterdam. I had a steak the size of a hot water bottle, went for
a long walk around the town, stood impressed in the shadow of
the cathedral, returned to the hotel, showered steamily, and went
to bed a happy man.

In the morning I returned to Amsterdam. I used to love walking
in cities on Sunday mornings, but it gets more and more dispiriting.
All the things left over from Saturday night—vomit slicks, litter,
twisted beer cans—are still lying around, and everywhere now there
are these depressing grilles and iron shutters on all the storefronts.
They make every street look dangerous and forbidding, which is
just absurd in Europe. On an innocuous pedestrian street called
Heiligeweg, almost every storefront was completely hidden behind
a set of iron blinds—even the Aer Lingus office. What on earth is
anyone going to steal from an Aer Lingus office—the little model
airplane in the window?

I found my way to the canals—the Singel, Herengracht, Keizers-
gracht, and Prinsengracht—and things were immediately better. I
roamed along the canals in a happily random way, shuffling through
leaves and litter, cocooned by the tall, narrow houses and old trees.
Along its canals Amsterdam is an immensely beautiful city, especially on a Sunday morning when there is almost no one about. A
man sat in a patch of sun on his stoop with a cup of coffee and a
newspaper, another was returning from somewhere with a bottle of
wine, a young couple passed entwined in a postcoital glow, and the
occasional unhurried cyclist crossed from one side street to another
somewhere up ahead, like extras employed to lend the scene color,
but in two hours of wandering around I saw not another soul but
them.

Again and again, I found myself leaning on a railing on a small
humpbacked bridge, just gazing into the shimmering green water,
lost in a simpleminded reverie until a tour boat would chunter by,
full of tourists with cameras, slicing through the mirrored street
scene below me to break the spell. In its wake there would be a little
festival of bestirred litter—a bottle of dishwashing liquid, some cig-

arette packets, assorted cartons from McDonald's and Burger King—and I would be reminded that Amsterdam is also a dirty city. It is full of dog shit and litter and graffiti. The graffiti is everywhere—on phone boxes, on park benches, on the walls of almost every building, even on the marbled vaults of the passageway that runs like a tunnel beneath the Rijksmuseum. I have never seen so much graffiti. And it's not even good graffiti. It's just random squiggles, sprayed by people with brains the size of a Cheerio. The Dutch seem to have a problem with mindless crime. You may never get mugged in Amsterdam, but I'm told you cannot park a car on the streets anywhere in the central area of the city in the evening without a strong probability of someone scoring the paintwork from end to end with a screwdriver.

When I was twenty I liked Amsterdam—indeed, admired it passionately—for its openness, its tolerance, its relaxed attitude to dope and sex, and all the other sins that one can't get enough of at twenty. But I found it oddly wearisome now. The people of Amsterdam were rather stuck with their tradition of tolerance, like people who take up a political stance and then have to defend it no matter how untenable it gets.

Because the Dutch have been congratulating themselves on their intelligent tolerance for all these centuries, it is now impossible for them not to be nobly accommodating to graffiti and burned-out hippies and dog shit and litter. Of course, I may be completely misreading the situation. They may like dog shit and litter. I sure hope so, because they've certainly got a lot of it.

HERE AND there I passed a house braced with timbers, awaiting urgent repairs. Amsterdam was built on a swamp, and just keeping the canalside houses from sinking into it is an unending task. My Dutch colleague's brother bought a house on one of the lesser canals and discovered after moving in that the pilings on which it had been built three hundred years earlier were rotting away, and that the house was sinking into the underlying ooze at a rate that would make most of it basement within a short while. Putting new pilings under several tons of existing structure is not the easiest job in the world, and it cost him almost twice as much to have the house shored up as it did to buy it in the first place. This was almost twenty years ago, and he still wears socks with holes in them because of the debt.

I suppose the same story has been repeated in countless buildings all over the city, so you have to admire the people of Amsterdam for keeping the houses standing, and even more for having the uncommon sense to keep the canal streets residential. In Britain the ground floors would long ago have been filled with kebab houses and banks and dry cleaners, all with big picture windows, as if anybody in the world cares to see what's going on inside a dry cleaner or a bank.

I've never understood why the first thing a bank does when it acquires a Victorian building in Britain is to gut the ground floor and put in a lot of plate glass. Why? Banks in Britain have nothing to put in their windows. So they make a fan-shaped arrangement of brochures informing you that you can borrow money there—"Jeez, thanks, I thought you sold sausages"—and insert some dreadful watercolors by the manager's wife. So I am full of admiration for the Dutch for preserving their finest streets and insisting that people live on them.

The one problem is that it makes the occasional catastrophe all the more unbearable, as I discovered with a cry of pain as I reached the far end of Nieuwezijds Voorburgwal. There, where once a fine gabled house must have stood, squatted a new Holiday Inn, a building so ugly, so characterless, so *squat* that it stopped me in my tracks. Everything about it was cheap and unimaginative—the cardboard-box shape, the empty, staring windows, the acrylic canopy over the entrance, the green plastic signs, the wall-mounted video cameras peering at every passerby. It looked like a parking ramp. Not the tiniest effort had been made to give it any distinction.

The building would have been painful enough out by an airport, but it was in the heart of one of the great cities of Europe, on a street otherwise lined with handsome, patrician houses. How could an architect walk through such a city and allow himself to design a building of such utter indistinction? How could the city authorities let him? How could anyone sleep in it? I found myself turning dumb-struck to people passing on the sidewalk as if to say, "Do you see this building here?" but they all just hunched past, quite unmoved by its existence. I just don't understand the world.

*   *   *

EVENING CAME. A light rain began to fall. Pulling my collar up to my ears, I walked to the dark streets of the red light district and squinted through rain-spattered glasses at the goods on offer. The red light district had changed considerably since my day. In 1973, the most outspoken thing was a club with a sign that said: LIVE ON STAGE—REAL FOCKY-FOCKY SHOW. Now everything was much more explicit. The shop windows were filled with a mind-boggling array of plastic phalluses, vibrators, whips, erotic video tapes, unguents, love potions, magazines, leatherwear, and other exotica not to be found in your average Kmart. One window contained a plastic, life-sized, astonishingly realistic woman's reproductive region, completely with dilated labia. It was *awful*. It looked like something that would be used in an anatomy lesson, and even then you could imagine students fainting.

The magazines were even grosser. They showed every variety of couple doing messy and urgent things to each other—heterosexuals, gays, mixed races, sado-masochists, grotesquely fat people (a little comic relief, I guess), and even animals. The cover of one magazine showed a woman providing—how shall I put this?—a certain oral service to a horse that a horse wouldn't normally expect to get, even from another horse. And this was just the stuff in the windows. God knows what they keep under the counters.

The whores were still there. They sat in luminous body stockings in windows lit with a pinkish glow, and winked at me as I passed. ("Hey, they like me!" I thought until I realized that they do this for everybody.) Behind them, I could sometimes glimpse the little cells where they conduct their business, looking white and clinical, like places you would go to have your hemorrhoids seen to. Twenty years ago the prostitutes were all Dutch. They were friendly and sweet-natured and often heartbreakingly attractive. But now the prostitutes were Asian or African, and they looked mean and weathered, even when they were pouting and blowing kisses in their most coquettish, come-hither manner.

The amazing thing was that there was a whole street of this stuff, several blocks long, with a spillover into the side streets. I couldn't believe that there could be that many people in Amsterdam—that many people in the *world*—requiring this sort of assistance just to get their rocks off. Whatever happened to personal initiative?

I S P E N T the morning of my last day in the Rijksmuseum. Its most famous painting, "The Night Watch," wasn't on view because a few days earlier some crazy person had attacked it with a knife, and both he and it had been taken away for rehabilitation, but the museum is so massive—250 rooms—and so filled with wonderful pictures that there was plenty else to look at.

Afterward I strolled on to the Anne Frank House on Prinsengracht. It was packed with visitors, but moving nonetheless. Eight people, including Otto Frank, his wife, and two daughters, spent three years of the war hiding in a secret apartment above Mr. Frank's spice business. Now an endless line of visitors shuffles through the building every day to see the famous bookcase that hid the secret entrance to their attic flat and the five rooms in which they lived. The tragic part is that when the Franks and their companions were anonymously betrayed and finally captured, in August 1944, the Allies were on the brink of liberating Holland. A couple of more weeks and they would have been saved. As it was, seven of the eight died in concentration camps. Only Anne's father, Otto, survived.

The Anne Frank museum is excellent at conveying the horror of what happened to the Jews, but it is a shame that it doesn't give even a passing mention to the Dutch people who risked their own lives in helping the Franks and others like them. Miep Gies, Otto Frank's secretary, had to find food each day for eight people, as well as herself and her husband, for three years at a time of the strictest rationing. It must have been extremely trying, not to mention risky. Yet it was hardly a rare act. Twenty thousand people in Holland sheltered Jews during the war at considerable peril to themselves. They deserve to be remembered too.

What must it have been like to be a Jew in Europe in the 1930s? From the beginning they were subjected to the grossest indignities: forced to wear yellow stars, forbidden to sit in parks or cafés or to ride on trams, required to give up their cars and bicycles, even their children's bicycles, bullied with impunity by thugs. If matters had ended there, it would have redounded to Germany's shame forever, but of course the situation grew unspeakably worse, as photographs and documents in the museum's other rooms gruesomely testify—people being herded onto cattle trains, piles of sticklike corpses, the gaunt faces of the living dead, all the pictures you have seen a thousand times.

One picture I hadn't seen transfixed me. It was a blurry photo of a German soldier taking aim with a rifle at a woman and the baby she was clutching as she cowered beside a trench filled with bodies. I couldn't stop staring at it, trying to imagine what sort of person could do such a thing.

It probably wasn't the best picture to look at just before heading to the station and catching a train to Germany.

9

HAMBURG

I CAUGHT an afternoon train to Hamburg, by way of Osnabrück and Bremen, and arrived in the early evening. I hadn't been to Hamburg before. Katz and I had passed through it by train on our way to Scandinavia, but it was late at night and all I recalled was a dark city and a dark station where we stopped for half an hour while more carriages were hooked on. The station was much as I remembered it, vaulted and echoing, but brighter and busier at six in the evening. People were everywhere, hurrying to catch trains.

I threaded my way through the crowds to the tourist information desk and, having had so much trouble finding a room in Amsterdam, gladly paid a handsome fee to have accommodation found for me, then was chagrined to discover that the Hotel Popp, the establishment to which the pleasant and well-spoken young man directed me after relieving me of a handful of money, was directly opposite the station. I could have found it on my own in thirty seconds and applied the money to a night of abandon in the Reeperbahn. Still, it was convenient and had a bar and restaurant, so I couldn't complain. Actually, I could. The room was tiny and depressingly basic, with a twenty-watt bulb in the reading light, no carpet, no television, and a bed that could have passed for an ironing board. But at least with a place called the Hotel Popp, I wouldn't forget the name and end up, as I often do in strange cities, asking a cabbie to just drive around until I spotted it.

I went out for a stroll before dinner. Lounging at intervals along the side streets around the station were some of the most astonishingly unattractive prostitutes I had ever seen—fifty-year-old women in miniskirts and black fishnet stockings, with crooked lipstick and tits that grazed their kneecaps. Where on earth they got their trade from I couldn't begin to guess. One of them gave me a "Hello, dearie" look and I was nearly crushed by a bus as I faltered backward into the street. However, within a block or two things improved considerably. I had left my city map behind in the hotel, so I had no idea where I was going, but it looked inviting in every direction. It was a warm spring evening, with dusk settling cozily over the city, like a blanket around one's shoulders, and people were out walking aimlessly and browsing in shop windows. I was pleased to find myself among them.

I had expected Hamburg to be grimmer, a sort of German Liverpool, full of crumbling overpasses and vacant lots—I already knew that it had the highest unemployment rate in Germany, over 12 percent, half as high again as the national average, so I expected the worst—but Hamburg proved to be anything but struggling, at least on the surface. The department stores along the Mönckebergstrasse, the main shopping street, were bright and spotless and full of fancy goods—much finer than anything on Oxford Street in London—and the side streets glowed with restaurants and bistros through whose golden windows I could see people dining elegantly and well.

I walked through the big town hall square, around the darkened streets of the warehouse district, handsome and silent, then rounded a corner to find one of the more arresting city sights—the Inner Alster, the smaller of the two lakes around which Hamburg is built. I knew from maps that Hamburg had these lakes, but nothing I had read or seen in photographs had prepared me for just how beautiful they were. The Inner Alster is much the smaller of the two, but it is still large enough to present a great rectangular pool of silence and darkness in the midst of the city. The lakeside is agreeably lined with trees and benches, overlooked by office buildings and a couple of hotels of the old school, where the doormen are dressed like Albanian admirals and rich old ladies in furs constantly go in and out with little dogs under their arms.

I sat on a bench in the darkness for perhaps half an hour just watching the lights shimmering on the surface and listening to the lapping of water, then stirred myself enough to walk over to the Kennedybrücke, a bridge across the point where the two lakes meet.

The Outer Alster, seen from here, was more massive and irregular and even more fetching, but I would leave that for tomorrow.

Instead, famished, I strolled back to the welcoming glow of the Popp, where I dined amply and surprisingly well for what was after all just a small station hotel, bloating my cheeks with bread rolls and salad and meat and potatoes till I could eat no more, and then filled all the remaining space inside me with good German beer and read half a book until at last, at about half-past midnight, I arose from the table, nodded genteelly to the six Turkish waiters, who had been waiting hours for me to leave, and ascended in a tiny slow-motion elevator to the fourth floor, where I spent no more than thirty minutes stabbing at the keyhole with my key before bursting unexpectedly into the room, pushing the door shut with the back of my foot, shedding some clothes (one sock, half a shirt), and falling onto the bed, where I dropped more or less immediately into a deep, contented and, I daresay, grotesquely blubbery sleep.

I awoke in a square of sunshine, too hot and bright to sleep through, and stumbled to the window to find a gorgeous morning blazing away outside, much too gorgeous to waste. The Hauptbanof concourse and the street below, the Kirchenallee, were so brightly bathed in sunlight that I had to shield my eyes. I had a hangover you could sell to science, but after two cups of strong coffee at a sunny table outside the Popp, a handful of aspirins, two cigarettes, and a cough so robust that I tapped into two new seams of phlegm, I felt tolerably human and was able to undertake a gentle stroll to the waterfront through the dappled sunshine of Saint Pauli Park. There wasn't much to see upon arrival, just cranes and dockyards and the broad, sluggish estuary of the Elbe. I thought of what Konrad Adenauer used to say: "You can smell Prussia when you get to the Elbe." I could only smell dead fish, or at least I assumed it was dead fish. Maybe it was Prussians.

In the 1930s, the docks at Hamburg employed 100,000 people. Now the number is barely twelve hundred, though it is still the second busiest port in Europe, after Rotterdam, with a volume of trade equal to the whole of Austria's. Until just a couple of weeks before, I could have witnessed the interesting sight of freighters unloading grain from their aft holds and redepositing it in their forward holds as a way of extracting additional funds from the ever-beneficent EEC. With its flair for grandiose screwups, the EEC for years paid special subsidies to shippers for grain that was produced in one part of the Common Market and re-exported from another, so shippers taking a consignment from, say, France to Russia, discovered that they could make a fortune by stopping off at Hamburg en route, and pointlessly unloading the cargo, and then reloading it. This little ruse enriched the shippers by a mere $75 million before the bureaucrats of the EEC realized that that money could be much better spent on something else—themselves, say—and put a stop to the practice.

I walked a few hundred yards inland and uphill to the Reeperbahn, that famed mile-long avenue of sin. It looked disappointingly unlusty. Of course, sinful places never look their best in daylight. I remember thinking in Las Vegas that it looked rather endearingly pathetic when viewed over a cup of coffee and a doughnut. All that noise and electric energy that is loosed at dusk vanishes with the desert sun and everything suddenly seems as thin and one-dimensional as a film set. But even allowing for this, the Reeperbahn looked tame stuff, especially after Amsterdam. I had envisioned a narrow pedestrian street packed on both sides with bars, sex shops, peep shows, strip clubs, and all the other things a sailor needs to revive a salty dick, but this was almost a normal city street, busy with traffic flowing between the western suburbs and the downtown. There was a fair sprinkling of seamy joints, but also a lot of more or less normal establishments—restaurants, coffee shops, souvenir stores, jeans stores, even a furniture store and a theater showing the inescapable *Cats*. Almost the only thing that told you this was a neighborhood of dim repute was the hard look on people's faces. They all had that gaunt, washed-out look of people who run fun-fair stalls.

The really seedy attractions were on the side streets, like Grosse Freiheit, which I turned up now. I walked as far as the Kaiserkeller at number 36, where the Beatles used to play. Most of the other businesses along the street were given over to live sex shows, and I was interested to note that the photos of the artistes on display outside were unusually—and perhaps a little unwisely—candid. In my experience, places such as these usually show pictures of famously beautiful women like Christie Brinkley and Raquel Welch, which I daresay even the most inexperienced sailor from Tristan da Cunha must realize is not what he's likely to encounter inside, but at least they leave you wondering what you *are* going to find. These photographs, however, showed gyrating women of frightfully advanced years—women with maroon hair and thighs that put me in mind of flowing lava. These ladies must have been past their best when the Beatles were playing. They weren't just over the hill; they were pinpricks on the horizon.

The sex shops, too, were as nothing compared with those of Amsterdam, though they did do a nice line in inflatable dolls, which I studied closely, never having seen one outside of a Benny Hill sketch. I was particularly taken with an inflatable companion called the Aphrodite, which sold for 129 marks. The photograph on the box was of a delectably attractive brunette in a transparent negligee. Either this was cruelly misleading or they had made more progress with vinyl in recent years then I had realized.

In large, lurid letters, the box listed Aphrodite's many features: "LIFE-SIZE!" "SOFT FLESHLIKE SKIN!" "INVITING ANUS!" (Beg pardon?) "MOVABLE EYES!" (Ugh!) "LUSCIOUS VAGINA!" and, for those who missed it the first time around, "LUSCIOUS VAGINA THAT VIBRATES AT YOUR COMMAND!"

"Yeah, but can she cook?" I thought.

There was another one called a Chinese Love Doll 980. "FOR A LONG-LASTING RELATIONSHIP," it promised sincerely and in bolder letters added: "EXTRA-THICK VINYL RUBBER." This was clearly a model for the more practical types. On the other hand, it also had a "VIBRATING VAGINA AND ANUS" and "TITS THAT GET HOT!!" Below this it promised: "SMELLS LIKE A REAL WOMAN."

All these claims were given in a variety of languages. It was interesting to see that the German versions all sounded coarse and bestial: "Lebengroße," "Volle Junge Bruste," "Liebender Mund." The same words in Spanish sounded curiously delicate and romantic: "Ano Tentador," "Deliciosa Vagina que Vibra a Tu Orden," "Labios Amorosos."

I was fascinated. Who buys these things? Presumably the manufacturers wouldn't include a vibrating anus or tits that get hot if the demand wasn't there. How does anyone bring himself to make the purchase? Do you tell the person behind the counter you're getting it for a friend? Can you imagine taking the doll home on the tram and worrying all the way that the bag will split and that the doll will flop out or self-inflate or, worse still, that you'll be killed in a crash and all the next week the papers will be full of headlines like POLICE IDENTIFY RUBBER-DOLL MAN above a smiling picture of you from your high school yearbook? I couldn't handle the tension. Imagine having friends drop in when you were just about to pop the champagne cork and settle down for a romantic evening with your vinyl companion and having to shove her up the chimney and worry that you've left the box on the bed or some other giveaway clue lying around. ("By the way, who's the other place setting for, Bill?")

Perhaps it's just me. Perhaps these people aren't the least embarrassed about their abnormal infatuations. Perhaps they talk about it freely with their friends, sit around bars saying: "Did I tell you I just traded up to an Arabian Nights Model 280? The eyes don't move, but the anus gives good action." Maybe they even bring them along. "Helmut, I'd like you to meet my new 440. Careful of her tits. They get hot."

With this distracting thought to chew on, I strolled back to the city center past the massive law courts and concert hall and along an avenue interestingly named Gorch-Fock-Wall (which sounded to me like the answer to a riddle: "What does Gorch do when he can't find his inflatable doll?"), and had a look around the shopping streets and classy arcades packed into the area between the huge town hall and the Inner Alster.

It was getting on for midday, and people were sitting out in the sunny plazas having lunch or eating ice cream. Almost without exception they looked healthy and prosperous and often were strikingly good-looking. I remembered German cities almost twenty years ago being full of businessmen who looked just as Germans were supposed to look—fat and arrogant. You would see them gorging on piles of sausages and potatoes and gulping with full mouths from liter tankards of beer at all hours of the day, but now they seemed to be picking delicately at salads and fish, and looking fit and tanned—and, more than that, friendly and happy. Maybe this was just a Hamburg trait. Hamburg is after all closer to Denmark and Sweden and even England than it is to Munich, so perhaps it is atypical of Germany.

At all events, this relaxed and genial air was something that I hadn't associated with Germans before, at least not those aged over twenty-five. There was no whiff of arrogance here, just a quiet confidence, which was clearly justified by the material wealth around them. Those little doubts we've all had about the wisdom of letting the Germans become the masters of Europe evaporated in the Hamburg sunshine. Forty-five years ago Hamburg was rubble. Virtually everything around me was new, even when it didn't look it. The people had made their city, and even themselves, rich and elegant and handsome through their cleverness and hard work, and they had every right to be arrogant about it, but they were not, and I admired them for it.

I don't think I can altogether forgive the Germans their past, not as long as I can wonder if that friendly old waiter who brings me my coffee might once have spent his youth bayoneting babies or herding Jews into gas ovens. Some things are so monstrous as to be unpardonable. But I don't see how anyone could go to Germany now and believe for a moment that that could ever happen again. The Germans are becoming the new Americans—rich, ambitious, hardworking, health-conscious, sure of their place in the world. Seeing Hamburg now, I was happy to hand them my destiny—happier, at any rate, than leaving it to those who had spent the last forty years turning Britain into a kind of nation-state equivalent of Kmart.

One thing hadn't changed. The women still don't shave their armpits. This has always puzzled me. The women all look so beautiful and stylish, and then they lift up their arms and there's a Brillo pad hanging there. I know some people think it's earthy, but so are turnips and I don't see anyone hanging turnips in their armpits. Still, if this is the worst trait the Germans take with them into the closing years of the century, then I for my part shall be content to let them lead us into the new millennium.

*   *   *

ALL THOSE lithe and attractive bodies began to depress me, especially after I caught sight of my reflection in a store window and realized that I was the fat one now. After spending the first twenty-five years of my life looking as if my mother had mated with a stick insect, I am still shocked by these sudden reflected glimpses of rolling blubber. Even now I have to stop myself from giving a good morning smile to the fat guy every time I get into a mirrored elevator. I tried to diet once, but the trouble is diets so easily get out of control. I lost four pounds in the first week and was delighted until it occurred to me that at this rate in only a little over a year I would vanish altogether. So it came as something of a relief to discover that in the second week I put all the weight back on (I was on a special diet of my own devising called the Pizza and Ice Cream Diet), and I still draw comfort from the thought that if there is ever a global famine, I will still be bounding around, possibly even playing a little tennis, while the rest of you are lying there twitching your last.

I devoted the afternoon to a walk around the immense Outer Alster. I hadn't intended to spend the whole afternoon there, but it was so beautiful that I couldn't pull myself away. Sailboats dotted the water and little red and white ferries plied endlessly beneath a sky of benign clouds, taking passengers between the rich northern quarters of the city and the distant downtown. A narrow park, full of joggers and lovers and occasional benchloads of winos (who looked remarkably fit and prosperous, considering their vocation), encircled the lake and offered one enchantment after another. Every view across the water was framed by sturdy oaks and trembling willows, and provided distant prospects of the city: the space-needle eminence of a TV tower, a few scattered skyscrapers and, for the rest, copper roofs and church spires that looked as if they had been there forever.

On the streets around the perimeter of the lake, and as far back into the surrounding streets as you cared to wander, stood huge houses of every architectural style, with nothing in common but their grandness. Where the lake occasionally wandered off into placid backwaters, the houses had immense shady lawns running down to the water's edge, with gazebos and summer houses and their own jetties. It must be very agreeable to live on a lake in a grand house and go to work by foot or bike around the lake or by ferry across it or even aboard your own boat, and to emerge at the other end at such a rich and handsome city center. What a perfect life you could lead in Hamburg.

1 0 .

COPENHAGEN

I TOOK a train to Copenhagen. I like traveling by train in Denmark because you are forever getting on and off ferries. It takes longer, but it's more fun. I don't know how anyone could fail to experience that frisson of excitement that comes with pulling up alongside a vast white ship that is about to sail away with you aboard it. I grew up a thousand miles from the nearest ocean, so for me any sea voyage, however brief, remains a novelty. I noticed, however, that even the Danes and Germans, for whom this must be routine, were peering out the windows with an air of expectancy as we reached the docks at Puttgarden and our train was shunted onto the ferry, the *Karl Carstens*.

Here's a tip for you if you ever travel on a Scandinavian ferry. Don't be the first off the train, because everyone will follow you, trusting you to find the way into the main part of the ship. I was in a group of about three hundred people following a flustered man in a gray trilby who led us on a two-mile hike around the cargo deck, taking us up and down long avenues of railway carriages and huge canvas-sided trucks, casting irritated glances back at us as if he wished we would just go away, but we knew that our only hope was to stick to him like glue and sure enough he eventually found a red button on the wall, which when pressed opened a secret hatch to the stairwell.

Overcome with new frissons of excitement, everyone clambered hurriedly up the metal stairs and made straight for the buffet. You could tell the nationality of the people by what they went for. The Germans had plates piled high with meat and potatoes, the Danes had Carlsbergs and cream cakes, the Swedes one piece of crispbread with a little dead fish on it. The lines were too much for me, so I went up on the top deck and stood out in the sunshine and gusty breeze as the boat cast off and, with a sound oddly like a washing machine on its first cycle, headed across twelve miles of mildly turbulent water between northern Germany and the Danish island of Lolland. There were about eight of us, all men, standing in the stiff breeze, pretending we weren't perishing. Slowly, Puttgarden receded in a wake of foam, and before long Lolland appeared over the horizon and began to glide toward us, like a huge low-lying sea monster.

You cannot beat sea travel, but there's not much of it left these days. Even now grand plans are under way to run bridges or tunnels between all the main islands of Denmark and between Copenhagen and Sweden, and even across this stretch of water between Puttgarden and Rødbyhavn, so that people will be able zip across it in ten minutes and scarcely notice that they have moved from one country to another. This new European impulse to blur the boundaries between countries seems a mite misguided to me.

At Rødbyhavn, our frissons spent, we all reboarded the train and rode listlessly through the rest of the afternoon to Copenhagen. Denmark was much neater and emptier than northern Germany had been. There were no factories, as there had been in Germany, and none of the farmyard clutter of abandoned tractors and rusting implements that you see in Belgium and Holland. Big electricity-generating wind turbines, their three-bladed fans spinning sluggishly, were dotted around the low hillsides and stood in ranks in the shallow coastal bays. It was a pity, I thought with that kind of distant casualness that comes with looking at things that are already sliding from view, that they hadn't made them more attractive—like scaled-up Dutch windmills perhaps.

It struck me as odd and sad that man could for centuries have so effortlessly graced the landscape with structures that seemed made for it—little arched bridges and stone farmhouses, churches, windmills, winding roads, hedgerows—and now appeared quite unable to do anything to the countryside that wasn't like a slap across the face. These days everything has at best a sleek utility, like the dully practical windmills slipping past with the scenery outside my train window, or else it looks cheap and temporary, like the tin sheds and concrete hangars that pass for superstores on the edge of every mid-sized town. We used to build civilizations. Now we build shopping malls.

WE REACHED Copenhagen's central station at a little after five, but the station tourist office was already closed. Beside it stood a board with names of thirty or so hotels and alongside each name was a small red light to indicate whether it was full or not. About two thirds of the lights were lit. There was no map to show where the hotels stood in relation to the station. I considered for a moment jotting down some of the names and addresses, but I didn't alto-gether trust the board, and in any case the addresses were meaning-less unless I could find a map of the city.

Perplexed, I turned to find a Danish bag lady clasping my forearm and addressing me in cheerful babbles. These people have an un-canny way of knowing when I hit town. They must have a news-letter or something. We wandered together through the station, I looking distractedly for a map of the city on a wall, she holding on to my arm and sharing demented confidences with me. We must have looked an odd sight. A businessman stared at us over the top of a newspaper as we wandered past. "Blind date," I explained confi-dentially, but he just kept staring.

I could find no map of the city, so I allowed the lady to accompany me to the front entrance, where I disengaged her grip and gave her some small coins of various nations. She took them and wandered off without a backward glance. I watched her go and wondered why crazy people like train and bus stations so much. I can never under-stand why they don't go to the beach or the Alps or someplace more agreeable.

I went to half a dozen hotels in the immediate neighborhood of the station, but they were all full. "Is there some reason for this?" I asked at one. "Some convention or national holiday or something?"

"No, it's always like this," I was assured.

Am I wrong to find this exasperating? Surely, it shouldn't be too much, on a continent that thrives on trade and tourism, to arrange things so that a traveler can arrive in a city in late afternoon and find a room without having to traipse around for hours like a boat person. I mean, here I was, ready to spend freely in their hotels and restaurants, subsidize their museums and trams, shower them with foreign exchange, and pay an extortionate value-added tax of 22 percent, all without a quibble, and all I asked in return was a place to lay my head.

I walked the length of the old part of the city without luck and was about to trudge back to the station to begin again when I came across a hotel by the waterfront called the Sophie Amalienborg. It was large, clean, modern, and frightfully expensive, but they could give me a single room for two nights and I took it without hesitation. I had a steamy shower and a change of clothes and hit the streets a new man.

Is there anything, apart from a really good chocolate cream pie and receiving a large unexpected check in the mail, to beat finding yourself at large in a foreign city on a fair spring evening, loafing along unfamiliar streets in the long shadows of a lazy sunset, pausing to gaze in shop windows or at some church or lovely square or tranquil stretch of quayside, hesitating at street corners to decide whether that cheerful and homey restaurant you will remember fondly for years is likely to lie down this street or that one? I just love it. I could spend my life arriving each evening in a new city.

You could certainly do worse than Copenhagen. It is not an especially beautiful city, but it's an endlessly appealing one. It is home to one and a half million people—more than one in four of the entire Danish population—but it has the pace and ambience of a university town. Unlike most great cities, Copenhagen is refreshingly free of any delusions of self-importance. It has no monuments to an imperial past and very little to suggest that it is the capital of a country that once ruled Scandinavia. Other cities put up statues of generals and potentates. In Copenhagen they give you a little mermaid. I think that's swell.

I walked along Nyhavn, a three-block-long street with a canal in the middle filled with tall-masted ships and lined with narrow, step-gabled seventeenth- and eighteenth-century houses, looking for all the world like a piece of Amsterdam gone astray. The neighborhood was in fact originally settled by Dutch sailors and remained the haunt of jolly tars until recent times. Even now it has a vaguely raffish air in parts—a tattoo parlor and one or two of the sort of dive bars through whose windows you expect to see Popeye and Bluto trading blows—but these are fading relics. For years, restaurateurs have been dragging Nyhavn almost forcibly upmarket, and most of the places now are yuppie bars and designer restaurants, but very agreeable places for all that, since the Danes don't seem to be the least bit embarrassed about living well, which is after all how it should be.

The whole length of Nyhavn was lined with outdoor tables, with young, blond, gorgeous people drinking, eating, and enjoying the unseasonably warm weather. I always wonder what they do with their old people in Copenhagen—they must put them in cellars or send them to Arizona—because everyone, without exception, is youthful, fresh-scrubbed, healthy, and immensely good-looking. You could cast a Pepsi commercial in Copenhagen in fifteen seconds. And they all look so happy.

The Danes are so full of *joie de vivre* that they practically sweat it. In a corner of Europe where the inhabitants have the most blunted concept of pleasure (in Norway, three people and a bottle of beer is a party; in Sweden, the national sport is suicide), the Danes' relaxed attitude to life is not so much refreshing as astonishing. Do you know how long World War II lasted for Denmark? It was over in a day—actually less than a day. Hitler's tanks crossed the border under cover of darkness and had taken control of the country by dawn. As a politician of the time remarked: "We were captured by telegram." By evening they were all back in the bars and restaurants.

Copenhagen is also the only city I've ever been in where office girls come out at lunchtime to sunbathe topless in the city parks. This alone earns it my vote for European City of Culture for any year you care to mention.

I dined in a crowded, stylish basement restaurant halfway along Nyhavn. I was the only person who didn't look as if he had just come from the set of *Miami Vice*. All the men wore shirts buttoned to the throat and the women had big earrings and intentionally distressed hair, which they had to shove out of the way each time they went to their plate. Every one of them was beautiful. I felt like Barney Rubble. I kept expecting the manager to come to the table and say, "Excuse me, sir, but would you mind putting some of this mousse on your hair?" In any event, the staff treated me like an old friend, and the food was so superb that I didn't mind parting with the six-inch wad of kroner that any meal in Copenhagen occasions.

When I climbed the steps to the street, darkness had fallen and the air had chilled, but people still sat outside at tables, drinking and talking enthusiastically, jackets draped over their shoulders. I crossed Kongens Nytorv, one of the city's principal squares, sleepy and green, passed beneath the soft lights of the Hotel d'Angleterre, full of yet more happy diners, and headed up Strøget, Copenhagen's main shopping street. Strøget means strolling place, and it is the world's longest pedestrian street. Actually, it's five streets that run together for 1.2 miles between Kongens Nytorv and the city's other main square, Rådhuspladsen, at the Tivoli end. Every travel article on Copenhagen talks rapturously about Strøget, but I always feel vaguely disappointed. Every time I see it, it seems to have grown a tiny bit seedier. There are still many swish and diverting stores down at the Kongens Nytorv end—Georg Jensen for silver, Brødrene Andersen for clothes, Holmegaard for china and glass—but as you pass the halfway point, Strøget swiftly deteriorates into tacky gift shops and McDonald's, Burger Kings, and other brightly lighted temples of grease. The whole area could do with a lot more benches and flagstones (it's all patched asphalt now), and even—dare I say it?—the odd tub of geraniums. It's a shame that in a country as wealthy and design-conscious as Denmark they can't make the whole street—the words tumble involuntarily from my lips—more picturesque.

Still, it is pleasant to walk from one end of the downtown to the other without encountering cars, and just as you reach the western end, when you think that this is too, too dreary and you really should turn back, you step into the large and colorful Rådhuspladsen, or Town Hall Square. One of the things they do in Europe that impresses me is to let advertisers put colorful neon signs all over the roofs and top floors of the buildings around the main squares. You don't notice the signs in the daytime because they are so high up, so the buildings preserve that air of stern magnificence appropriate to their function, but when darkness falls and you could do with a little gaiety, the same buildings suddenly light up with bright advertisements that illuminate the square and color the faces of the people below. Wonderful.

I walked across to Tivoli, even though I could see from a distance that it was shut and darkened, as if under dust sheets. A sign on the gate said it wouldn't open for a couple of weeks. As I walked back across the square toward Strøget, I encountered a small crowd by the town hall and stopped to have a look.

Two police officers, a man and a woman, both young and blond and gorgeous, were talking softly and with sympathy to a boy of about seventeen who had clearly ingested the sort of drugs that turn one's brain into an express elevator to Pluto. Disoriented by his sudden zip through the cosmos, he had apparently stumbled and cracked his head; a trickle of blood ran from above his hairline to his downy cheek. The police officers were wearing the smartest commando-style uniforms I have ever seen—navy blue jump suits with lots of zippers and Velcro pockets and loops for holding flashlights and notebooks and portable telephones, and, for all I know, grappling hooks and rocket launchers. They looked as if between them they could handle any contingency, from outbreaks of Lassa fever to disarming a nuclear submarine.

And the thing is, this was probably the biggest thing they would have to deal with all evening. The Danes are almost absurdly law-abiding. The most virulent crime in the country is bike theft. In 1982, a year for which I happen to have the facts at my fingertips, there were 6 murders in Copenhagen, compared with 205 in Amsterdam, a city of similar size, and 1,688 in New York. The city is so safe that Queen Margrethe used to walk from Amalienborg Palace to the shops every morning to buy flowers and vegetables just like a normal citizen. I once asked a Dane who guarded her in such circumstances, and he looked at me with surprise and replied, "Why, we all do," which I thought was rather sweet. All that changed, alas, when Olof Palme was gunned down in Stockholm.

The police officers helped the boy to his feet and led him to the patrol car. The small crowd dispersed, but I found myself following the officers, almost involuntarily. I don't know why I was so fascinated except that I had never seen such gentle police. At the patrol car, I said in English to the female officer, "Excuse me, what will you do with the boy?"

"We'll take him home," she answered simply, then raised her eyebrows a fraction and added: "I think he needs his bed."

I was impressed. I couldn't help thinking of the time I was stopped by police in America, made to stand with my arms and legs splayed against a wall and frisked, then taken to a police station and booked because of an unpaid parking ticket. I was about seventeen myself at the time. God knows what the cops would have done to me if they had found me in a drugged stupor on a city bench. I suppose I'd be getting out of jail about now. "Will he be in trouble for this?" I asked.

"With his father, I think so, yes. But not with us. We are all young and crazy sometimes, you know? Good night. Enjoy your stay in Copenhagen."

"Good night," I said and with the deepest admiration watched them go.

I AWOKE in a mood to take in some museums. Copenhagen has splendid museums, but they are often strangely neglected, even by the Danes. I went first to the immense National Museum, opposite Christiansborg Palace, and had it more or less to myself. National museums, especially in small countries, are often feeble affairs—department store mannequins dressed in sixteenth-century peasant costumes and a display case containing six Roman coins found in somebody's backyard. But the Danish National Museum is both vast and richly endowed, and I spent an entire morning happily wandering through its miles of echoing rooms.

Afterward I went to the Ny Carlsberg Glyptotek. Some museums have great treasures but are dull buildings and some have dull treasures but are great buildings, but the Glyptotek succeeds on both counts. It has an outstanding collection of Roman statuary and some of the finest Impressionist paintings to be seen anywhere, and the building itself is a joy—light, airy, impeccably decorated, with a warm and tranquil palm court full of gently dozing old people. (So that's where they put them!)

The best museum of all I saved for last—the Hirschsprung Collection in Østre Anlaeg Park. Everything about it is wonderful. It's a pleasant and gentle stroll from the city center, and Østre Anlaeg is the best park in the city, in my experience (which is short but in this case attentive), for seeing secretaries sunning their breasts. But even without these novel inducements, the museum is worth seeking out because it is so terrific and so little visited. It contains 884 paintings, assembled over forty years by one man, almost all of them from the nineteenth-century Skagen school of Danish painting, and packed densely into twenty or so mostly small rooms. The paintings are all concerned with simple themes—summer landscapes, friends enjoying a casual dinner, a view of the sea from an open window, a woman at a sink—but the effect is simply enchanting, and you come away feeling as if you have spent the afternoon in some kind of marvelous and refreshing ionizer.

Afterward, my spirits lifted, I had a long, happy walk through the surrounding park, moving methodically from one sunbathing blonde to another, inquiring if they needed any assistance with their suntan lotion. Actually, it wasn't warm enough for sunbathing, and it was four in the afternoon and all the secretaries in Copenhagen were tucked away in their dark offices, their lovely breasts bagged away for at least another day, so I just walked around the park and imagined.

Early in the evening, I went for a stroll along the city's curiously uninspiring waterfront: a dull vista of fish-processing factories and industrial cranes. Far away across the still water a ship-repair yard was working late doing something shrill and drastic to a rusted freighter, which fought back with hideous shrieks and a shower of sparks. I walked as far as the statue of the Little Mermaid, perched forlornly but rather prettily on her rock at the harbor's edge, and then strolled around a neighboring park called Castellet, named for its star-shaped fortress guarding the harbor mouth, before finally stopping for a light and cheapish dinner at a café/bistro on Stockholmsgade.

The food was not remarkable, but the beer was good and the service was excellent because I was the only customer in the place. I had only to look up and smile hopefully and a fresh beer would be hustled to me. After a while I didn't even have to look up. A new bottle would magically appear as the last drop fell from the old one. This was my kind of bistro.

So I sat contentedly for two hours looking at some Danish newspapers that had been left on the table, trying to discern from the mass of unfamiliar words whether Margaret Thatcher had perchance fallen out of a moving car or World War III had started yet. But Planet Earth seemed to be much as I had left it three weeks ago, so instead I gazed out the window at the passing traffic and lost myself in those aimless reveries that are the lone traveler's equivalent of a night on the town.

Eventually I rose, paid the enormous bill, and tottered a trifle wobbily out into the night. It was a fair hike back to my hotel, but I sustained myself en route by stopping at any place that looked bright and friendly and dispensed beer, of which Copenhagen possesses a gratifying plenitude, and thus passed the evening sitting alone in a series of corners, drinking far too many beers, smiling inanely at strangers, and dribbling ash down my shirt. Sometime around 1:00 A.M., as I was weaving down Strøget, suppressing the urge to break into song, I encountered an Irishman reeling down the street toward me, swearing crazily at anyone who passed.

"You fucking cunts!" he screamed at a genteel-looking couple, whose pace immediately quickened. "You shit head! You great Danish turd!" he shouted at a young man, who lowered his head and hurried on.

The odd thing was the Irishman was dressed in a dapper gray suit. He looked like a successful businessman. God knows what was going on inside his addled head. He caught sight of me, but seemed to recognize me as a fellow drunk and let me pass with a listless wave of the hand, but immediately perked up to rain obscenities on a middle-aged man. "You're a piece of crap for sure, you stupid old twat!" he said to the man's considerable surprise, then added mysteriously, "And I bet you're staying in a fucking posh hotel!" I stood with my arms crossed and watched as the Irishman reeled off down the street, shouting abuse at the buildings, before he lurched abruptly to the left, as if yanked on a long rope, and disappeared down a side street, taking his expletives into the night.

*   *   *

I A W O K E the next day feeling as if I had spent the night with my head attached to one of those machines they use to test shock absorbers. I looked at my watch. It was a quarter to ten. I had intended to catch a train to Sweden at half past ten, and I had yet to pack and check out. I went to the bathroom to struggle through the morning hygiene and make low death noises, then wandered around the room dealing with personal effects as I chanced upon them—a sock went on my foot, a map was forced into the rucksack, a Big Mac box that I had no recollection of acquiring went into the wastebasket—until at last I had assembled my possessions. I needed coffee the way Dan Quayle needs help with an I.Q. test.

I arrived at the front desk just in time to take up a position behind twenty-seven Italian visitors who, in that interesting way of the Italians, were all trying to check out at once. This didn't help my fragile mood. Finally, the Italians departed, moving across the lobby as if surgically linked, and the last I saw of them they were all trying to go out the revolving door together. I gave my key to the young woman and waited as the computer hummed for a minute, as if getting up steam, and then abruptly spewed out several feet of paper, which was shorn of its sprocket holes and separated into sixteen sheets, the faintest of which was presented to me for inspection.

I was surprised to see that the bill contained a charge for phone calls. The night before—it all seemed so long ago now—I had tried to phone home, but all I got was a recording in Danish, which I presumed was telling me that the international lines were busy or that I was dialing wrong or possibly that I should just go and screw myself. In any case, I couldn't get anywhere with it, and after three tries gave up. So I was taken aback to see I was billed for three phone calls. I explained this to the girl.

"Yes," she said. "But you must pay for any phone calls you try to make, whether or not you are connected."

"But that's insane."

She shrugged, as if to say, maybe it is, maybe it isn't.

"You're telling me," I said slowly, my head feeling like the gong in a J. Arthur Rank movie, "that I have to pay for phone calls I didn't make?"

"Yes, that is correct."

"I didn't use the spare blanket in the cupboard. Do I have to pay you for that, too?" She looked steadily at me, clearly unaware that she was dealing with a person who could tip over the edge into violent insanity at any moment. "I didn't use the shower cap," I went on. "Shall I give you a little something for that? And I didn't use one of the bars of soap or the trouser press. This is going to cost me a fortune, isn't it?"

The girl continued to gaze levelly at me, though with a certain noticeable diminishment of good will. She had obviously weathered these storms before. "I am sorry you find these small charges inconvenient, but it is the normal practice in Copenhagen."

"Well, I think it stinks!" I barked, then caught a glimpse of a seriously demented person in the mirror—wild hair, red face, Parkinsonlike shakiness—and recognized myself. I gave her my credit card, scratched a wild signature on the bill, and with a haughty turn exited, regretting only that I didn't have a cape to sling over my shoulder and an ebony stick with which to scatter the doormen.

I should have gone immediately and had two cups of coffee and caught a later train. That would have been the sensible thing to do. Instead, still steaming, I proceeded toward the station at a pace that did my body no good at all, stopping en route at a bank on Strøget to cash a travelers' check. It was for only fifty dollars—a trifling amount in Scandinavia, mere pocket money until I reached Sweden in the evening and would require some serious cash—but for this I was charged the whopping sum of thirty-five kroner, well over 10 percent of the total. I suddenly realized why the Irishman from the night before had been swearing at everyone. He had paid one Danish bill too many. "That's an outrage," I said, clutching the bank receipt like bad news from a doctor. "I don't know why I don't just pin money to my jacket and let you people pick it off me!" I shrilled, leaving a row of clerks and customers looking at each other as if to say, "What's his problem? Not enough coffee?"

And it was in this dim and unfortunate frame of mind that I

boarded the morning express to Gothenburg, abused a hapless young conductor for giving me the unwelcome news that it had no buffet car, and sat morosely in a corner, watching the gardenlike suburbs of Copenhagen slip past, every nerve ending in my body tingling for caffeine.

GOTHENBURG

O N T H E ferry across the Øresund between Denmark and Sweden, I drank a cup of coffee and began to feel human again. I passed the time staring out at the slate-gray sea and studying my Kümmerly and Frey *Südskandinavien* map. Denmark looks like a plate that has been dropped onto a hard floor. It is fractured into a thousand pieces, forming deep bays and scorpion-tail peninsulas and seas within seas. The villages and towns sounded inviting—Aerøskøbing, Skærbaek, Holstebro, the intriguingly specific Middelfart—and from dozens of them dotted red lines led out to cozily forlorn islands like Anholt and Endelave and above all Bornholm, adrift in the Baltic, closer to Poland than to Denmark. I had a sudden strong urge to visit them all. There would never be enough time. There never is in life. There wasn't even time for another cup of coffee.

A reddish-brown train was waiting at Helsingborg to take us on to Gothenburg, 243 kilometers to the north along Sweden's west coast. We traveled through a landscape of low hills, red barns, small towns with mustard-colored town halls, impenetrable pine forests, scattered lakes dotted with clapboard holiday cottages, jetties, upturned rowing boats. Occasionally, the train would swing near the coast and give a glimpse through the trees of a cold sea. After a while rain began to streak the window.

I shared a compartment with a tanned young man, blond as only a Swede can be, in wire-rimmed glasses and a pony tail, who was returning to Gothenburg from Agadir, where he had been visiting a girlfriend. Actually, she was a former girlfriend and he hadn't exactly visited her because upon arriving he discovered she was living with a Moroccan rug merchant—she had somehow neglected to mention this in her postcards—who had pulled out a scimitar and threatened to send the Swede home with his nuts in a Baggie if he didn't clear off instantly. Considering that he had just made a pointless journey of a couple of thousand miles, the young man seemed remarkably equable and spent almost the entire journey sitting cross-legged spooning purple yogurt into his mouth from an enormous jar and reading a novel by Thomas Mann.

At Angelholm we were joined by two more people, a grim-looking older woman all in black who looked as if she hadn't smiled since 1937 and who spent the entire journey watching me as if she had seen my face on a wanted poster, and by a fastidious older man who I guessed to be a recently retired schoolmaster and to whom I took an instant dislike.

The young Swede was sitting in the schoolmaster's reserved seat. Not only did the schoolmaster make him move, but instructed him to transfer all his personal effects from the luggage rack above the seat to the rack on the other side, which takes a particular kind of pettiness. The schoolmaster then spent an endless period fussily sorting out his things—extracting a folded newspaper and a small bag of plums from his case, arranging the case on the rack, examining the seat minutely for anything unpleasant and giving it a brush with the back of his hand, folding his jacket and his sweater with ritualistic care, adjusting the window in consultation with the lady but without reference to me or the young Swede, getting his case down again for some forgotten item, checking his hankie, readjusting the window. Every time he bent over, his ass bobbed in my face. How I longed for a Smith & Wesson. And every time I looked around there would be that old crone watching me like the Daughter of Death.

And so the morning passed.

I fell into one of those drooly, head-lolling dozes that seem to be more and more a feature of my advancing years. When I awoke, I discovered that my companions were also snoozing. The schoolmaster was snoring raspily, his mouth hugely agape. I noticed that my swaying foot had rubbed against him, leaving a dusty mark on his navy blue pants. I further discovered, with cautious movements of my foot, that it was possible to extend the mark from just above his knee almost to his ankle, leaving an interesting streak on the trouser leg. In this means I amused myself for some minutes until I turned my head a fraction and discovered that the old lady was watching me. Immediately, I pretended to be asleep, knowing that if she uttered a sound I would have to smother her with my jacket. But she said nothing.

And so the afternoon passed.

I hadn't eaten since my snack supper of the night before, and I was so hungry that I would have eaten almost anything, even a plate of my grandmother's infamous creamed ham and diced carrots, the only dish in history to have been inspired by vomit. Late in the afternoon, a porter came along with a creaking food cart carrying a coffee urn and snackstuffs, and everyone stirred to a kind of frisky wakefulness and examined the fare keenly. I had twenty-four kronor of Swedish money, which I thought a handsome sum, but it proved sufficient to buy just one hopelessly modest open-faced sandwich, like the bottom half of a hamburger bun, with a withered piece of lettuce and eight marble-sized meatballs on top of it. Eating in Sweden is really just a series of heartbreaks.

I bought the sandwich and carefully peeled away the plastic wrap, but just as I lifted it to my mouth the train lurched violently over a siding, making the bottles clatter in the food cart, and causing all the meatballs to jump off the bun, like sailors abandoning a burning ship. I watched with dismay as they hit the floor and bounced to eight dusty oblivions.

I'd have scarcely thought it possible, but the lady in black gave me a look of even deeper contempt. The schoolmaster skittishly slid his feet out of the way, lest a meatball come to rest against his glossy brogues. Only the young Swede and the food attendant took a sympathetic interest and pointed helpfully as I gathered up the meatballs and deposited them in the ashtray. This done, I nibbled bleakly on my piece of lettuce and dry bun and dreamed of being almost anywhere else in the universe. Only another two and a half hours to go, I told myself, and fixed the old lady with a hard stare that I hoped somehow conveyed to her what pleasure, what deep and lasting pleasure, it would give me to haul her off her seat and push her out the window.

*   *   *

WE REACHED Gothenburg just after six. Rain was pelting down, drumming on the pavements and coursing in torrents through the gutters. I sprinted across the open square outside the station, jacket over head, dodging trams with split-second, if largely inadvertent, precision, skirted a large puddle, feinted between two parked cars, head-faked a lamppost and two startled elderly shoppers (once I start running, I can't stop pretending I'm returning a kickoff for the Chicago Bears. It's a compulsion—a sort of Tourette's syndrome of the feet), and darted breathless and sodden into the first hotel I came to.

I stood in the lobby, a vertical puddle, wiped the steam from my glasses with a corner of shirttail, and realized with a touch of horror as I hooked my glasses back around my ears that this was much too grand a place for me. It had potted palms and everything. For a moment I considered bolting, but I noticed that a reptilian young reception clerk was watching me narrowly, as if he thought I might roll up a carpet and try to carry it out under my arm, and I became instantly obstreperous. I was damned if some nineteen-year-old pipsqueak with zits and a clip-on tie was going to make me feel loathsome. I marched to the front desk and inquired the price of a single room for one night. He quoted me the sort of sum that would necessitate a trip to the bank with a wheelbarrow if paid in cash.

"I see," I said, trying to sound casual. "I assume it has a private bath and color TV?"

"Of course."

"Free shower cap?"

"Yes, sir."

"Assortment of complimentary bath gels and unguents in a little wicker basket by the sink?"

"Certainly, sir."

"Sewing kit? Trouser press?"

"Yes, sir."

"Hair dryer?"

"Yes, sir."

I played my trump card. "Magic-wipe disposable shoe sponge?"

"Yes, sir."

Shit. I had been counting on him saying no to at least one of these so that I could issue a hollow guffaw and depart shaking my head, but he did not and I had no choice but to slink away or sign in. I signed in.

The room was pleasant and businesslike, but small, with a twenty-watt reading light—when will Europeans learn that this is just not good enough?—a small TV, a clock radio, a good bath with a shower. I tipped all the lotions from the bathroom into my rucksack, then tossed in the little wicker basket, too—well, why not?—and went through the room harvesting matchbooks, stationery, and all the other items that were either complimentary or portable. This done, I ventured out into Gothenburg, still famished.

The rain was still falling in sheets. I had thought I might stroll out toward the famous Liseberg Gardens, but I got no more than a couple of hundred yards before I was turned back by the pitiless downpour. I trudged back to the city center and tried to have a look around the main shopping district, sprinting squelchily from doorway to doorway and from one dripping awning to another, but it was hopeless. I wanted a restaurant, one simple wholesome restaurant, but there seemed to be none. I was soaked and shivering, and was about to return in a desultory spirit to my hotel to take whatever food was offered there at whatever price, when I noticed an indoor shopping center and darted in, shaking myself like a dog. The shops were mostly dreary Woolworth's-type places and they were all shut, but there was a surprising number of people wandering around, as if this were a marvelous place to take an evening stroll. There were a lot of young drunks staggering about, too, most of them at that noisy and unattractive stage where they might want to be your pal or pick a fight or just throw up on you, so I gave them a wide berth.

One of the more striking features of Sweden and Norway is how much public drunkenness there is. I mean, here you have two countries where you cannot buy a beer without taking out a bank loan, where successive governments have done everything in their power to make drinking not worth the cost and effort, and yet everywhere you go there are grossly intoxicated people—in train stations, on park benches, in shopping centers. I don't understand it.

But then I don't begin to understand a lot of things about Sweden and Norway. It's as if the inhabitants are determined to squeeze all the pleasure out of life. They have the highest income tax rates, the highest VAT rates, the harshest drinking laws, the dreariest bars, the dullest restaurants, and television that is like two weeks in Nebraska. Everything costs a fortune. Even the purchase of a bar of chocolate leaves you staring in dismay at your change and anything larger than that brings tears of pain to your eyes. It's bone-crackingly cold in the winter and it does nothing but rain the rest of the year. The most fun thing to do in Sweden is walk around a semidarkened shopping center after it has closed, looking in the windows of stores that sell wheelbarrows and plastic garden furniture at prices no one can afford.

On top of that, the Swedes and Norwegians have shackled themselves with some of the most inane and restrictive laws imaginable, laws that leave you wondering what on earth they were thinking about. In Norway, for instance, it is illegal for a bartender to serve you a fresh drink until you have finished the previous one. Does that sound to you like a matter that needs to be covered by legislation? It is also illegal in Norway for a bakery to bake bread on a Saturday or Sunday. Well, thank God for that, say I. Think of the consequences if some ruthless Norwegian baker tried to foist fresh bread on people on the weekend. But the most preposterous law of all, a law so pointless as to scamper along the outer margins of the surreal, is the Swedish one that requires motorists to drive with their headlights on during the daytime, even on the sunniest summer afternoon. I would love to meet the guy who thought up that one. He must be head of the Department of Dreariness. It wouldn't surprise me at all if on my next visit to Sweden all the pedestrians are wearing miners' lamps.

I ended up dining in a Pizza Hut in the basement of the shopping center, the only customer in the place. I had forgotten to bring anything to read, so I passed the time waiting for my pizza by staring thoughtfully at the emptiness around me, sipping a glass of water, and making up Scandinavian riddles—

Q.: How many Swedes does it take to paint a wall?
A.: Twenty-seven. One to do the painting and twenty-six to organize the spectators.

Q.: What does a Norwegian do when he wants to get high?
A.: He takes the filter off his cigarette.

Q.: What is the quickest way in Sweden of getting the riot police to your house?
A.: Don't take your library book back on time.

Q.: There are two staples in the Swedish diet. One is herring. What is the other?
A.: Herring.

Q.: How do you recognize a Norwegian on a Mediterranean beach?
A.: He's the one in the snowshoes.

—and chuckling quietly in the semidemented manner of someone who finds himself sitting alone in damp clothes in an empty restaurant in a strange country waiting for a twenty-five-dollar pizza.

Afterward, just to make an evening of it, I went to the train station to purchase a ticket on the next morning's express to Stockholm. You cannot just hop onto a train in Sweden, but must think about it carefully and purchase a ticket in advance. The ticket hall had one of those systems where you take a number from a machine by the door and wait for it to appear above one of the ticket windows. My number was 415, and the highest number presently seeing action was 391. I waited for twenty minutes, yet the numbers advanced only to 393, so I wandered off to the station newsstand to look at girlie magazines. The newsstand, alas, was closed, so I looked at a couple of travel posters, and then wandered back. Not entirely to my surprise, I discovered that there had been a frenzy of activity in my absence, and number 415 had come and gone. So I took another number—432 this time—and a seat and waited for half an hour. When at last my number came, I presented myself at the window and asked the man for a ticket on the 10:05 to Stockholm the next morning.

He regarded me sadly. "I'm sorry, I do not speak English," he said.

I was taken aback. "Everybody in Sweden speaks English," I protested feebly.

His sadness grew. "I don't. Please you must to go to window sree." He indicated a window farther down the line. "She speaks vair good English."

I went to window three and asked for a ticket to Stockholm the next morning. The woman, seeing the number 432 crumpled in my fist, pointed to the number above her window. "You have the wrong number. This window is for number 436." Even as she spoke, a ferocious-looking lady with gray hair and a dicky hip was hoisting herself out of her chair and charging toward me. I tried to explain my problem with the monoglot at window five, but the ticket lady just shook her head and said: "You must take another ticket. Then maybe I will call you. Now I must deal with this lady."

"You are at zer wrong window!" the old lady announced in the bellow of someone whose hearing is going. "This is *my* window," she added and tossed a haughty look to the rest of the room as if to say, "Are foreigners stupid as shit, or *what?*"

Forlornly, I shuffled over to the machine and took another number. In fact, I took three—I figured this would give me some insurance—then retired to a new seat to watch the board. What a lot of fun I was having! Eventually, my number came around again. It directed me to return to window five—home of the only man in Sweden who speaks no English. I crumpled this ticket and waited for the next to be called. But he called the next one, too. I scampered to his window and begged him not to call my remaining number, but he did.

I couldn't bear to start the whole thing all over again. "Please," I said, speaking carefully, "I just want a one-way ticket to Stockholm for tomorrow morning at ten-oh-five."

"Certainly," he said, as if he had never seen me before, took my money and gave me a ticket. It's no wonder so many Swedes kill themselves.

~~~~~~

STOCKHOLM

~~~~~~

I N T H E morning it was still raining, and I gave up hope of exploring Gothenburg before catching my train. Instead, I went to the station and spent my children's inheritance on two cups of coffee and a leaden iced bun. The train left promptly at 10:05, and after four hours and twenty minutes of riding through the endless pine forest that is Sweden, I was making my way through the throngs at Stockholm's pleasantly gloomy central station.

I went to the station tourist office to have a room found for me. I had to fill out a form with about seven hundred questions on it, but it was worth it, because the hotel, the Castle on Riddargatan, about a mile from the station, was a charming little find, friendly, clean, and reasonably priced, insofar as that statement can be made about anything in Sweden.

After a wash and a change into dry socks and a coffee at a café around the corner, I was ready for Stockholm. I headed across the Strömbron Bridge to Gamla Stan, the old town. The area had an oddly Central European feel to it: narrow, hilly streets lined by severe, heavy buildings, the color of faded terra-cotta, sometimes with chunks of plaster missing, as if they had been struck a glancing blow by tank fire, and often with pieces knocked off the corner plinths where trucks had carelessly backed into them. The old town had a kind of knocked-about charm, but it was surprisingly lacking in any air of prosperity. Most of the windows were dirty, the brass nameplates and door knockers were generally unpolished, and almost every building was in serious need of a good coat of paint. It looked much as I would expect Cracow or Bratislava to look. Maybe it was just the rain, which was falling steadily again, bringing its inevitable gray gloom to the city. Did it never stop raining in Sweden?

I walked with shoulders hunched and eyes cast down, avoiding the water that rushed down the steep, slickly cobbled lanes, browsing in the windows of antique shops, wishing I had a hat or an umbrella or a ticket to Bermuda. I retreated into a dark coffee shop, where I sat shivering, drinking a three-dollar cup of coffee with both hands, watching the rain through the window, and realized I had a cold coming on.

I returned to the hotel, had a lavishly steamy bath and a change of clothes and felt marginally better. I spent the closing hours of the afternoon studying a map of Stockholm and waiting for the weather to clear. At about five the sky brightened. I immediately pulled on my damp sneakers and went out to explore the streets between Norr-malmstorg, a nearby square, and Kungsgården, a small rectangular park that ran down to the waterfront. Everything was much better now. It was Saturday evening, and the streets were full of people meeting friends or partners and repairing in high spirits to the little restaurants and bistros scattered around the neighborhood.

Starving as ever, I looked carefully at several and finally selected what looked to be the cheeriest and most popular of all, a cavernous bistro overlooking Norrmalmstorg called Matpalatset. It was friendly and crowded and wonderfully warm and snug, but the food was possibly the worst I've ever had outside a hospital cafeteria—a gray salad with watery cucumber and mushrooms that tasted of old newspaper, and a lasagna that was not so much cooked as scorched. Each time I poked it with my knife and fork, the lasagna recoiled as if I were tormenting it. Nowhere else in Europe could a place serve food this bad and stay in business, and yet people were lining up at the door. I ate it all because I was hungry and because it was costing me as much as a weekend in Brighton, but seldom have I felt more as if I were engaged in a simple refueling exercise.

Afterward I went for a long walk and felt more charitably disposed to Stockholm now that the rain had stopped. It really is an excep-tionally beautiful city, more watery even than Venice, and with more parkland per person than any other city in Europe. It is built on 14 islands, and within a few miles of the city there are 25,000 more, almost all of them dotted with cottages into which the city drains its population every weekend. I walked far out onto the broad and leafy avenues and narrower side streets to the north of the downtown, all of them lined with six-story nineteenth-century apartment buildings, stern and stolid and yet oddly homey, and at least three quarters of the windows were darkened. It must be a burglar's paradise between Friday evening and Sunday afternoon.

I grew up wanting to live in a building like one of these. It needn't necessarily have been in Europe—it could have been in Buenos Aires or Dar-es-Salaam, say—but it had to be in the center of a big foreign city, full of noises and smells and sights unknown in Iowa. Even now I find myself drawn to such neighborhoods, and I am able to walk for hours through their anonymous streets, which is what I did now. I returned to the city center feeling pleased with Stockholm and content everywhere but in my stomach.

I passed the movie house on Sveavägen where Olof Palme, the prime minister, was gunned down in March 1986. He had walked, unguarded, with his wife from their flat nearby to see a movie about Mozart, and they had just emerged from the theater to stroll home when some madman stepped from the shadows and shot him. It seemed to me one of the tragedies of our age because this must have been almost the last important place in the world where a prime minister could walk the streets and stand in movie lines just like a normal person.

The killing of a politician was such an unexpected event that the police responded as if they had been trained by Mack Sennett. Palme was killed at 11:21 P.M., but the order to watch the roads didn't go out until 12:50 A.M., and even then the police in patrol cars weren't told what they were looking for, and the airports were not closed until 1:05 A.M. The police cordoned off a large area outside the movie house and brought in forensic experts to make a minute search of the scene, but both of the assassin's bullets were picked up and handed in by passersby. A 300-member police unit spent 11 months and $6 million investigating the murder before finally arresting an innocent man. They still don't know who did it.

I strolled aimlessly along Kungsgatan, one of the main shopping streets, past the PUB department store where Greta Garbo used to work in millinery, and down the long pedestrian shopping street called Drottninggatan, and felt as if I were entering a different city. Drottninggatan is a mile and a half of concrete charmlessness, awash with rain-sodden litter. There were drunks everywhere, too, stumbling about. I paused to gaze in some shop window and realized after a moment that a middle-aged man a few yards to my right was peeing down the front of it, as discreetly as he could on a lighted street, which wasn't very discreetly at all. He was seriously intoxicated, but he had a suit on and looked prosperous and educated, and I felt immensely disappointed in him, and in all the hundreds of people who had dropped hamburger boxes and potato-chip wrappers all over the streets. This was unworthy of the Swedes. I expected better than that from them.

I grew up admiring Sweden because it managed to be rich and socialist at the same time, two things I believe everyone ought to be. Coming from a country where no one seemed to think it particularly disgraceful that a child with a brain tumor could be allowed to die because his father didn't have the wherewithal to pay a surgeon, or where an insurance company could be permitted by a state insurance commissioner to cancel the policies of its fourteen thousand sickest patients because it wasn't having a very good year (as happened in California in 1989), it seemed admirable beyond words that a nation could dedicate itself to providing equally and fairly for everyone, whatever the cost.

Not only that, but the Swedes managed to be rich and successful as well, unlike Britain, say, where the primary goal of socialists seemed to be to make everyone as poor and backward as a shop steward in a British Leyland factory. For years, Sweden was to me the perfect society. It was hard enough to come to terms with the fact that the price to be paid for this was a scandalously high cost of living and an approach to life that had all the gusto of an undertakers' convention, but to find that there was litter everywhere and educated-looking people peeing on shopfronts was almost too much.

Still starving, I stopped at a mobile fast-food stand near the waterfront and paid a small fortune for the sort of hamburger that leaves you wondering if this could mark the start of a long period on a life-support machine. I ate a third of it and dropped the rest in a bin. The rain began to fall again. On top of that my cold was growing worse. I returned to my room in grim spirits.

*　　*　　*

I AWOKE with my head full of phlegm and my sneakers full
of water, but at least Stockholm looked better. The sun was out, the
air was clean and crisp, more like late October than early April, and
the water of the harbor sparkled, as blue as a swimming pool. I
walked out along Strandvägen, a grand residential boulevard with a
boat-lined harbor on one side and imposing apartment houses on the
other, out toward Djurgården, an island given entirely over to parkland in the midst of the city. It is the most wonderful place.

Essentially, Djurgården is just a city park full of grassy knolls and
woodlands, but scattered through it are all kinds of enchanting
diversions—a museum of Nordic life, an amusement park, a permanent circus, a "Komedie Teatern," a biological museum, a vast open-
air museum called Skansen, a technological museum, and much else.
Everything was just stirring to life when I arrived. Kiosk awnings
outside Skansen were being cranked into place, chairs were being set
out at little open-air cafés, ticket booths readied for the happy crowds
that would soon be arriving.

I pushed on into the depths of the island, warmed by the morning
sunshine. Every couple of hundred yards the road would branch into
three or four side roads, and whichever one I took would lead
through some new and captivating landscape—a view across the
water to the green copper roofs of the downtown, a statue of some
hero named Gustavus or Adolphus, or both, astride a prancing horse,
a wooded dell full of infant leaves and shafts of golden sunshine.
Occasionally, I would pass things I would never have expected to
find in a public park—a boarding school, the Italian embassy, even
some grand and very beautiful wooden houses on a hill above the
harbor. I don't know who lives in those places, but what lucky
people they are.

One of the many wonderful things about European cities is how
often they have parks—like Denmark's Tivoli Gardens, the Bois de
Boulogne, the Prater in Vienna—that are more than just parks, that
are places where you can not only go for fresh air and a stroll, but
also for a decent meal or to visit an amusement area or explore some
interesting observatory or zoo or museum. Djurgården is possibly

the finest of them all. I spent half a day there, making a lazy circuit of the island, constantly pausing, knuckles on hips, to survey the views, having a coffee outside Skansen, watching the families arriving, and I came away admiring Stockholm all over again.

I walked back into the city to Drottninggatan, and it didn't look half so bad in the spring sunshine. Two street-sweeping machines were collecting up the Saturday night litter, which I was heartened to see, though in fact they were only just playing at it because anything that was in a doorway or under a bench or trapped against a wall was beyond the reach of the machines' brushes, so they left behind as much as they gathered up. And people passing by were already depositing fresh litter in their wake.

I thought I would treat myself to an English newspaper and I needed some Kleenex for my leaking nose, but there were no shops open anywhere that I could see. Stockholm must be the deadest city in Europe on a Sunday. I stopped for coffee at a McDonald's and helped myself to seventy-five napkins, then strolled over a low bridge to Skeppsholmen and Kastellholmen, two lovely, sleeping islands in the harbor offering classic views of the city from their small, rounded hilltops. Afterward I wandered back to Gamla Stan, also much improved by the sunshine. Now the mustard and ocher-colored buildings seemed to positively glow, and the deep shadows in the doorways and windows gave everything a texture and richness it entirely lacked the day before.

I made a circuit of the colossal royal palace (and I mean colossal—it has six hundred rooms), which may be one of the most boring buildings ever constructed. It's not ugly or unpleasant, just boring, featureless, like the buildings children make by cutting window holes in cardboard boxes. Still, I enjoyed the sentries, who must be the most engagingly wimpish-looking in the world. Sweden has been at peace for 150 years and remains determinedly unmilitaristic, so I suppose they don't want their soldiers to look too macho and ferocious, and as a result they make them wear a white helmet that looks disarmingly like a bathing cap and white spats straight out of Donald Duck. It's very hard not to go up to one and say, out of the side of the mouth, "You know, Lars, you look *quite* ridiculous."

I walked back down the hill to the waterfront and crossed the

Strömbron Bridge, stopping midway across to lean on the railing and be hypnotized once more by the view of bridges, islands, and water. As I stood there, a raindrop from out of nowhere struck me on the head, and then another and another.

I looked up to see a turmoil of gray clouds rolling in from the west. Within seconds the sky was black and the rain was in a sudden free fall. People who a moment before had been walking lazily hand in hand in the mild sunshine were now dashing for cover with newspapers over their heads. I stayed where I was, too dumbfounded by the fickleness of the Swedish weather to move, staring out over the now gray, rain-studded water, blowing my nose expansively on McDonald's napkins. At length I gazed up at the unkind sky and took an important decision.

I was going to Rome.

~~~~~~

ROME

~~~~~~

WELL, I'M sorry. I had intended to reach Rome as you would expect me to, in a logical, systematic way, progressing diligently down the length of Germany, through Austria and Switzerland, across a corner of France, and finally arriving, dusty and weary and in desperate need of a Laundromat, by way of Lombardy and Tuscany. But after nearly a month beneath the endlessly damp skies of northern Europe, I longed for sunshine. It was as simple as that. I wanted to walk down a street in shirtsleeves, to sit out of doors with a cappuccino, to feel the sun on my face. So it was with only the odd wrenching spasm of guilt that I abandoned my planned itinerary, caught an airplane, and bounded with a single leap across fifteen hundred miles of Europe. Traveling is more fun—hell, life is more fun—if you can treat it as a series of impulses.

I hadn't been to Rome before, but I had wanted to go there for about as long as I could remember, certainly since I first saw *La Dolce Vita* as a teenager. I love Italian movies, especially the truly crummy ones—the ones that are only shown on television in the middle of the night and are dubbed by actors who refuse to let a total absence of acting skill stand in the way of a career in the movies. These films all seem to star Giancarlo Giannini and the delectable Ornella Muti and have titles that tell you just how bad the film is going to be—*A Night Full of Rain, That Summer in Naples, When Spring Comes*—so you know you will not be distracted by plots and can concentrate instead on the two important things, namely, waiting for Ornella Muti to shed her clothes, and looking at the scenery. Italian films are always full of good background shots—usually of Ornella and Giancarlo riding a buzzing Vespa past the Colosseum and the Piazza Navona, and the other tourist sights of Rome, on the way to having either a brisk bonk or a soulful discussion about how they can't go on like this, usually because one of them is living with Marcello Mastroianni.

Movies everywhere used to be full of this kind of local color—every film shot in Britain in the 1960s was required by law, if I am not mistaken, to show four laughing swingers in an open-topped Morgan roadster crossing Tower Bridge, filmed from a helicopter at a dizzy angle—but now everyone but the Italians seems to have abandoned the practice, which is a huge pity because my whole notion of the world was shaped by the background scenes in films like *To Catch a Thief* and *Breathless* and *Three Coins in a Fountain,* and even the Inspector Clouseau movies. If I hadn't seen these pictures, I would be living in Peoria now and thinking that that was about as rich as life gets.

Rome was as wonderful as I had hoped it would be, certainly a step up from Peoria. It was everything Stockholm was not—warm, sunny, relaxed, lively, full of good food and cheap drink. I went to dinner on the first night with an American expatriate friend who had lived there for twenty years and he complained the whole time about how expensive and impossible it had become, but it seemed wonderfully cheap after Stockholm and in any case, as I asked him, how could you sit in the open air on a warm evening eating a splendid meal and bitch about anything at all?

"Sure, sure, but you should try to get your plumbing fixed," he said, as if that settled everything. After dinner he took me on a brisk walk around the city and showed me how everything had deteriorated—how the bars on the Via Veneto had no class any longer and were full of German and American tourists too stupid and sluggish to know that they were being mercilessly ripped off; how Rugantino's, the nightclub near the Spanish Steps made famous by *La Dolce Vita,* is now a McDonald's; how some once-charming restaurant or hotel had been vandalized by tasteless proprietors whose only motivation was greed.

I listened, but I didn't hear. Everything seemed wonderful to me, even the monumentally impassive waiters, even the cab drivers, even the particular cab driver who bilked me out of the better part of thirty thousand lire—the price he quoted to take me from the Stazione Termini to my hotel, without bothering to inform me that it was two and a half blocks away and could be walked in thirty seconds—because he did it with such simplicity and charm, forgiving me my stupidity for letting him do this to me. I was so touched that I tipped him.

My hotel was in a battered, out-at-the-elbow district just off the Via Cavour—it was the sort of neighborhood where it would be all right to pee on the buildings—but it had the compensating virtue of being central. You could walk anywhere in the city from there, and that's what I did, day after day, walked and walked. I arose each morning just after dawn, during that perfect hour when the air still has a fresh, unused feel to it, and watched the city come awake— whistling shopkeepers slopping out, sweeping up, pulling down awnings, pushing up shutters.

I walked through the gardens of the Villa Borghese, up and down the Spanish Steps, window-shopped along the Via dei Condotti, admired the Colosseum and Forum, crossed the river by the Isola Tiberina to tramp the hilly streets of Trastevere, and wandered up to the lofty heights of Monte Gianicolo, where the views across the city were sensational and where young couples were entwined in steamy embraces on the narrow ledges. The Italians appear to have devised a way of having sex without taking their clothes off, and they were going at it hammer and tongs up there. I had an ice cream and watched to see how many of the lovers tumbled over the edge to be dashed on the rocks below, but none did, thank goodness. They must wear suction cups on their backs.

For a week, I walked till my feet steamed. And when I tired I sat with a coffee or sunned myself on a bench until I was ready to walk again.

Having said this, Rome is not an especially good city for walking. For one thing, there is the constant danger that you will be run over. Zebra crossings count for nothing in Rome, which takes some getting used to. It is a shock to be strolling across an expansive boulevard, lost in an idle fantasy involving Ornella Muti and a vat of Jell-O, when suddenly you become aware that the six lanes of cars bearing down on you at speed have no intention of stopping.

It isn't that they *want* to hit you, as they do in Paris, but more that they just will hit you. This is partly because Italian drivers pay no attention to anything happening on the road ahead of them. They are too busy tooting their horns, gesturing wildly, preventing other vehicles from cutting into their lane, making love, smacking the children in the backseat, and eating a sandwich the size of a baseball bat, often all at once. So the first time they are likely to notice you is in the rearview mirror as something lying in the road behind them.

Even if they do see you, they won't stop. There is nothing personal in this. It's just that they believe that if something is in the way they must move it, whether it is a telephone pole or a visitor from the Middle West. The only exception to this is nuns. Even Roman drivers won't hit a nun—you see groups of them breezing across eight-lane arteries with the most amazing impunity, like scraps of black and white paper borne along by the wind—so if you wish to cross some busy place like the Piazza Venezia, your only hope is to wait for some nuns to come along and stick to them like a sweaty T-shirt.

I love the way the Italians park. You turn any street corner in Rome and it looks as if you've just missed a parking competition for blind people. Cars are pointed in every direction, half on the sidewalks and half off, facing in, facing sideways, blocking garages and side streets and phone booths, fitted into spaces so tight that the only possible way out would be through the sun roof. Romans park their cars the way I would park if I had just spilled a beaker of hydrochloric acid on my lap.

I was strolling along the Via Sistina one morning when a Fiat Croma shot past and screeched to a smoky halt a hundred feet up the road. Without pause the driver lurched into reverse and came barreling backward down the street in the direction of a parking space that was *precisely* the length of his Fiat, less two and a half feet. Without slowing even fractionally, he veered the car into the space and crashed resoundingly into a parked Renault.

Nothing happened for a minute. There was just the hiss of escaping steam. Then the driver leaped from his car, gazed in profound disbelief at the devastation before him—crumpled metal, splintered taillights, the exhaust pipe of his own car limply grazing the pavement—and regarded it with as much mystification as if it had dropped on him from the sky. Then he did what I suppose almost any Italian would do. He kicked the Renault in the side as hard as he could, denting the door, punishing its absent owner for having the gall to park it there, then leaped back in his Fiat and drove off as madly as he had arrived, and peace returned once again to the Via Sistina, apart from the occasional clank of a piece of metal dropping off the stricken Renault. No one but me batted an eye.

All over the city you see drivers bullying their cars into spaces about the size of a sofa cushion, holding up traffic and prompting every driver within three miles to lean on his horn and give a passable imitation of a man in an electric chair. If the opening is too small for a car, the Romans will decorate it with litter—an empty cigarette packet; a wedge of half-eaten pizza; twenty-seven cigarette butts; half an ice cream cone with an ooze of old ice cream emerging from the bottom, danced on by a delirium of flies; an oily tin of sardines; a tattered newspaper; and something truly unexpected, like a tailor's dummy or a dead goat.

Even the litter didn't greatly disturb me. I know Rome is dirty and crowded and the traffic is impossible, but in a strange way that's part of the excitement. Rome is the only city I know, apart from New York, that you can say that about. In fact, New York is just what Rome reminds me of—it has the same noise, dirt, volubility, honking, the same indolent cops standing around with nothing to do, the same way of talking with one's hands, the same unfocused electric buzz of energy. The only difference is that Rome is so wondrously chaotic. New York is actually pretty well ordered. People stand patiently in line, and for the most part obey traffic signals and observe the conventions of life that keep things running smoothly.

Italians are entirely without any commitment to order. They live their lives in a kind of pandemonium, which I find very attractive. They don't line up, they don't pay their taxes, they don't turn up for appointments on time, they don't undertake any sort of labor without a small bribe, they don't believe in rules at all. On Italian trains every window bears a label telling you in three languages not to lean out the window. The labels in French and German instruct you not to lean out, but in Italian they merely suggest that it might not be a good idea. It could hardly be otherwise.

Even kidnappers in Italy can be amazingly casual. In January 1988, a gang kidnapped an eighteen-year-old named Carlo Celadon. They put him in a six-foot-deep pit in the earth where they fed him, but didn't bother sending a ransom demand until—listen to this—the following October, nine months after they took him. Can you believe that? The kidnappers demanded five billion lire (about $4 million) and the desperate parents immediately paid up, but the kidnappers then asked for more money. This time the parents balked. Eventually, two years and one hundred days after they took him, the kidnappers released him.

At the time of my visit, the Italians were working their way through their forty-eighth government in forty-five years. The country has the social structure of a banana republic, yet the amazing thing is that it thrives. It now has the fifth biggest economy in the world, which is a simply staggering achievement in the face of such chronic disorder. If the Italians had the work ethic of the Japanese they could be masters of the planet. Thank goodness they don't. They are too busy expending their considerable energies on the pleasurable minutiae of daily life—on children, on good food, on arguing in cafés—which is just how it should be.

I was in a neighborhood bar on the Via Marsala one morning when three workmen in blue boiler suits came in and stopped for coffees at the counter. After a minute one of them started thumping the other emphatically on the chest, haranguing him about something, while the third flailed his arms, made mournful noises, and staggered about as if his airway were obstructed. I thought at any moment knives would come out and there would be blood everywhere, until it dawned on me that all they were talking about was the quality of Schillaci's goal against Belgium the night before or about the mileage on a Fiat Tipo or something equally innocuous, and after a minute they drained their coffees and went off together as happy as anything.

What a wonderful country.

I WENT one morning to the Museum of the Villa Borghese. I knew from a newspaper clipping that it had been shut in 1985 for two years of repairs—the villa was built on catacombs and for years had been slowly collapsing in on itself—but when I got there the building was still covered in scaffolding and fenced off with warped and flimsy sheets of corrugated iron and looked to be nowhere near ready for the public, this a mere five years after it was shut and three years after its forecast reopening. This is the sort of constant unreliability that must be exasperating to live with (especially if you left your umbrella in the cloakroom the day before the museum shut), but you quickly take it as an inevitable part of life, like the weather in England.

The care of the nation's cultural heritage is not, it must be said, Italy's strong suit. The country spends $200 million a year on maintenance and restoration, which seems a reasonable sum until it is brought to your attention that that is less than the cost of a dozen new miles of highway, and a fraction of what was spent on stadiums for the 1990 World Cup soccer tournament. Altogether it is less than 0.2 percent of the national budget. As a result, two thirds of the nation's treasures are locked away in warehouses or otherwise denied to the public and many others are crumbling away for want of attention—in March 1989, the nine hundred-year-old civic tower of Pavia collapsed, just keeled over, killing four people—and there are so many treasures lying around that thieves can blithely walk off with them. In 1989 alone, almost thirteen thousand works of art were taken from the country's museums and churches, and as I write, some ninety thousand works of art are missing. Eighty percent of all the art thefts in Europe take place in Italy.

This casual attitude toward the national heritage is something of a tradition in Rome. For a thousand years, usually with the blessings of the Roman Catholic Church (which had a share in the profits and a lot to answer for generally, if you ask me), builders and architects looked upon the city's ancient baths, temples, and other timeless monuments as quarries. The Colosseum isn't the hulking ruin it is today because of the ravages of time, but because for hundreds of years people knocked chunks from it with sledgehammers and carted them off to nearby lime kilns to turn into cement. When Bernini needed a load of bronze to build his sumptuous *baldacchino* in St. Peter's, it was stripped from the roof of the Pantheon. It's a wonder that any of ancient Rome survives at all.

*　　*　　*

DEPRIVED OF the opportunity to explore the interior of the Borghese, I wandered instead through the surrounding gardens, now the city's largest and handsomest public park, full of still glades and piercing beams of sunlight, and enjoyed myself immensely except for one startled moment when I cut through a wooded corner and encountered a rough-looking man squatted down crapping against a tree, regarding me dolefully. I hadn't thought about this much before, but Europeans do seem to have a peculiar fondness for alfresco excretion. Along any highway in France or Belgium you can generally see somebody standing beside a parked car having a whizz in the bushes only a foot from the road. In America these people would be taken away and beaten. And in Paris you can still find the extraordinary *pissoirs,* gun-metal gray barriers that are designed to let the world see who's in there and what he's doing. I could never understand why passersby had to be treated to the sight of the occupant's lower legs and upper body.

I remember once watching a man and two women—office colleagues on their way to lunch, I guess—carrying on an animated three-way conversation while the man was standing in one of these contraptions. It seemed very odd to me that they were talking as if nothing extraordinary was going on. In England, if such a thing as a *pissoir* existed, the women would have turned away and talked between themselves, affecting not to be aware of what their colleague was up to in there. But then, according to Reay Tannahill's *Sex in History,* in eighteenth-century France, aristocratic men and women thought nothing of going to the toilet together, and sometimes would repair en masse to the privy after dinner in order not to interrupt their lively discussions. I think this explains a lot about the French.

And at the end of that enlightening digression, let us make our way to Vatican City and St. Peter's—the world's largest church in its smallest country, as many a guidebook has observed. I had always thought of Vatican City as being ancient, but in fact as an institution it dates only from 1929, when Mussolini and the pope signed the Lateran Treaty. I arrived wondering vaguely if I would have to pass through some sort of border control and pay a steep fee, but the only obstacle I encountered were two dozen jabbering men all trying to

sell me slide strips or to take my photograph with a Polaroid. I
directed them to a lady in a Denver Broncos warm-up jacket fifteen
feet away, saying that she was my wife and had all my money, and
they all rushed off to her and I was thus able to cross the great piazza
unmolested, pausing only to attach myself briefly to an American
tour group, where I learned the aforementioned fact about Mussolini
and the Lateran Treaty, and was informed which balcony the pope
would come out on if he were going to come out, which he wasn't.
This was interesting stuff, and I would have stayed with them longer,
but the guide quickly spotted me because I wasn't wearing a baseball
cap and warm-up jacket and trousers in one of the livelier primary
colors. She informed me that this was a private party, and clearly
wasn't going to continue until I had slunk off.

St. Peter's doesn't look all that fabulous from the outside, at least
not from the piazza at its foot, but step inside and it is so sensational
that your mouth falls open. St. Peter's is a marvel, so vast and
beautiful and cool and filled with treasures and airy heights and pale
beams of heavenly light that you don't know where to place your
gaze. It is the only building I have ever entered where I have actually
felt like sinking to my knees, clasping my hands heavenward, and
crying, "Take me home, Lord." No structure on earth would ever
look the same to me again.

I wandered down the wide central aisle, agog at the scale of the
place. It is 730 feet long, 364 feet wide, and 438 feet from the floor
to the top of the dome. But as Mark Twain noted in *The Innocents
Abroad,* the trouble is that because every bit of it is built to such a
scale, you have to remind yourself continually of its immensity. The
four grand pillars that support the dome don't look so mighty in
such a setting until you back up to one and abruptly realize that it is
fifty feet wide, and the *baldacchino* does indeed look, as Twain said,
like nothing more than a magnified bedstead, but it is more than half
as high as Niagara Falls. It was only when I looked down at the
length of the church where more visitors were coming in, and saw
that they looked like insects, that I had a sudden, crushing sense of
just how big this place was. It occurred to me, too, that although the
building was nearly silent and seemed almost empty—every clutch
of visitors had an area of floor space about the size of a football

field—there were nonetheless hundreds and hundreds of us in there.

I had a look at the "Pieta"—in a side vault behind a glass screen and with a barrier that keeps you so far back you can barely see it, which seems a bit harsh just because some madman attacked it once years ago—then went to the Sistine Chapel and the museums, and they were naturally impressive, but I confess that all the other visual experiences were largely wasted on me after the spacious grandeur of St. Peter's.

I walked back toward the neighborhood of my hotel along the Via della Conciliazione and was pleased to find the street crowded with souvenir shops. I have a certain weakness for tacky memorabilia, and in my experience no place is more reliable in this regard than shops specializing in religious curios. Once in Council Bluffs, Iowa, I agonized for an hour over whether to pay $49.95 for a backlit electric portrait of Christ, which when switched on gave the appearance of blood flowing perpetually from his wounds, before finally concluding that it was too tasteless even for me, and at any rate I couldn't afford it. So I thought I might find some suitably tasteless compensation here—crucifix corn-on-the-cob holders or a Nativity pen-and-pencil set or a musical Last Supper toilet paper holder, or at the very least a crucifix paperweight that said: "My Dad Went to Vatican City and All He Brought Me Was This Lousy Crucifix." But all the shops sold a more or less identical assortment of rosary beads, crucifixes in 120 sizes, plaster models of the basilica, and Pope John Paul dinner plates, none of them in remotely bad taste (unless you really went to town and bought a dozen papal plates for use at dinner parties, but that would cost a fortune), and so I trudged on. One of the worst parts about living in the 1990s is that crappy souvenirs are so hard to find these days.

O N M Y final morning I called at the Capuchin monks' mausoleum in the church of Santa Maria della Concezione off the busy Piazza Barberini. This I cannot recommend highly enough. In the sixteenth century some monk had the inspired idea of taking the bones of his deceased fellow monks and using them to decorate the place. Is that rich enough for you? Half a dozen gloomy chambers along one side of the church were filled with such attractions as an altar made of rib cages, shrines meticulously concocted from skulls and leg bones, ceilings trimmed with forearms, wall rosettes fashioned from vertebrae, chandeliers made from the bones of hands and feet. In the occasional corner stood the complete skeleton of a Capuchin monk dressed like the Grim Reaper in his hooded robe, and ranged along the outer wall were signs in six languages with such cheery sentiments as WE WERE LIKE YOU. YOU WILL BE LIKE US. and a long poem engagingly called "My Mother Killed Me!!" These guys must have been a barrel of laughs to be around. You can imagine every time you got the flu some guy coming along with a tape measure and a thoughtful expression.

Four thousand monks contributed to the display between 1528 and 1870, when the practice was stopped for being just too tacky for words. No one knows why or by whom the designs were made, but the inescapable impression is that the Capuchins once harbored in their midst a half-mad monk with time on his hands and a certain passion for tidiness. It is certainly a nice little money-spinner for the Church. A constant stream of tourists comes in, happy to hand over a stack of lire for the morbid thrill of it all. My only regret, predictably, was that they didn't have a gift shop where you could purchase a boxed set of vertebrae napkin rings, say, or backscratchers made from real arms and hands, but it was becoming obvious that in this respect I was to be thwarted.

14

NAPLES,
SORRENTO, AND
CAPRI

I CHECKED out of my hotel and walked to Rome's central station. It was, in the way of most public places in Italy, a madhouse. At every ticket window, customers were gesturing wildly. They didn't seem so much to be buying tickets as pouring out their troubles to the monumentally indifferent and weary-looking men seated behind each window. It is amazing how much emotion the Italians invest in even the simplest transactions.

I had to wait in line for forty minutes while a series of people ahead of me tore their hair and bellowed and eventually were issued a ticket and came away looking suddenly happy. I couldn't guess what their problems were, and in any case I was too busy fending off the many people who tried to cut in front of me, as if I were holding a door open for them. One of them tried twice. You need a pickax to keep your place in a Roman line.

Finally, with only a minute to spare before my train left, my turn came. I bought a second-class single to Naples—it was easy; I don't know what all the fuss was about. Then I raced around the corner to the platform and did something I've always longed to do: jumped onto a moving train—or, to be slightly more precise, fell into it, like a mailbag tossed from the platform.

The train was crowded, but I found a seat by a window, caught my breath, and mopped up the blood trickling down my shins as we lumbered slowly out through the endless tower-block suburbs of

Rome, picked up speed, and moved on to a dusty, hazy countryside full of half-finished houses and small apartment buildings with no sign of work in progress. It was a two-and-a-half-hour journey to Naples, and everyone on the train, without apparent exception, passed the time by sleeping, stirring to wakefulness only to note the location when we stopped at some drowsing station or to show a ticket to the conductor when he passed through. Most of the passengers looked poor and unshaven (even several of the women), which was a notable contrast to the worldly elegance of Rome. These people, I supposed, were mostly Neapolitan laborers who had come to Rome for the work and were now heading home to see their families.

I watched the scenery—a low plain leading to mountains of the palest green and dotted with occasional lifeless villages, all bearing yet more unfinished houses—and filled the hours dreamily embroidering my Ornella Muti fantasy, which had now grown to include a large transparent beach ball, two unicycles, a trampoline, and the massed voices of the Mormon Tabernacle Choir. The air in the carriage was warm and still, and before long I fell into a doze myself, but was startled awake after a few minutes by a baleful wailing. A Gypsy woman, overweight and in a head scarf, was passing along the carriage carrying a filthy baby, loudly orating to everyone the tale of her troubled life and asking for money, but no one gave her any. She pushed the baby in my face—he was covered in chocolate drool and so startlingly ugly that it was all I could do to keep from going "Aiieee!" and throwing my hands in front of my face—and I gave her a thousand lire as fast as I could drag it out of my pocket before Junior loosed a string of gooey brown dribble onto me. She took the money with the indifference of a conductor checking a ticket and without thanks proceeded on through the train shouting her troubles anew. The rest of the journey passed without incident.

At Naples, I emerged from the train and was greeted by twenty-seven taxi drivers, all wanting to take me someplace nice and probably distant, but I waved them away and transferred myself by foot from the squalor of the central station to the squalor of the nearby Circumvesuviana station, passing through an uninterrupted stretch of squalor en route. All along the sidewalks people sat at wobbly tables selling packets of cigarettes and cheap novelties. All the cars parked along the street were dirty and battered. All the stores looked gloomy and dusty, and their windows were full of items whose packaging had faded, sometimes almost to invisibility, in the brilliant sunshine. The city had a strange, knocked-about appeal to it—a tantalizing surfeit of grubbiness and commotion, quite unlike any city I had seen before—but the heat was terrible and I longed for a quiet day or two in a small place by the sea. Naples would have to wait.

It was getting on for rush hour by the time I got to Circumvesuviana and bought a ticket to Sorrento. The train was packed with sweating people and very slow. I sat between two fat women, all wobbling flesh, who talked across me the whole time, making it all but impossible for me to read my book or do any useful work on the Ornella Muti fantasy, but I considered myself lucky to have a place to sit, even if it was only six inches wide, and the women were marvelously soft, it must be said. I spent most of the journey with my head on one or the other of their shoulders, gazing up adoringly at their faces. They didn't seem to mind at all.

We traveled out of the slums of Naples and through the slums of the suburbs and onward into a slummy strip of countryside between Vesuvius and the sea, stopping every few hundred feet at some suburban station, where 100 people would get off and 120 would get on. Even Pompeii and Herculaneum, or Ercolano as they call it nowadays, looked shabby, all washing lines and piles of crumbled concrete, and I could see no sign of the ruins from the train. But a few miles farther on, we climbed higher up a mountainside and into a succession of tunnels. The air was suddenly cool and the villages—sometimes no more than a few houses and a church in a gap between tunnels—were stunningly pretty with long views down to the blue sea.

I fell in love with Sorrento in an instant. Perhaps it was the time of day, the weather, the sense of relief at being out of Naples, but it seemed perfect: a compact town tumbling down from the station to the Bay of Naples. At its heart was a small, busy square called the Piazza Tasso, lined with outdoor cafés. Leading off the square at one end was a network of echoing alleyways, cool and shadowy and richly aromatic, full of shopkeepers gossiping in doorways and children playing and the general tumult of Italian life. For the rest, the town appeared to consist of a dozen or so wandering streets lined with agreeable shops and restaurants and small, pleasant, old-fashioned hotels hidden away behind heavy foliage. It was lovely, perfect. I wanted to live here, starting now.

I got a room in the Hotel Eden, a medium-sized 1950s establishment on a side street, expensive but spotless, with a glimpse of sea above the rooftops and through the trees, and paced the room manically for five minutes, congratulating myself on my good fortune, before abruptly switching off the lights and returning to the streets. I had a look around, explored the maze of alleyways off the Piazza Tasso, and gazed admiringly in the neat and well-stocked shop windows along the Corso Italia, then repaired to an outdoor seat at Tonino's snack bar on the square, where I ordered a Coke and watched the passing scene, radiating contentment.

The town was full of middle-aged English tourists having an off-season holiday (i.e., one they could afford). Wisps of conversation floated to me across the tables and from couples passing on the sidewalk. It was always the same. The wife would be in noisemaking mode, that incessant, pointless, mildly fretful chatter that overtakes Englishwomen in midlife. "I was going to get tights today and I forgot. I asked you to remind me, Gerald. These ones have a ladder in them from here to Amalfi. I suppose I *can* get tights here. I haven't a clue what size to ask for. I knew I should have packed an extra pair. . . ." Gerald was never listening to any of this, of course, because he was secretly ogling a braless beauty leaning languorously on a lamppost and trading quips with some hoods on Vespas, and appeared to be aware of his wife only as a mild, chronic irritant on the fringe of his existence. Everywhere I went in Sorrento I kept seeing these English couples, the wife looking critically at everything, as if she were working undercover for the Ministry of Sanitation, the husband dragging along behind her, worn and defeated.

I had dinner at a restaurant just off the square. The place was packed, but friendly and efficient, and the food was generous and superb—ravioli in cream, a heap of scallopine alla Sorrentino, a large but simple salad, and an overample bowl of homemade ice cream that caused tears of pleasure to well in my eye sockets.

Afterward, as I sat bloated with a coffee and a cigarette, resting my stomach on the tabletop, an interesting thing happened. A party of eight people came in, looking rich and self-important and distinctly shady, the women in furs, the men in cashmere coats and sunglasses, and within a minute a brouhaha had erupted, sufficiently noisy to make the restaurant fall silent as everyone, customers and waiters alike, looked over.

Apparently the new arrivals had a reservation, but their table wasn't ready—there wasn't an empty table in the place—and they were engaged in various degrees of making a stink about it. The manager, wringing his hands, soaked up the abuse and had all his waiters dashing around like scene shifters, with chairs and tablecloths and vases of flowers, trying to assemble a makeshift table for eight in an already crowded room. The only person not actively involved in this was the head of the party, a man who looked uncannily like the actor Adolfo Celli and stood aloof, a thousand-dollar coat draped over his shoulders. He said nothing except to make a couple of whispered observations into the ear of a pock-faced henchman, which I assumed involved concrete boots and the insertion of a dead fish in someone's mouth.

The headwaiter dashed over and fawningly reported that they had so far assembled a table for six, and hoped to have the other places shortly, but if in the meantime the ladies would like to be seated. . . . He touched the floor with his forehead. But this was received as a further insult. Adolfo whispered again to his henchman, who departed, presumably to get a machine gun or to drive a bulldozer through the front wall.

Just then I said, "Scusi" (for my Italian was coming on a treat), "you can have my table. I'm just going." I drained my coffee, gathered my change, and stood up. The manager looked as if I had saved his life, which I would like to think I may have, and the headwaiter clearly thought about kissing me full on the lips, but instead covered me with obsequious *grazies*. I've never felt so popular. The waiters beamed and many of the other diners regarded me with, if I say it myself, a certain lasting admiration. Even Adolfo inclined his head in a tiny display of gratitude and respect. As my table was whipped away, I was escorted to the door by the manager and headwaiter, who bowed and thanked me and brushed my shoulders with a whisk broom and offered me their daughters' hands in marriage or even just for some hot sex. I turned at the door, hesitated for a moment, suddenly boyish and good-looking, a Hollywood smile on my face, tossed a casual wave to the room and disappeared into the evening.

WEIGHTED DOWN with good pasta and a sense of having brought peace to a troubled corner of Sorrento, I strolled through the warm twilight along the Corso Italia and up to the coast road to Positano, the high and twisting Via del Capo, where hotels had been hacked into the rockface to take advantage of the commanding view across the Bay of Naples. All the hotels had names that were redolent of another age—the Bel Air, the Bellevue Syrene, the Admiral, the Caravel—and looked as if they hadn't changed a whit in forty years. I spent an hour draped over the railings at the roadside, staring transfixed across the magical sweep of bay to Vesuvius and distant Naples and, a little to the left, floating in the still sea, the islands of Procida and Ischia. Lights began to twinkle on around the bay, and were matched by early evening stars in the grainy blue sky. The air was warm and kind and had a smell of fresh-baked bread. This was as close to perfection as anything I had ever encountered.

On the distant headland overlooking the bay was the small city of Pozzuoli, really a suburb of Naples and the hometown of Sophia Loren. The citizens of Pozzuoli enjoy the dubious distinction of living on the most geologically unstable piece of land on the planet, the terrestrial equivalent of a Vibro-Bed. They experience up to four thousand earth tremors a year, sometimes as many as a hundred in a day. People in Pozzuoli are so used to having pieces of plaster fall into their ragù and tumbling chimneystacks knock off their grannies that they hardly notice it anymore.

This whole area is like an insurance man's worst nightmare. Earthquakes are a way of life in Calabria—Naples had one in 1980 that left 250,000 people homeless, and another even fiercer one could come at any time. The towns are built on hills so steep that they look as if the tiniest rumble would send them sliding into the sea. And on top of that, quite literally, there's always Vesuvius grumbling away in the background, still dangerously alive. It last erupted in 1944, which makes this its longest period of quiescence since the seventeenth century. Doesn't sound very promising, does it?

I stared for a long time out across the water at Pozzuoli's lights and listened intently for a low boom, like scaffolding collapsing, or the sound of the earth tearing itself apart, but I heard nothing, only the mosquito buzz of an airplane high above, a blinking red dot moving steadily across the sky, and the soothing background hum of Sorrento traffic.

I N T H E morning I walked through bright sunshine down to the Sorrento marina along a perilously steep and gorgeous road called the Via da Maio, in the shadow of the Grand Hotel Excelsior Vittoria, and took a nearly empty hover-ferry to Capri, a mountainous outcrop of green ten miles away off the western tip of the Sorrentine Peninsula.

Up close, Capri didn't look much. Around the harbor stood a dozing, unsightly collection of shops, cafés, and ferry booking offices. All of them appeared to be shut, and there was not a soul about except for a sailor with Popeye arms lazily coiling rope at the quayside. A road led steeply off up the mountain. Beside it stood a sign saying: CAPRI 6 KM.

"Six kilometers!" I squeaked.

I had with me two incredibly useless guidebooks to Italy, so useless that I'm not even going to dignify them by revealing their titles here, except to say that one of them should have been called *Let's Go Get Another Guidebook* and the other was Fodor's (I was lying a minute ago). Neither of them so much as hinted that Capri town was miles away up a vertical mountainside. They both made it sound as if all you had to do was spring off the ferry and there you were. But from the quayside, Capri town looked to be somewhere up in the clouds.

The *funicolare* up the mountainside wasn't running. (Natch.) I looked around for a bus or a taxi or even a burro, but there was nothing, so with a practiced sigh I turned and began the long trek up. It was a taxing climb, mollified by some attractive villas and sea views. The road snaked up the mountain in a series of long, lazy

S-bends, but a mile or so along, some steep and twisting steps had been hewn out of the undergrowth and they appeared to offer a more direct, if rather more precipitate, route to Capri town. I ventured up them. I have never seen such endless steps. They just went on and on. They were closed in by the whitewashed walls of villas on both sides and overhung by tumbling fragrant shrubs—highly fetching, but after about the three hundredth step I was gasping and sweating so much that the beauty was entirely lost on me.

Because of the irregular geography of the hillside, it looked as if the summit might be just ahead, but then I would round a turning to be confronted by another expanse of steps and yet another receding view of the town. I stumbled on, reeling from wall to wall, gasping and wheezing, shedding saliva, watched with silent interest by three women in black coming down the steps with the day's shopping. "Buon giorno, aaargh, oh God oh God oh God, aargh!" I sputtered as I stumbled past them. The only thing sustaining me was the thought that clearly I was going to be the only person tenacious enough to make the climb to Capri. Whatever lay up there was going to be mine, all mine. Eventually, the houses grew closer together until they were interconnected, like blocks of Lego, and the steps became a series of steep cobbled alleyways. I passed beneath an arch and stepped out into one of the loveliest squares I have ever seen. It was packed with German and Japanese tourists. The tears streamed down my cheeks.

I GOT a room in the Hotel Capri. "Great name! How long did it take you to come up with it?" I asked the manager, but he just gave me the look of studied disdain that European hotel managers reserve for American tourists and other insects. I don't know why he was so snooty because it wasn't a great hotel. It didn't even have a bellboy, so the manager had to show me to my room himself, though he left me to deal with my baggage. We went up a grand staircase, where two workmen were busy dribbling a nice shade of ocher on the marble steps and occasionally putting some of it on the wall, and to a tiny room on the third floor. As he was the manager, I wasn't sure whether to give him a tip, as I would a bellboy, or whether this would be an insult to his lofty position. In the event, I settled on what I thought was an intelligent compromise. I tipped him, but I made it a very small tip. He looked at it as if I had dropped a ball of lint into his palm, leading me to conclude that perhaps I had misjudged the situation. "Maybe you'll laugh at my jokes next time," I remarked cheerfully, under my breath, as I shut the door on him.

Capri town was gorgeous, an infinitely charming little place of villas and tiny lemon groves and long views across the bay to Naples and Vesuvius. The heart of the town was a small square, the Piazza Umberto I, lined with cream-colored buildings and filled with tables and wicker chairs from the cafés ranged around it. At one end, up some wide steps, stood an old church, dignified and white, and at the other was a railinged terrace with an open view to the sea far below.

I have never seen a more beguiling place for walking. The town consisted almost entirely of a complex network of white-walled lanes and passageways, many barely wider than your shoulders, and all of them interconnected in a wonderfully bewildering fashion, so that I would constantly find myself returning to a spot I had departed from in an opposing direction ten minutes before. Every few yards an iron gate would be set in the wall through which I could glimpse a white cottage in a jungle of flowery shrubs and, usually, a quarry-tiled terrace overlooking the sea. Every few yards a cross passageway would plunge off down the hillside or a set of steps would climb halfway to the clouds to a scattering of villas high above. I wanted every house I saw.

There were no roads at all, apart from the one leading from the harbor to the town and onward to Anacapri, on the far side of the island. Everywhere else had to be got to on foot, often after an arduous trek. Capri must be the worst place in the world to be a washing machine delivery man.

Most of the shops lay beyond the church up the steps from the central piazza, in yet another series of lanes and little squares of unutterable charm. They all had names like Gucci and Yves Saint Laurent, which suggested that the summertime habitués must be rich and insufferable, but mercifully most of the shops were still not open for the season, and there was no sign of the yachting-capped assholes and bejeweled crinkly women who must make them prosper in the summer.

A few of the lanes were enclosed, like catacombs, with the upper stories of the houses completely covering the passageways. I followed one of these lanes now as it wandered upward through the town and finally opened again to the sky in a neighborhood where the villas began to grow larger and enjoy more spacious grounds. The path meandered and climbed, so much so that I grew breathless again and propelled myself onward by pushing my hands against my knees, but the scenery and setting were so fabulous that I was dragged on, as if by magnets. Near the top of the hill the path leveled out and ran through a grove of pine trees, heavy with the smell of rising sap. On one side of the path were grand villas—I couldn't imagine by what method furniture got there when people moved in or out—and on the other was a giddying view of the island; white villas strewn across the hillsides, half buried in hibiscus and bougainvillea and a myriad other types of shrub.

It was nearly dusk. A couple of hundred yards farther on, the path rounded a bend through the trees and ended suddenly, breathtakingly, in a viewing platform hanging out over a precipice of rock—a little patio in the sky. It was a lookout built for the public, but I had the feeling that no one had been there for years, certainly no tourist. It was the sheerest stroke of luck that I had stumbled on it. I have never seen anything half as beautiful—on one side the town of Capri spilling down the hillside, on the other the twinkling lights of the cove at Anacapri and the houses gathered around it, and in front of me a sheer drop of—what?—two hundred feet, three hundred feet, to a sea of the lushest aquamarine washing against outcrops of jagged rock. The sea was so far below that the sound of breaking waves reached me as the faintest of whispers. A sliver of moon, brilliantly white, hung in a pale blue evening sky, a warm breeze teased my hair, and everywhere there were scents of lemon and honeysuckle and pine. Ahead of me there was nothing but open sea, calm and seductive, for 150 miles to Sicily. I would do anything to own that view, anything. I would sell my mother to Donald Trump. I would renounce my citizenship and walk across fire. I would trade eyelashes—yes!—with Tammy Bakker.

Just above me, I realized after a moment, overlooking this secret place was the patio of a villa set back just out of sight. Somebody *did* own that view, could sit there every morning with his Grape-Nuts and orange juice, in his Yves Saint Laurent bathrobe and Gucci slippers, and look out on this sweep of Mediterranean heaven. It occurred to me that it probably was owned by Donald Trump, or the Italian equivalent, some guy who only uses it for about two minutes a decade and then is too busy making deals and screwing people by telephone to notice the view. Isn't it strange how wealth is always wasted on the rich? And with this discouraging thought I returned to the town.

I HAD a dinner in a splendid, friendly, almost empty restaurant on a back street, sitting in a windowseat with a view over the sea, and had the chilling thought that I was becoming stupefied with all this ease and perfection. I began to feel that queasy guilt that you can only know if you have lived among the English—a terrible suspicion that any pleasure involving more than a cup of milky tea and a chocolate digestive biscuit is somehow irreligiously excessive. I knew with a profound sense of doom that I would pay for this when I got home—I would have to sit for whole evenings in an icy draft and go for long tramps over wild, spongy moors and eat at a Wimpy's at least twice before I began to feel even the tiniest sense of expiation. Still, at least I was feeling guilty for enjoying myself so much, and that made me feel slightly better.

It was after eight when I emerged from the restaurant, but the neighboring businesses were still open—people were buying wine and cheese, picking up a loaf of bread, even having their hair cut. The Italians sure know how to arrange things. I had a couple of beers in the Caffè Funicolare, then wandered idly into the main square. The German and Japanese tourists were nowhere to be seen, presumably tucked up in bed or, more probably, hustled back to the mainland on the last afternoon ferry. Now it was just locals, standing around in groups of five or six, chatting in the pleasant evening air, beneath the stars, with the dark sea and far-off lights of Naples as a backdrop. It seemed to be the practice of the townspeople to congregate here after supper for a half hour's conversation. The teenagers lounged on the church steps, while the smaller children raced among the grownups' legs. Everyone seemed incredibly happy. I longed to be part of it, to live on this green island with its wonderful views and friendly people and excellent food, and to stroll nightly to this handsome square with its incomparable terrace and chat with my neighbors.

I stood off to one side and studied the dynamics of the scene. People wandered about from cluster to cluster, as they would at a cocktail party. Eventually, they would gather up their children and wander off home, but then others would come along. No one seemed to stay for more than half an hour, but the gathering itself went on all evening. A young man, who was obviously a newcomer to Capri, stood shyly on the fringe of a group of men, smiling at their jokes. But after a few moments he was brought into the conversation, literally pulled in with an arm, and soon he was talking away with the rest of them.

I stood there for ages, perhaps for an hour and a half, then turned and walked back toward my hotel and realized that I had fallen spectacularly, hopelessly, and permanently in love with Italy.

I AWOKE to a gloomy day. The hillsides behind the town were obscured by a wispy haze, and Naples across the bay appeared to have been taken away in the night. There was nothing but a plain of dead sea and beyond it the tumbling fog that creatures from beyond the grave stumble out of in B-movies. I had intended to walk to the hilltop ruins of Tiberius's villa, where the old rascal used to have guests who displeased him hurled over the ramparts onto the rocks hundreds of feet below—what charming people the Romans were—but when I emerged from the hotel, a cold, slicing rain was falling, and I spent the morning wandering from café to café, drinking cappuccinos and scanning the sky. Late in the morning, out of time to see Tiberius's villa unless I stayed another day, which I could scarce afford to do, I reluctantly checked out of the Hotel Capri and walked down the steep and slippery steps to the quay, where I purchased a ticket on a slow ferry to Naples.

The rain had stopped by the time we docked, but the sky was still threatening. Naples looked even worse after Sorrento and Capri than it had before. I walked for half a mile along the waterfront, but there was no sign of happy fishermen mending their nets and singing "Santa Lucia," as I had fervently hoped there might be. Instead there were just menacing-looking derelicts and mountains—and I mean mountains—of garbage on every corner and yet more people selling lottery tickets and trinkets from cardboard tables.

I had no map and only the vaguest sense of the geography of the city, but I turned inland, hoping that I would blunder onto some shady square lined with small but decent hotels. Surely even Naples must have its finer corners. Instead, I found precisely the sort of streets that you automatically associate with Naples—mean, cavernous, semipaved alleyways with plaster peeling off walls and washing hung like banners between balconies that never saw sunlight. The streets were full of overplump women and unattended toddlers, often naked from the waist down, in filthy T-shirts.

I felt as if I had wandered onto another continent. In the center of Naples some seventy thousand families live even now in cramped *bassi*—tenements without baths or running water, sometimes without even a window, with up to fifteen members of an extended family living together in a single room. The worst of these districts, the Vicaria, in which I was walking, is said to have the highest population density in Europe. And it has crime to match—especially for the pettier crimes like car theft (29,000 in one year) and muggings. Yet I felt safe enough. No one paid any attention to me except occasionally to give me a stray smile or, among the younger people, to shout some smart-ass but not especially hostile wisecrack. I was clearly a tourist with my rucksack and I confess I clutched the straps with a certain firmness, but there was no sign of the *scippatori,* the famous bag snatchers on Vespas, who doubtless sensed that all they would get was some dirty underpants, half a bar of chocolate, and a tattered copy of H. V. Morton's *A Traveller in Southern Italy.*

They are used to having a hard time of it in Naples. After the war, people were so starving that they ate everything alive in the city, including all the fish in the aquarium, and an estimated one third of the women took up prostitution, at least part time, just to survive. Even now the average worker in Naples earns only a third of what he would receive in Milan. However, the city has also brought a lot of problems on itself, largely through corruption and incompetence.

As of 1986, according to *The Economist,* Naples had not paid its own street-lighting bill for three years and had run up a debt of $1.1 billion. Every service in the city is constantly on the brink of collapse. It has twice as many garbage men as Milan, a bigger city, but the streets are filthy and the service is appalling. Naples has become effectively ungovernable.

I passed the Istituto Tecno Commerziale, where a riot seemed to be in progress both inside and outside the building. Students were hanging out the upstairs windows, tossing down books and papers, and holding shouted exchanges with their colleagues on the ground. Whether this was some sort of protest or merely part of the daily routine I couldn't tell. All I know is that everywhere I went there were rubbish and pandemonium—people shouting, horns honking, ambulances bleating.

After Capri the din and filth were hard to take. I walked and walked, but things never got any better. I found the main shopping street, the Via Roma, and though the shops were generally smart, it was thronged with people and litter and all but impossible to walk along without stepping down off the sidewalk and into the fringes of the lunatic traffic. Not once did I see a hotel that looked as if its beds were occupied for more than twenty minutes at a time.

Eventually, to my considerable surprise, I found myself in the Piazza Garibaldi, in front of the central railway station. I had walked right across Naples. Sweat-streaked and footsore, I looked back at the city I had just walked through and thought about giving it one more try. But I couldn't face it. Instead, I went into the station, waving off the twenty-seven cab drivers, and bought a ticket to Florence. Things would have to be better there.

FLORENCE

I **WENT** to Florence on the world's slowest train. It limped across the landscape like a runner with a pulled muscle, and it had no buffet car. At first it was crowded, but as afternoon gave way to evening and evening merged into the inkiness of night, there were fewer and fewer people left, until eventually it was just a business-man buried in paperwork, and a guy who looked as if he were on his way to an Igor look-alike competition, and me. Every two or three miles the train stopped at some darkened station where no train had stopped for weeks, where grass grew on the platforms, and where no one got on and no one got off.

Sometimes the train would come to a halt in the middle of no-where, in the black countryside, and just sit. It would sit for so long that you began to wonder if the driver had gone off into the sur-rounding fields for a pee and fallen down a well. After a time the train would roll backward for perhaps thirty yards, then stop and sit again. Then suddenly, with a mighty *whoomp* that made the carriage rock and the windows sound as if they were about to implode, a train on the parallel line would fly past. Bright lights would flash by—you could see people in there dining and playing cards, having a won-derful time, moving across Europe at the speed of a laser—and then all would be silence again and we would sit for another eternity before our train gradually gathered the energy to creep onward to the next desolate station.

It was well after eleven when we reached Florence. I was starving and weary and felt that I deserved any luxury that came my way. I saw with alarm, but not exactly surprise, that the restaurants around the station were all closed. One snack bar was still lighted and I hastened to it, dreaming of a pizza the size of a trash-can lid, drowning in mushrooms and salami and olive oil, but the proprietor was just locking up as I reached the door.

Dejected, I went to the first hotel I came to, a modern concrete box half a block away. I could tell from the outside that it was going to be expensive, and it contravened all my principles to patronize a hotel of such exquisite ugliness, especially in a city as historic as Florence, but I was tired and hungry and in serious need of a pee and a face wash and my principles were just tapped out.

The receptionist quoted me some ludicrous figure for a single room, but I accepted with a weary wave and was shown to my room by a 112-year-old porter who escorted me into the world's slowest elevator and from whom I learned, during the course of our two-day ascent to the fourth floor, that the dining room was closed and there was no room service—he said this with a certain smack of pride—but that the bar would be open for another thirty-five minutes and I might be able to get some small snack stuff there. He waggled his fingers cheerfully to indicate that this was by no means a certainty.

I was desperate for a pee and to get to the bar before it shut, but the porter was one of those who feel they have to show you everything in the room and required me to follow him around while he demonstrated the shower and television and showed me where the closet was. "Thank you, I would never have found that closet without you," I said, pressing thousand-lire notes into his pocket and more or less bundling him out the door. I don't like to be rude, but I felt as if I were holding back Hoover Dam. I barely made it, but, oh my, the relief. I washed my face, grabbed a book, and hastened to the elevator. I could hear it still descending. I pushed the DOWN button and looked at my watch. Things weren't too bad. I still had twenty-five minutes till the bar closed, time enough for a beer and whatever snacks they could offer. I pushed the button again and passed the time by humming the "Waiting for an Elevator Song," puffing my cheeks for the heck of it, and wondering again why hotel carpet is always *so* ugly.

Still the elevator didn't come. I decided to take the fire stairs. I bounded down them two at a time, the whole of my existence dedicated to the idea of a beer and a sandwich, and at the bottom found a padlocked door and a sign in Italian that said: IF THERE IS EVER A FIRE HERE, THIS IS WHERE THE BODIES WILL PILE UP." Without pause, I bounded back up to the second floor. The door there was locked, too. Through a tiny window I could see the bar: dark and cozy and still full of people. Somebody was playing a piano. What's more, there were little bowls of peanuts and pistachios on each table. I'd settle for that! I tapped on the door and scraped it with my fingernails, but nobody could hear me, so I bounded up to the third floor and the door there was unlocked, thank goodness. I went straight to the elevator and jabbed the DOWN button. An instant later the UP light dinged on and the doors slid open to reveal three Japanese men in identical blue suits. I indicated to them, as best as I could in my breathless state, that they were going the wrong direction for me and that my reluctance to join them had nothing to do with Pearl Harbor or anything like that. We exchanged little bows and the door closed.

I pushed the DOWN button again and immediately the doors popped open to reveal the Japanese men. This was repeated four times until it dawned on me that I was somehow canceling out their instructions to ascend, so I stood back and let them go away. I waited a full two minutes: caught my breath, counted my remaining travelers' checks, hummed the Elevator Song, glanced at my watch—ten minutes till closing!—and pushed the DOWN button.

Immediately the doors opened to reveal the Japanese men still standing there. Impulsively I jumped on with them. I don't know if it was the extra weight that kick-started it, but we began to rise, at the usual speed of about one foot every thirty seconds. The elevator was tiny. We were close enough together to be arrested in some countries and as I was facing them, all but rubbing noses, I felt compelled to utter some pleasantry.

"Businessmen?" I asked.

One of them gave a small, meaningless bow from the shoulders.

"In Italy on business?" I elaborated. It was a stupid question. How many people go on vacation in blue suits?

The Japanese man bowed again and I realized he had no idea what I was saying.

"Do you speak English?"

"Ahhhr . . . No," said the second man, as if not certain, swaying just a tiny bit, and it dawned on me that they were all extremely drunk. I looked at the third man and he bowed before I could say anything.

"You guys been to the bar?" A small, uncomprehending bow. I was rather beginning to enjoy this one-way conversation. "You look like you've had a few, if you don't mind my saying so. Hope nobody's going to be sick!" I added jauntily.

The elevator crept on and eventually thudded to a halt. "Well, here we are, gentlemen, eighth floor. Alight here for all stations to Iwo Jima."

They turned to me in the hallway and said simultaneously, "Buon giorno."

"And a very buon giorno to you," I riposted, jabbing button number one anxiously.

I got to the bar two minutes before it shut, though in fact it was effectively shut already. An overzealous waiter had gathered up all the little dishes of nuts and the pianist was nowhere to be seen. It didn't really matter because they didn't serve snacks there anyway. I returned to my room, rummaged in the minibar and found two tiny foil bags containing about fourteen peanuts each. I searched again, but this was the only food among the many bottles of soft drinks and intoxicants. As I stood eating the peanuts one at a time, to make the pleasure last, I idly looked at the minibar tariff card and discovered that this pathetic little snack was costing me $4.80. Or at least it would have if I'd been foolish enough to tell anyone about it.

IN THE morning I transferred to the Hotel Corallo on the Via Nazionale. The room had no TV, but there was a free showercap and it was fifty thousand lire a day cheaper. I have never seen a smaller bathroom. The bathroom and shower stall were effectively one and the same. There was a nozzle on the wall and no curtain. You just shut the door to the bedroom and let the shower spray all over everything—over the toilet, over the sink, over yesterday's copy of *The Guardian*, over your fresh change of underwear. It took some getting used to.

I went first to the cathedral, or Duomo, the centerpiece of the town. I defy anyone to turn the corner into the cathedral piazza and not have his little heart leap. It is one of Europe's great sights. But it was packed with tourists and with people trying to sell them things. When I was there in 1972, Florence was crowded, but it was August and you expected it. This was a weekday in April, in the middle of the working year, and it was far worse.

I walked down to the Uffizi Palace and around the Piazza della Signoria and the other fixtures of the old part of town and it was the same everywhere—throngs of people, almost all of them from abroad, shuffling about in that aimless, exasperating way of visitors, in groups of five and six, always looking at something about twenty feet above ground level. What is it they see up there?

In my adolescent years whenever I was in crowded places, I often pretended I had a ray gun with me, which I could use to vaporize anyone I didn't like the look of—dawdlers, couples in matching outfits, children called "Junior" and "Chip." I always imagined striding through the crowd, firing the gun at selected targets, and shouting: "Make way, please! Culling!" I felt a little like that now.

There were hundreds of Japanese—not just the traditional busloads of middle-aged camera-toters but also students and young couples and backpackers. They were at least as numerous as Americans, and Americans were everywhere, plus hordes of Germans and Australians and Scandinavians and Dutch and British and on and on. You wonder how many people one city can absorb.

Here's an interesting statistic for you: In 1951, the year I was born, there were seven million international airline passengers in the world. Now that many people fly to Hawaii every year. The more popular tourist places of Europe routinely receive numbers of visitors that dwarf their own populations. In Florence the annual ratio of tourists to locals is 14:1. How can any place preserve any kind of independent life when it is so manifestly overwhelmed? It can't. It's as simple as that.

It is of course hypocritical to rail against tourists when you are one yourself, but nonetheless mass tourism is ruining the very things it comes to celebrate. And it can only get worse as the Japanese and other rich Asians become bolder travelers. When you add in the tens of millions of Eastern Europeans who are free at last to go where they want, we could be looking back on the last thirty years as a golden age of travel. God help us all.

Nowhere is the decline in quality in Florence more vivid than the Ponte Vecchio, the shop-lined bridge across the Arno River. Twenty years ago the Ponte Vecchio was home to silversmiths and artisan jewelers and it was quiet enough, even in August, that you could take a picture of a friend (or in my case a picture of Stephen Katz) sitting on the bridge rail. Now it's like the stowage deck of the *Lusitania* just after somebody said, "Say, is that a torpedo?" The bridge was covered with Senegalese immigrants selling semicrappy items of jewelery and replica Louis Vuitton luggage, spread out on blankets or pieces of black velvet. And the crowds of tourists pushing among them were unbelievable. It took me half an hour to bulldoze my way through, and I didn't try it again for the rest of the week. Far easier, I concluded, to make a quarter-mile detour to the Ponte Santa Trinità, the next bridge downriver, and cross from there.

The city fathers of Florence could do a good deal more to ease the pressures—for example, allow museums to be open for more than a couple of hours a day, so that everybody doesn't have to go at once. I went to the Uffizi and had to stand in line for forty minutes and then had to shuffle around amid crowds of people straining to see the paintings. Several rooms were roped off and darkened. Again, surely, they could spread the crowds around by opening more rooms and showing more paintings. In 1900, the Uffizi had 2,395 paintings on display. Today it shows just five hundred. The others are locked away, almost never seen.

Still, few galleries are more worth the frustration. The Uffizi must have more perfect paintings than any other gallery on the planet— not just Tintorettos and Botticellis, but the most sumptuous and arresting works by people till now quite unknown to me, like Gentile da Fabriano and Simone Martini. It struck me as odd that the former artists could be so much more famous than the latter ones. Then again, a hundred years from now it could easily be the other way around. Old masters come and go. Did you know, for instance, that Piero della Francesca was all but unknown a century ago? It seems impossible to look at his portraits of the Duke of Urbino and not see them instantly as masterpieces, but Ruskin in all his writings mentioned him only once in passing, and Walter Pater mentioned him not at all, and the bible of the nineteenth-century art world, Heinrich Wölfflin's *Classic Art,* appeared to be unaware of his existence. It wasn't until 1951, with a study by Kenneth Clark, that people really began to appreciate him again. The same was true of Caravaggio and Botticelli, whose works spent much of two centuries tucked away in attics, quite unloved. Caravaggio's "Bacchus" was found in an Uffizi storeroom in 1916.

I SPENT four days wandering around Florence, trying to love it, but generally failing. The famous view of the rooftops from the Boboli Gardens—the one that graces a thousand postcards—was splendid, and I liked the long walks along the Arno, but mostly I was disappointed. Even when making allowances for the hordes of tourists, I couldn't help feeling that much of Florence was tawdrier than any city so beautiful and historic and lavishly subsidized by visitors had any right to be. There was litter everywhere, and Gypsy beggars constantly importuning passersby, and Senegalese street vendors cluttering every sidewalk with their sunglasses and Louis Vuitton luggage, and cars parked half on the narrow sidewalks so that you constantly had to step in the road to get past them. You don't so much walk around Florence as pick your way among the obstacles. Everything seemed dusty and in need of a wash. The trattorias were crowded and expensive and often unfriendly, especially in the center of town. Nobody seemed to love the city. Even rich people dropped litter without qualm. The buildings around the Duomo seemed to grow progressively dustier and shabbier each time I walked past them.

Why is it that the cities that people most want to see are the ones that so often do the least to make it agreeable to do so? Why can't the Florentines see that it would be in their own interest to sweep up the litter and put out some benches and force the Gypsies to stop being so persistent in panhandling and spend more on brightening the place up? Florence has more treasures than any city in the world—twenty-one palaces, fifty-five historic churches, eight galleries, twenty museums—more than the whole of Spain, according to a UNESCO report, and yet the annual restoration budget for the entire city is less than $10 million. (The Archaeological Museum alone has ten thousand pieces still waiting to be cleaned from the great flood of 1966.) It's no wonder so much of it looks unloved.

Where neglect doesn't come into play, incompetence and corruption often do. In 1986, the long-overdue decision was taken to restore the cobbles of the Piazza della Signoria. The ancient stones were dug up and taken away for cleaning. When they were returned they looked brand-new. They were brand-new. The originals, or so it was alleged, had been taken away and sold for a fortune and could now be found as driveways to rich people's houses.

It was the Gypsies who got to me the most. They sit along almost every street, calling out to passersby, with heartbreakingly filthy children of three and four stuck on their laps, made to sit there for hour after hour just to heighten the pathos. It's inhuman, as scandalous as making the children work in a sweatshop, and yet the *carabinieri*, who strut through the streets in groups of three and four, looking smart and lethal in their uniforms, pay them not the slightest notice.

The only Gypsy I didn't mind, curiously enough, was the little girl who picked my pocket as I was leaving the city. The kid was magic. It was a Sunday morning, brilliantly sunny. I had just checked out of the hotel and was heading for the station to catch a train to Milan. As I reached the street opposite the station, three children carrying wrinkled, day-old newspapers approached, trying to sell them to me. I waved them away. One, a jabbering and unwashed girl of about eight, was unusually persistent and pressed the paper on me to such an extent that I stopped and warned her off with a firm voice and a finger in her face and she slunk off, abashed. I walked on, with the cocksure strut of a guy who knows how to handle himself on the street, and ten feet later knew without even feeling my pockets that something was missing. I looked down and the inside breast pocket of my jacket was unzipped and gaping emptily. In the time it had taken me to give the kid a five-second lecture on street etiquette, she had managed to reach into my jacket, unzip the pocket, dip a hand inside, withdraw two folders of travelers' checks, and pocket them. I wasn't angry. I was impressed. I couldn't have been more im-

pressed if I had found myself standing there in my underpants. I took
inventory of my rucksack and other pockets, but nothing else had
been disturbed. The girl, who of course was now nowhere to be
seen—who was probably at that moment sitting down to a feast of
truffles and Armagnac with her seventy-four nearest relatives at a
campground somewhere in the hills—had got fifteen hundred dollars' worth of travelers' checks, not bad for five seconds' work.

I went to the police office at the train station, but the policeman
there, sitting with his feet evidently nailed to the desk, did not want
his Sunday morning disturbed and indicated that I should go to the
Questura, the central police office. It never entered his mind to go
out and try to find the little culprit. Only with reluctance did he
write down the Questura's address on a scrap of paper I found
for him.

I climbed into a cab and told the driver where to take me. "Peek-
pockets?" he asked, looking at me in the rearview mirror as we
whizzed through the streets. This Questura run was obviously part
of his Sunday morning routine.

"Yes," I said, a bit sheepishly.

"Geepsies," he added with disgust and made a spitting sound, and
that was the end of our conversation.

I presented myself at the guardroom of the Questura and was
directed upstairs to a waiting room, a bare cell with gray, flaking
walls and a high ceiling. There were three others ahead of me. Occasionally, a policeman or policewoman would come and summon
one of them. I waited an hour. Others came and were seen ahead of
me. Eventually, I presented myself at one of the cubicles around the
corner and was told curtly to return to the waiting room.

I had with me a Fodor's guide to Italy, which contained an ap-
pendix of Italian-English phrases, and I looked through it now to see
if it offered anything applicable to encounters with sticky-fingered
Gypsy children. But it was only full of the usual guidebook type of
sentences, like "Where can I buy silk stockings, a map of the city,
films?" (my shopping list exactly!) and "I want: razorblades, a haircut, a shave, a shampoo, to send a telegram to England (America)."
The utter uselessness of the language appendices in guidebooks never
fails to fascinate me. Take this sentence from Fodor's, which I quote

here verbatim: "Will you prepare a bath for seven o'clock, ten o'clock, half-past ten, midday, midnight, today, tomorrow, the day after tomorrow?" Think about it. Why would anyone want to order a bath for midnight the day after tomorrow? The book doesn't tell you how to say "good night" or "good afternoon," but it does tell you how to ask for silk stockings and get baths drawn around the clock. What sort of world do they think we're living in?

Not only are you unlikely ever to need the things described, but they overlook the somewhat elementary consideration that even if you do by some wild chance require tincture of paregoric, three opera tickets, and water for your radiator, and even if you sit up all night committing to memory the Italian for these expressions, you are not going to have the faintest idea what the person says to you in reply.

Yet I find myself studying them with an endless sense of wonder. Take this sentence: "We would like a bathing cabin for two, a beach umbrella, three deck chairs." Why three deck chairs, but a bathing cabin for two? Who is being made to change outside? It must be the old roué in the party who used the book for private purposes and shamed the family by going into a pharmacy and saying leeringly to the lady behind the counter, "I'd like these two enlarged," then adding with a suggestive whisper: "Will you put some air in my tires?"

I always end up trying to imagine the person who compiled the list. In this case, it was obviously one of those imperious, middle-aged, mannish Englishwomen with stout shoes and Buster Brown haircuts often seen at foreign hotels, banging the desk bell and demanding immediate attention. They despise all foreigners, assume that they are being cheated at every step, and are forever barking out orders: "Take this to the check room." "Come in!" "I want this dress washed (ironed)." "Bring me soap, towels, iced water." "How much, including all taxes?" The evidence also clearly pointed to a secret drinking problem: "Is there a bar in the station?," "a glass (a bottle) of beer to take away?" "Bring a bottle of good local wine." "Twenty liters."

The only phrase book I've ever come across that was of even the remotest use was a nineteenth-century volume for doctors, which I found years ago in the library of the county hospital in Des Moines. (I worked there part time while I was in college and used to go into the library on my dinner break to see if I could find a medical condition that would get me excused from Phys. Ed.) In five languages the book offered such thoughtful expressions as "Your boils are septic. You should go to a hospital without delay" and "Do you have difficulty in passing water?" Knowing that I was about to summer in Europe, I committed several of these phrases to memory, thinking they might come in handy with truculent waiters. At the very least, I thought it might be useful, upon finding myself on a crowded train or in a long line, to be able to say in a variety of languages, "Can you kindly direct me to a leprosy clinic? My skin is beginning to slough." But I never found a use for any of them and sadly they are forgotten to me now.

Eventually, with the waiting room empty and nothing happening, I presented myself at the nearest interrogation cubicle. A young policeman, who was taking down details from a woman with a bruised face, looked at me irritably for disturbing him twice in two hours. "Do you speak Italian?" he said.

"No."

"Then come back tomorrow. There will be an English-speaking policeman here then." This rather overlooked the fact that his own English seemed entirely adequate to the task.

"Why didn't you tell me this two hours ago?" I inquired with the semishrill voice of someone challenging an armed person.

"Come back tomorrow."

I checked back into the Hotel Corallo and spent a festive afternoon dealing with the Italian telephone system and trying to get through to the claims offices in London. I had two types of travelers' checks, Visa and American Express, which meant that I got to do everything twice. I spent the afternoon on telephone lines that sounded as if they were full of water reading out lists of serial numbers:

"R H two-five-nine—"

I would be interrupted by a tiny voice shouting at me from a footlocker at the bottom of a very deep lake: "Is that R A two-nine-nine—?"

"No, it's R *H* two-five-nine—"

"Can you speak up, please?"

"IT'S R H TWO-FIVE-NINE!!"

"Hello? Are you still there, Mr. Byerson? Hello? Hello?"

And so the afternoon went. American Express told me I could get my refund at their Florence office in the morning. Visa wanted to sleep on it.

"Look, I'm destitute," I lied. They told me they would have to wire the details to an associate bank in Florence, or elsewhere in Europe, and I could have my money once the paperwork was sorted out at my end. I already knew from experience how byzantine Italian banks were—you could have a heart attack in an Italian bank and they wouldn't call an ambulance until you had filled out a Customer Heart Attack Form and had it stamped at at least three windows—so I unhesitatingly told her to give me the name of a bank in Geneva. She did.

In the morning I returned to the Questura and after waiting an hour and a half was taken into a room called the Ufficio Denunce. The Office of Denunciations! I just loved that. I was introduced to a young lady in blue jeans who sat at a desk behind a massive and ancient manual typewriter. She had a kind, searching face and asked me lots and lots of questions—my name and address, where I came from, my passport number, what I did for a living, my ten favorite movies of all time, that sort of thing—and then typed each response with one finger and inordinate slowness, searching the half-acre keyboard for long minutes before tentatively striking a key, as if fearful of receiving an electric shock. After each question she had to loosen the typewriter platen and move the sheet of paper around to get the next answer in the vicinity of the blank space for it. (This was not her strongest skill.) The whole thing took ages. Finally, I was given a carbon copy of the report to use in securing a refund. The top copy, I have no doubt, went straight into a wastebasket.

I walked a couple of miles to the American Express office—I was now out of money—wondering if I would be lectured like a schoolboy who had lost his lunch money. There were seven or eight people, all Americans, in the single line, and it became evident, as we chatted together in that friendly, open way of Americans, that we had all had our pockets picked by children of roughly the same description, though at different places in the city. And this of course was just the American Express checks. If you added in all the Visa and other kinds of travelers' checks taken, and all the cash, then it was obvious that these Gypsies must clear at a minimum $25,000 or $30,000 every Sunday afternoon. Presumably the checks are then laundered through friendly exchange bureaus around the country. The whole thing must be an enormous racket. Why did the police care so little about it (unless of course they get a cut)? At all events, American Express replaced my checks with commendable dispatch, and I was back on the street fifteen minutes later.

Outside, a Gypsy woman with a three-year-old on her lap asked me for money. "I gave already," I said and walked on to the station.

MILAN AND COMO

I ARRIVED in Milan in midafternoon, expecting great things. It is after all the richest city in Italy, the headquarters of many of the most famous names of Italian commerce: Campari, Benetton, Armani, Alfa-Romeo, the Memphis design group, and the disparate empires of Silvio Berlusconi and Franco Maria Ricci. But this, as I should have realized beforehand, is the problem. Cities that are dedicated to making money, and in Milan they appear to think about little else, seldom have much energy left for charm.

I got a room in an expensive but nondescript hotel across from the monumental white marble central railway station—it looks like something built for Mussolini to give a strutting address to massed crowds—and embarked on a long, hot walk into town along the Via Pisani, a broad, modern boulevard, more American-looking than European. It was lined with sleek glass-and-chrome office buildings, but the central grass strip was scrubby and uncared for, and the few benches where you could rest had syringes scattered beneath them.

As I moved farther into the city, the buildings became older and more pleasing, but there was still something lacking. I paused to consult my map in a tiny park on a pleasant residential street near the cathedral square. The park was squalid—grassless and muddy, with broken benches and pigeons picking among hundreds of cigarette butts and disused tram tickets. I find that hard to excuse in a rich city.

Two blocks farther on and Milan blossomed. Clustered together were the city's three glories: La Scala, the cathedral, and the Galleria Vittorio Emanuele II. I went first to the cathedral—cavernous and Gothic, the third largest church in the world—begrimed on the outside and covered in scaffolding, and so gloomy within that it took me whole minutes to find the ceiling. It was quite splendid in a murky sort of way, and entirely free of tourists, which was a happy novelty after Florence. Here you had just a constant stream of locals popping in to add a candle to the hundreds already burning and to whisper a quick Ave Maria before heading home for supper. I liked that. It is such an unusual sight to find a grand church being used for its intended purpose.

Afterward I crossed the cathedral square to the Galleria Vittorio Emanuele II and spent a happy hour wandering through it, hands behind my back, browsing in the windows and noting with unease the occasional splats from the pigeons that had managed to sneak in and were now leading a rewarding life gliding among the rafters and shitting on the people below. The Galleria is an imposing shopping arcade, four stories high, built in the grandiose style of the 1860s, and still probably the most handsome shopping mall in the world, with floors of neatly patterned tiles, a vaulted latticework roof of glass and steel, and a cupola rising 160 feet above a rotunda where the two interior avenues intersect. It has the loftiness and echoing hush, and even shape, of a cathedral, but with something of the commercial grandness of a nineteenth-century railway station thrown in. Every shopping center should be like this.

Needing my afternoon infusion of caffeine, I took a table outside one of the three or four rather elegant cafés scattered among the shops. It was one of those typically European places with seventy tables and one hopelessly overworked waiter, who dashes around trying to deliver orders, clear the tables, and take money all at the same time, and who has the cheerful, nothing's-too-much-trouble attitude that you would expect of someone in such an interesting and remunerative line of work. You don't get a second chance in these places. I was staring at nothing in particular, chin in hand, idly wondering if Ornella Muti had ever done any mud wrestling, when it filtered through to my consciousness that the waiter was making one of his rare visits to my vicinity and had actually said to me, "Prego?"

I looked up. "Oh, an espres—" I said, but he was gone already, and I realized that I was never going to get this close to him again unless I married his sister. So, with a sigh of resignation I pulled myself up, moved sideways through the tiny gaps between the tables, grimacing apologetically as I caused a succession of unforgiving people to slop their coffee or plunk their noses into their dolci, and returned unrefreshed to the streets.

I strolled along the Corso Vittorio Emanuele, a wide pedestrian shopping street, looking for an alternative café and finding none. For a moment I thought I had died and been sent by mistake to yuppie heaven. Unlike the Galleria Vittorio Emanuele, where at least there were a couple of bookshops and an art gallery or two, here and on the neighboring streets there was nothing to sustain the mind or soul, just boutiques selling expensive adornments for the body: shoes, handbags, leather goods, jewelry, designer clothing that hung on the body like sacking and cost a fortune. Things reached a kind of understated intensity on the Via Montenapoleone, an anonymous-looking side street, but nonetheless the most exclusive shopping artery in the country and lined with ritzy stores where the password was clearly "Money's no object." Apart from the old shopping arcade, Milan appeared to have no café life at all. There were a few establishments, but they were all hole-in-the-wall stand-up places, where people would order a small coffee, toss it back, and return to the street, all in five seconds. This wasn't what I was looking for.

After southern Italy, Milan seemed hardly Italian at all. People walked quickly and purposefully, swinging shopping bags with names like Gucci and Ferragamo on them. They didn't dawdle over espressos and tuck into mountainous plates of pasta, napkins bibbed into their collars. They didn't engage in passionate arguments about trivialities. They held meetings. They made deals. They talked into car phones. They drove with restraint, mostly in BMWs and Porsches, and parked neatly. They all looked as if they had just stepped off the covers of *Vogue* or *GQ*. It was like an outpost of southern California. I don't know about you, but I find southern California hard enough to take in southern California. This was Italy—I wanted pandemonium and street life, people in sleeveless T-shirts on front stoops, washing hanging across the streets, guys selling things in pushcarts, Ornella Muti and Giancarlo Giannini zipping past on a Vespa. Most of all, I wanted a cup of coffee.

*   *   *

IN THE morning, I went to the Brera Gallery, hidden away on a back street and reached through a courtyard in a palazzo covered in scaffolding. Big things were going on here: Plaster dust hung in the air and there was a commotion of hammering and drilling. The gallery seemed to be only half open. Several of the rooms were closed off, and even in the open rooms there were lots of rectangles of darker wallpaper where pictures had been lent out or sent away for restoration. But what remained was not only sensational but familiar—Mantegna's foreshortened body of Christ, a Bellini Madonna, two Cannalettos recently and glowingly restored, and Piero della Francesca's gorgeously rich but decidedly bizarre "Madonna with Christ Child, Angels, Saints, and the Adoring Federico da Montefeltro"—our old friend the Duke of Urbino.

I didn't understand this picture at all. If it was painted after the Duke died and he was now in heaven, why was Christ a baby again? On the other hand, were we to take it that the Duke had somehow managed to fly through the centuries in order to be present at Christ's birth? Whatever the meaning, it was a nifty piece of work. One man liked it so much that he had brought his own folding chair and was just sitting there with arms crossed looking at it. The best thing about the Brera was that there was hardly anyone there, just a few locals and no foreign tourists but me. After Florence it was bliss to be able to see the paintings without having to ask somebody to lift me up.

Afterward I walked a long way across the city to see Leonardo's "Last Supper" in the refectory beside the church of Santa Maria delle Grazie. You pay a load of money at a ticket window and step into a bare, dim hall, and there it is, this most famous of frescoes, covering the whole of the far wall. A railing keeps you from approaching any closer than about twenty-five feet, which seemed unfair since the painting is so faded that it can barely be seen from five feet and you must strain to the utmost to see anything at all from twenty-five feet. It's like a ghost image. If you hadn't seen it reproduced a thousand times, you probably wouldn't be able to recognize any of it. One end of the painting was covered with scaffolding and a great deal of gleaming Dr. Who-like restoration equipment. A lone technician was standing on a platform scratching away. They have been working on "The Last Supper" for years, but I couldn't see any sign that the thing was actually coming to life.

Poor old Leonardo hasn't been very well served by history. The wall began to crumble almost immediately (some of it had been built with loose dirt) after he finished painting the fresco, and some early friars cut a door into it, knocking off Christ's feet. Then, over time, the hall stopped being a refectory and became in turn a stable (can you imagine a roomful of donkeys with the greatest painting in history on the wall?), a storage room, a prison, and a barracks. Much of the earlier restoration work was not, to put it charitably, very accomplished. One artist gave Saint James six fingers. It is a wonder that the painting survived at all. In point of fact, it hasn't. I don't know what another ten or fifteen years of restoration work will do, but for now it would be more accurate to say that this is where "The Last Supper" used to be.

I slotted a thousand lire into a machine on the wall, knowing that it would be a mistake, and was treated to a brief and ponderous commentary about the history of the fresco, related by a woman whose command of English pronunciation was not altogether up to the task ("Da fresk you see in fronna you iss juan of da grettest worts of art in da whole worl. . . ."), then looked around for any other ways to waste my money and, finding none, stepped, blinking, out into the strong sunshine.

I strolled over to the nearby Museo Tecnico, where I paid another hefty fee to walk through empty halls. I was curious to see this museum because I had read that it had working models of all of Leonardo's inventions. It did—small wooden ones—but they were surprisingly dull and, well, wooden, and as for the rest, the museum was full of old typewriters and oddments of machinery that meant nothing to me because the labels were in Italian. And anyway, let's be frank, the Italians' technological contribution to humankind stopped with the pizza oven.

I TOOK a late-afternoon train to Como for no other reason than that it was nearby and on a lake, and I didn't wish to spend another night in a city. I remembered reading that it was near Lake Como that Mussolini was found hiding after Italy fell to the Allies, and I figured it must have something going for it if it was the last refuge of a desperate man.

It did. Como was a lovely little city, clean and perfect, in a cupped hand of Alpine mountains at the southern end of the narrow, thirty-mile-long lake of the same name. It is only a small place, but it boasts two cathedrals, two train stations (each with its own line to Milan), two grand villas, a fetching park, a lakeside promenade overhung with poplars and generously adorned with green wooden benches, and a maze of ancient pedestrian-only streets filled with little shops and secret squares. It was perfect.

I found a room in the Hotel Plinius in the heart of town, had two coffees at a café on the Piazza Roma overlooking the lake, ate a splendid meal in a friendly restaurant on a back street, and fell in love with Italy all over again. After dinner I spent a long, contented evening just walking, shuffling with hands in pockets, along the apparently endless lakeside promenade and lolling for long periods watching night fall. I walked as far as the Villa Geno, on a prom-ontory at a bend in the lake, strolled back round to the opposite bank to the small lakeside park with its museum, built in the likeness of a temple, in commemoration of Alessandro Volta, who lived in Como from 1745 to 1827, and there lolled some more. I walked back to the hotel through empty streets, browsing in shop windows, and retired to bed a happy man.

In the morning I visited the two main churches. The Basilica of San Fidele, begun in 914, was much the more ancient, but the domed ca-thedral, five hundred years younger, was larger and more splendid—indeed, more splendid than any provincial church I had seen since Aachen. It was dark inside, and I had to stand for a minute to adjust to the dimness for fear of walking into a pillar. Morning sunlight flowed through a lofty stained-glass window, but was swallowed al-most immediately by the gloom among the high arches. The church was not only surprisingly large for its community, but richly endowed—it was full of subtle tapestries and ancient paintings and some striking statuary, including a Christ figure that is said to weep. I spent an hour sitting, gazing at the interior and watching people lighting candles. Very restful. This done, I felt content to return to the station and climb aboard the first train to Switzerland.

The train went north, through steep and agreeable countryside, but without the lake views I had been hoping for. We left the country at Chiasso, at the southernmost tip of a pointed length of Switzerland that plunges into Italy like a diver into water. Chiasso looked an unassuming border town, but it was the setting of one of Europe's greatest bank frauds, when in 1979 five men at the small local branch of Crédit Suisse managed to siphon off the better part of $1 billion before anyone back at HQ in Zurich noticed this slight drain on the bank's liquidity.

Switzerland and Italy are threaded together like the fingers of clasped hands all along the southern Alps, and I spent much of the day passing from one to the other as I headed for the town of Brig. The train climbed sluggishly through ever higher altitudes to Lugano and thence Locarno.

At Locarno I had to change trains and had an hour to kill, so I went looking for a sandwich. The town was immaculate and sunny, with a lakeside promenade even finer than Como's. They still spoke Italian here, but you could tell you were in Switzerland just from the zebra crossings and the glossy red benches, which all looked as if they had been painted that morning, and the absence of even a leaf on the paths of the lakeside park. Street sweepers were at work everywhere, sweeping up leaves with old-fashioned brooms, and I had the distinct feeling that if I dropped a chewing-gum wrapper, someone in uniform would step out from behind a tree and sweep it up or shoot me or, more probably, both.

They don't seem to eat sandwiches in Locarno. I walked all around the business district and had trouble finding even a bakery. When at last I did find one, it seemed to sell nothing but gooey pastries, though they did have a pile of what I took to be sausage rolls. Starving, I ordered three, at considerable expense. They turned out to contain mashed figs—a foodstuff that only your grandmother would eat, and only then because she couldn't find her dentures— and tasted like tea leaves soaked in cough syrup. I gamely nibbled away at one of them, but it was awful, so I put the rolls in my rucksack with the idea that I might try them again later. In the event

I forgot all about them and didn't rediscover them until two days later when I pulled my last clean shirt from the rucksack and found the rolls clinging to it.

I went into the station buffet for a glass of mineral water to wash away the stickiness. It was possibly the unfriendliest place in Switzerland. It had eight customers, but it was so quiet you could hear the clock ticking. The waiter stood at the counter lazily reaming beer glasses with a cloth. He made no move to serve me until I held up a finger and called for a mineral water. He brought a bottle and a glass, wordlessly placed them on the table, and returned to his cloth and wet glasses. He looked as if he had just learned that his wife had run off with the milkman and taken all his Waylon Jennings albums, but then I noticed that the other customers were wearing the same sour expression. It was unsettling after the remorseless good humor of Italy. Across from me sat an old lady with a metal crutch, which clattered to the floor as she tried to get up. The waiter just stood there watching, clearly thinking: "Now what are you going to do, you old cripple?" I sprang to her aid and for my pains was given a withering look and the teeniest of *grazies,* then she got up and hobbled out.

Locarno, I decided, was a strange place. I bought a ticket on the two o'clock train to Domodossola, a name that can be pronounced in any of thirty-seven ways. The man in the ticket window made me try out all of them, furrowing his brow as if he couldn't for the life of him think what nearby community had a name that might cause an American difficulty, until finally I stumbled on the approximate pronunciation. "Ah, Domodossola!" he said, pronouncing it a thirty-eighth way. As a final act of kindness, he neglected to tell me that because of work on the railway lines service would be by bus for the first ten kilometers.

I waited and waited on the platform, but the train never came, and it seemed odd that no one else was waiting with me. There were only a couple of trains a day to Domodossola. Surely there would be at least one or two other passengers. Finally, I asked a porter, who indicated, in that friendly why-don't-you-go-fuck-yourself? way of railway porters the world over, that I had to take a bus and, when pressed as to where I might find this bus, motioned vaguely with the back of his hand in the direction of the rest of the world. I went outside just in time to see the bus to Domodossola pulling out. Fortunately, I was able to persuade the driver to stop by clinging to the windshield for two hundreds yards. I was desperate to get out of there.

A few miles outside of Locarno, we joined a waiting train at a little country station. It climbed high into the jagged mountains and took us on a spectacular ride along the lips of deep gorges and forbidding passes, where farmhouses and hamlets were tucked away in the most inaccessible places, on the edge of giddy eminences. It would be hard to imagine a more difficult place to be a farmer. One misstep and you could fall for a day and a half. Even from the train it was unnerving, an experience more akin to wing-walking than rail travel.

It struck me as inconceivable that anyone could be confronted by such grandeur and not be overwhelmed by the beauty of it, and yet, according to Kenneth Clark, almost no visitor to the Alps before the eighteenth century remarked on the scenery. Now, of course, the problem is the reverse. Fifty million tourists a year trample through the Alps, delighting in and despoiling its beauty at the same time. All the construction associated with tourism—resorts, hotels, shops, restaurants, holiday homes, ski runs, ski lifts, and new highways—is not only altering the face of the Alps irreparably but undermining their very foundations. In 1987, just a few miles east of where I was now, sixty people died when a flash flood raced through the Valtellina Valley, sweeping houses and hotels away like matchboxes before a broom. The same summer, thirty people died in a landslide at Annecy in France. If the mountainsides had not been denuded of trees for new housing and resorts, neither catastrophe would have happened.

I was sitting on the wrong side of the train to look at scenery—outside my window there was nothing but a wall of rock—but a pleasant, bespectacled lady sitting across the aisle saw me straining to see things, and invited me to take the empty seat opposite her. She was Swiss and spoke excellent English. We chatted brightly about the scenery and our modest lives. She was a bank clerk in Zürich, but was visiting her mother in a village near Domodossola and had just spent a day shopping in Locarno. She showed me some flowers she had bought there. It seemed like weeks—it *was* weeks—since I had held a normal conversation with someone, and it was wonderful. I was so taken with the novel experience of issuing sounds through a hole in my head that I chattered away about any little thing that flitted through my mind, and before long she was fast asleep and I was back once again in my own quiet little world.

~~~~~~~~~~~~~~~~~~~~~~~~~~~~~~~~

SWITZERLAND

~~~~~~~~~~~~~~~~~~~~~~~~~~~~~~~~

I REACHED Brig, by way of Domodossola and the Simplon Pass, at about five in the evening. It was darker and cooler here than it had been in Italy, and the streets were shiny with rain. I got a room in the Hotel Victoria overlooking the station and went straight out to look for food, having had nothing to eat since my two bites of Mashed Fig Delight in Locarno at lunchtime.

All the restaurants in Brig were German. You never know where you are in Switzerland. One minute everything's Italian, then you travel a mile or two and everyone is talking German or French or some variety of Romansch. Along an irregular line running the length of east-central Switzerland you find pairs of villages that are neighbors and yet are clearly from different linguistic groups—St. Blaise and Erlach, Les Diablerets and Gsteig, Delémont and Laufen—and as you head south toward Italy the same thing happens with Italian. Brig was a nipple of German speakers, so to speak, between the two.

I examined six or seven restaurants, mystified by the menus, wishing I knew the German for liver, pigs' trotters, and boiled eyeball, before chancing upon an establishment called the Restaurant de la Place at the top of the town. Now this is a nice surprise, I thought, and went straight in, figuring that at least I'd have some idea what I was ordering, but the name Restaurant de la Place was just a heartless joke. The menu here was in German, too.

It is really the most unattractive language for foodstuffs. If you want whipped cream on your coffee in much of the German-speaking world, you order it *mit Schlag*. Now, does that sound like a frothy and delicious pick-me-up, or does that sound like the sort of thing smokers bring up first thing in the morning? Here the menu was filled with items that brought to mind the noises of a rutting pig: Knoblauchbrot, Schweinskotelett ihrer Wahl, Portion Schlagobers (and that was a dessert).

I ordered entrecôte and frîtes, which sounded a trifle dull after Italy (and indeed so they proved), but at least I wouldn't have to hide most of the meal in my napkin rather than face the awful, embarrassing cry of disappointment that waiters always give when they find you haven't touched your goat's scrotum *en croûte*. In any event, it was an agreeable enough place, as much bar as restaurant: dark and plain, with a tobacco-stained ceiling. The waitress was friendly and the beer was large and cold.

In the middle of the table sat a large cast-iron platter, which I assumed was an ashtray, and then I had the unsettling thought that perhaps it was some kind of food receptacle and that the waitress would come along in a minute and put some bread in it. I looked around the room to see if any of the other few customers were using theirs as an ashtray, but no one seemed to be, so I snatched out my cigarette butt and dead match and secreted them in a pot plant beside the table, and then tried to disperse the ash by blowing, but the ash went all over the tablecloth. As I tried to brush it away, I knocked my glass with the side of my hand and slopped beer all across the table.

By the time I had finished, much of the tablecloth was a series of gray smudges outlined in a large, irregular patch of yellow that looked distressingly like a urine stain. I casually tried to hide this with my elbow and upper body when the waitress brought my dinner, but she saw instantly what a mess I had made of things and gave me a look not of contempt, as I had dreaded, but—worse—of sympathy. It was the look you might give a stroke victim who has lost control of the muscles in his mouth but is still gamely trying to feed himself.

For one horrible moment, I thought she might tie a napkin around my neck and cut up my food for me. Instead, she retreated to her station behind the bar, but she kept a compassionate eye on me throughout the meal, ready to spring forward if any pieces of cutlery should clatter from my grasp or if a sudden spasm cause me to tip over backward. I was very pleased to get out of there. The cast-iron platter was an ashtray, by the way.

Brig was a bit of a strange place. Historically it was a staging post on the road between Zürich and Milan, but now it looked as if it didn't quite know what to do with itself. It was a reasonably sized town but appeared to offer little in the way of diversion. It was the kind of place where the red-light district would be in a phone box. All the shops sold unarresting products like refrigerators, vacuum cleaners, and televisions from behind shiny plate-glass windows. Then I realized that shops in most countries sell unarresting items from behind plate-glass windows. It was simply that I was no longer in Italy, which caused me a passing pang of grief. This is the problem with traveling: One day you are sitting with a cappuccino on a terrace by the sea, and the next you are standing in the rain in the dullest town in Switzerland looking at Zanussis.

It dawned on me that I hadn't seen a refrigerator, vacuum cleaner, or other truly functional thing on sale anywhere in Italy. I presume they don't all drive to Brig to buy them, that they must be able to purchase them somewhere in Italy. In Brig, however, there was seemingly nothing else for sale. I walked the empty streets, trying to work up an interest in white goods, but the mood wouldn't take me, and I retired to the bar of my hotel, where I drank some beer and read Philip Ziegler's classic account of the Black Death, imaginatively entitled *The Black Death*—just the thing for lonely, rainy nights in a foreign country.

Actually, the book was fascinating, not least because it dealt with places I had just passed through—Florence, for instance, where a hundred thousand people, half the populace, lost their lives in just four months, and Milan, where the news from Florence so terrified the locals that families suspected of harboring a plague victim were walled up inside their houses.

There's nothing like reading about people being entombed alive to put your own problems in perspective. I tend to think of life as bleak when I can't find a parking space at the supermarket, but imagine what it must have been to be an Italian in the fourteenth century. For a start, in 1345 it rained nonstop for six months, turning much of the country into stagnant lake and making planting impossible. The economy col-

lapsed, banks went bust, and thousands died in the ensuing famines.
Two years later the country was rocked with terrible earthquakes—in
Rome, Naples, Pisa, Padua, Venice—which brought more death and
chaos. And then, just when people were surely thinking that things
had to get better now, some anonymous sailor stepped ashore at
Genoa and said, "You know, I don't feel so hot," and within days the
great plague was beginning its long sweep across Europe.

And it didn't stop there. The plague returned for a mop-up operation in 1360–61, and yet again in 1368–69, 1371, 1375, 1390, and
1405. The odd thing is that these terrible events coincided with one
of the great periods of church building in Europe. I don't know
about you, but if I lived in an age when God was zinging every third
person in my town with suppurating bubos, I don't think I'd look on
Him as being on my side.

IN THE morning I took a fast train to Geneva. We rattled
through a succession of charmless semiindustrial towns—Sierre,
Sion, Martigny—places that seemed to consist almost entirely of
small factories and industrial workshops fringed with oil drums,
stacks of wooden pallets, and other semiabandoned clutter. I had
forgotten that quite a lot of Switzerland is really rather ugly. And
everywhere there were pylons. I had forgotten about those, too. The
Swiss are great ones for stringing wires. They thread them across the
mountainsides for electricity and suspend them from endless rows of
gibbets along every railway track and hang them like washing lines
on all the city streets for the benefit of trams. It seems not to have
occurred to them that there might be a more attractive way of arranging things.

We found the shore of Lake Geneva at Villeneuve and spent the
next hour racing along its northern banks at a speed that convinced
me the driver was slumped dead on the throttle. We shot past the
castle of Chillon—*shoomp:* a picturesque blur—flew through the stations at Montreux and Vevey, scattering people on the platforms,
and finally screeched to a long, slow stop at Lausanne, where the
body of the driver was presumably taken away for recycling (I assumed the fanatically industrious Swiss don't bury their dead but use

them for making heating oil), and his place taken by someone in better health. At all events, the final leg into Geneva was made at a more stately pace.

Just outside my carriage were two young Australians who spent the passage from Lausanne to Geneva discussing great brawls they had taken part in over the years. I couldn't quite see them, but I could hear every breathless word. They would say things like, "D'ya remember the time Muscles Malloy beat the crap out of the Savage triplets with a claw hammer? There was blood and guts all over the place, man."

"I was picking pieces of brain out of my beer!"

"Yeah, it was fan-tas-tic! D'ya remember that time Muscles rammed that snooker cue up Jason Brewster's nose and it came out the top of his head?"

"That Muscles was an animal, wasn't he?"

"Not half!"

"Did you ever see him eat a live cat?"

"No, but I saw him pull the tongue out of a horse once."

It went on like this all the way to Geneva. These guys were serious psychopaths, in urgent need of a clinic. I kept expecting one of them to look in at me and say, "I'm bored. Let's hang this asshole out the window upside down and see how many times we can hit his head on the railway ties." Eventually, I peeked out. They were both about four feet two inches tall and couldn't have beaten up a midget in a blindfold. I followed them off the train at Geneva and out of the station, chattering excitedly as they went on about people having their heads stuck in a waffle iron or their tongues nailed to the carpet.

I watched them go, then turned and, with an instinct that seldom fails to let me down, checked into the dreariest and unfriendliest hotel in its class in Geneva, the aptly named Terminus.

Finding nothing to detain me there, I went straight to the Union Bank of Switzerland offices on the Rue du Rhône to claim my refund on my Visa travelers' checks. I was directed to a small room in the basement, where international transactions were dealt with. I had assumed that things would be painlessly efficient here, but I hadn't allowed for the fact that the Swiss national motto is "Trust No One." It took most of the afternoon.

First, I had to stand in a long line, full of veiled women and men in nightshirts, all involved in complicated transfers of funds from one Arab sandpit to another, requiring the production of parchment documents and the careful counting of huge stacks of brightly colored money. All of this was presided over by a blond woman who clearly hated her job and every living thing on the planet. It took an hour just to reach the window, where I was required to do no more than establish my identity and reveal, in a low voice and with significant sidelong glances, the secret reclaim number I had been given over the phone in Florence. This done, the woman told me to take a seat.

"Oh, thanks, but I'd never get it in my suitcase," I said with my best Iowa smile. "Can't I just have my checks?"

"You must take a seat and wait. Next."

I sat for three quarters of an hour before I was summoned to the windows, handed a claims form packed with questions, and sent back to my seat to fill them in. It was an irritating document. It required me not only to explain in detail how I had been so reckless as to have lost the travelers' checks that Visa had trustingly endowed me with, and to give all manner of trifling detail, including the number on the police report and the address of the police station at which the report was made, but also contained long sections of utterly irrelevant questions concerning my height, weight, and complexion. "What the hell does my complexion have to do with travelers' checks?" I said, a trifle wildly, prompting a pleasant-looking matron sitting next to me to put some space between us. Finally, the form instructed me to give two financial references and one personal reference.

I couldn't believe it. By what mad logic should I have to give references to reclaim something that was mine? "American Express doesn't ask for anything like this," I said to the matronly lady, who looked at me warily and shifted her butt another two inches toward safety. I lied on all the answers. I said I was four feet two inches tall, weighed four hundred pounds, was born in Abyssinia, and busted broncos for a living. I put "amber" for complexion and Michael Milken and Ivan Boesky for my financial references. For a personal reference, I gave myself, of course. Who better? I was spluttering with indignation when I rejoined the line, which now had grown to include a delegation of Rwandan diamond merchants and two guys with camels.

"Why do I have to answer all these stupid questions?" I demanded as I turned in my claim form. "This is the most stupid thing I've ever seen. It's really . . . *stupid.*" I get eloquent like that when I'm angry. The woman pointed out that it was nothing to do with her, that she was just following instructions. "That's what Eichmann said!" I cried, both feet leaving the ground at once. Then I realized it was pointless, that she would only make me take a seat again and wait there until Michaelmas if I didn't act calm and Swiss about it all, so I accepted my replacement travelers' checks with nothing stronger than sulky indignation.

But from now on it's American Express travelers' checks for me, boy, and if the company wishes to acknowledge this unsolicited endorsement with a set of luggage or a skiing holiday in the Rockies, then let the record show that I am ready to take it.

I SPENT two days in Geneva, wandering around with an odd, empty longing to be somewhere else. I don't know why exactly because Geneva is an agreeable enough place—compact, spotless, eminently walkable, with a steep and venerable old town, some pleasant parks, and a vast blue lake, glittering by day and even more fetching at night with the multicolored lights of the city scattered across it. But it is also dull, expensive, businesslike, buttoned up, impossible to warm to. Everyone walked with a brisk, hunched, out-of-my-way posture. It was spring on the streets, but February on people's faces. There seemed to be no young people enlivening the bars and bistros, as they do in Amsterdam and Copenhagen. The place had no exuberance, no sparkle, no soul. The best thing that could be said for it was that the streets were clean.

I suppose you have to admire the Swiss for their industriousness. Here, after all, is a country that is small, mountainous, has virtually no natural resources and yet has managed to become the richest nation on earth. (Its per-capita GDP is almost 25 percent higher than even Japan's and more than double Britain's.) Money is everything in Switzerland—the country has more banks than dentists—and the inhabitants' quiet passion for it makes them cunning opportunists. The country is landlocked, three hundred miles from the nearest sniff of sea, and yet it is home to the largest manufacturer of marine engines in the world.

The virtues of the Swiss are legion: They are clean, orderly, law-abiding, and diligent—so diligent that in a national referendum in the 1970s they actually voted against giving themselves a shorter work week.

This, of course, is the whole problem. The Swiss are so desperately dull, and wretchedly conservative. A friend of mine who was living in Geneva in 1968, when students all over Europe were tearing the Continent apart, once told me that the students of Geneva decided to hold a riot of their own, but called it off when the police wouldn't give them permission. My friend swears it's a true story. It is certainly true that women didn't get the vote in Switzerland until 1971, a mere half century after they got it almost everywhere else, and in one of the cantons, Appenzell Inner Rhoden, women were excluded from cantonal votes until 1990. The Swiss have a terrible tendency to be smug and ruthlessly self-interested. They happily bring in hundreds of thousands of foreign workers—one person in every five in Switzerland is a foreigner—but refuse to offer the workers the security of citizenship. When times get tough, they send the workers home—300,000 during the oil-embargo shocks of 1973, for instance—making them leave their homes, pull their children from schools, abandon their comforts until times got better. Thus the Swiss are able to take advantage of cheap labor during boom times without the inconvenient social responsibilities of providing unemployment benefits and health care during bad times. And by this means do they keep inflation low and preserve their own plump, complacent standard of living. I can understand it, but I don't have to admire it.

O N M Y second day in Geneva, I went for a long stroll along the lakeside—leafy, spacious, empty—past the old and largely derelict League of Nations Building, where young boys with stones were trying without much success to break the windows, through the tranquil Jardin Botanique, and to the gates of the vast Palais des Nations (larger than Versailles, according to the tourist brochures) and now home to the United Nations Organization. I hesitated by the gate, thinking about paying the multifranc entrance fee for a guided tour, and aren't you glad I didn't?

Instead, I noticed on my city map that just up the road was the Musée International de la Croix-Rouge et du Croissant-Rouge (the International Museum of the Red Cross and Red Breakfast Roll), which sounded much more promising to me. And so it proved to be. It really was a surprisingly nice place, if that isn't too inappropriate a term to apply to a museum dedicated to human suffering in all its amazing and manifold variety. It was thoughtfully laid out, with a confident and accomplished use of multimedia resources, as I believe they call it in the trade. It was virtually empty, too, and generally effective at putting its story across, considering that everything had to be explained in four languages and that they couldn't be too graphic in their depictions of disasters and human cruelty lest it unsettle young visitors.

Clearly, too, the organization's hands were tied by certain political considerations. One of the displays was a replica of a cell no bigger than a broom closet in which Red Cross workers had discovered seventeen prisoners being held in conditions of unspeakable discomfort, unable even to lie down, for no reason other than that their political views did not accord with those of the rulers. But nowhere did it hint in what country this cell had been found. At first I thought this constant discretion craven, but on reflection I supposed that it was necessary and prudent. To name the country would no doubt have jeopardized the Red Cross's operations there. The scary thing was to realize just how many countries might have been the culprits.

I spent the rest of the day shuffling around the city, wandering through department stores, fingering the merchandise (this drives Swiss sales assistants crazy), hanging out at McDonald's (the only remotely affordable food in Geneva), visiting the cathedral, exploring the old town, and gazing in the windows of antique shops that sold the sort of overornate objects you would expect to see in, say, a *House Beautiful* article on Barry Manilow's Malibu hacienda—

life-sized porcelain tigers, Oriental vases you could put a child into, oversized Louis Quatorze bureaus, and sideboards with gilt gleaming from every curl and crevice.

In the evening, having scrubbed the mashed figs of Locarno out of my last clean shirt, I went for a beer in a dive around the corner, where I waited weeks for service and then spent the next hour gaping alternately at the largeness of the bill and the smallness of the beer, holding the two side by side for purposes of comparison. Declining the advance of Geneva's only prostitute ("Thanks, but I've just been screwed by the management"), I moved to another semiseamy bar down the street, but found precisely the same experience, and so returned with heavy feet to my hotel room.

I went into the bathroom to see how my shirt was drying. The purply, mashed fig stains, I noted with the steady gaze of someone who knows his way around disappointment, were coming back, like disappearing ink. I dropped the shirt in the wastebasket, then went back to the bedroom, switched on the TV, and fell onto the bed in one movement and watched a 1954 film called *The Sands of Iwo Jima,* featuring John Wayne killing Japanese people while talking in French using someone else's voice—an acting skill I never knew he possessed.

It occurred to me, as I lay there watching this movie, of which I could understand barely a word apart from "bonjour," "merci bien" and "aaaaargh!" (what the Japanese said when John stuck them in the belly with his bayonet), that this was almost boring enough to cause brain damage, and yet at the same time—and here's the interesting thing—I was probably having as much fun as anyone else in Switzerland.

I TOOK a morning train to Bern, two hours away to the east. Bern was a huge relief. It was dignified and handsome, and full of lively cafés and young people. I picked up a city map at the tourist office at the railway station and with its aid found a room in the Hotel Kreuz. I dumped my bag and went straight back out, not only eager to see the town but delighted at my eagerness. In Geneva I had begun to fear that my enthusiasm for travel might be seeping away and that I would spend the rest of the trip shuffling through museums and along cobbled streets in my Willy Loman posture. But, no, I was perky again, as if I'd just been given a booster shot of vitamins.

Bern is built on a bluff above a broad loop of the river Aare, and the views from the bridges and vantage points are quite splendid, especially back toward the old town—a jumble of orangish tiled roofs broken up with church spires and towers that look like mutant cuckoo clocks. Most of the streets are arcaded in a way I've never seen before: The ground floors are set back with the upper floors jutting out over them, their heavy weight supported by thick arched buttresses, creating a covered walkway over the pavements. The shops along these arcaded streets were infinitely more varied and interesting—even more classy—than those in Geneva. There were antiquarian bookstores and art galleries and antique shops specializing in everything from windup toys to clocks and binoculars to Etruscan pottery.

Culturally, Bern is on the dividing line between French-speaking Switzerland and German-speaking Switzerland, and there is a mildly exotic blending of the two. Waiters greet you with "bitte," for instance, but thank you with "merci." Architecturally, it is stolidly Swiss-German, with severe (though not disagreeable) sandstone buildings that look as if they were built to withstand a thousand earthquakes. Bern has the air of a busy provincial market town. You would never guess that it is the national capital. This is partly because of the peculiar nature of Swiss politics. So many powers devolve to the cantons and to national referenda that Switzerland doesn't even feel the need to have a prime minister, and the presidency is such a nominal and ceremonial position that it changes hands every year. They wouldn't have a president at all except that they need somebody to greet visiting heads of state at the airport. The Bundeshaus, the national parliament, looks like a provincial town hall, and nowhere in the city—even in the bars on the nearby streets—do you have a sense of being among bureaucrats and politicians.

I spent a day and a half wandering through the old town and across the high bridges to the more modern, but still handsome, residential streets on the far side of the Aare. It was a wonderful city for random walking. There were no freeways, no industry, no sterile office parks, just endless avenues of fine homes and small parks.

I attempted just two touristy diversions and failed at both. I crossed the high, arched Nydegg Bridge to see the famous bear pits—the city's name derives from the German word for bear, so they keep several bears as mascots—but the pits were empty. There was no sign to explain why and locals who arrived with their children were clearly as surprised and perplexed as I was.

I tried also to go to the Albert Einstein museum, housed in his old flat on Kramgasse, one of the main arcaded streets. I walked up and down the street half a dozen times before I found the modest entrance to the building, tucked away between a restaurant and a ladies' boutique. The door was locked—it was dusty and looked as if it hadn't been opened for weeks, perhaps years—and no one answered the bell, though according to the tourist brochure it should have been open. It struck me as odd that nowhere in the town had I encountered any indication that Einstein had ever lived there: no statue in a park or square, no street named in his honor, not even his kindly face on postcards. There wasn't so much as a plaque on the wall to tell the world that in one year, 1905, while working as an obscure clerk in the Swiss patent office and living above this door, Einstein produced four papers that changed forever the face of physics—on the theory of Brownian motion, on the theory of relativity, on the photon theory of light, and on the establishment of the mass-energy equivalence. I have no idea what any of that means, of course—my grasp of science is such that I don't actually understand why electricity doesn't leak out of sockets—but I would have liked to see where he lived nonetheless.

In the evening I had a hearty meal, which is about as much as the visitor can aspire to in Switzerland, and went for another long walk. As I returned to the city center along Marktgassse, the main pedestrian venue, I discovered that all the bars were closing. Waiters were taking chairs and tables inside and lights were going out. It was 9:20 in the evening. This gives you some idea of what a heady nightlife Bern offers.

Quietly distraught, I wandered around and with relief found another bar still open a couple of blocks away on Kochegasse. It was crowded but had an amiable, smoky air, and I was just settling in with a tall glass of golden Edelweiss beer and the closing chapters of *The Black Death,* when I heard a familiar voice behind me say: "D'ya remember that time Blane Brockhouse got the shits and went crazy with an Uzi in the West Goolagong Working Men's Club?"

I turned around to find my two friends from the Geneva train sitting on booster seats behind frothy beers. "Hey, how you guys doing?" I said before I could stop myself.

They looked at me as if I were potentially insane. "Do we know you, mate?" asked one of them.

I didn't know what to say. These guys had never seen me before in their lives. "You're Australian, huh?" I burbled stupidly.

"Yeah. So?"

"I'm an American." I was quiet for a bit. "But I live in England."

There was a long pause. "Well, that's great," said one of the Australians with a measured hint of sarcasm, then turned to his friend and said: "Do you remember the time Dung-Breath O'Leary hacked that waitress's forearms off with a machete because there was a fly in his beer?"

I felt like an asshole, which of course is a pretty fair description of my condition. Something about their diminutive size and warped little minds heightened the sense of quiet humiliation. I turned back to my beer and my book, the tips of my ears warm to the touch, and took succor in the plight of the poor people of Bristol, where in 1349 the plague so raged through the city that "the living were scarce able to bury the dead" and the grass grew calf-high in the city streets.

Before long, with the aid of two more beers and 120,000 agonized deaths in the West Country of England, my embarrassment was past and I was feeling much better. As they say, time heals all wounds. Still, if you wake up with a bubo on your groin, better see a doctor all the same.

LIECHTENSTEIN

Y O U K N O W when you are entering the German-speaking part of Switzerland because all the towns have names that sound like someone talking with his mouth full of bread: Thun, Leuk, Bülach, Plaffeien, Flims, Gstaad, Pfäffikon, Linthal, Thusis, Fluelin, Thalwil.

According to my rail ticket, I was headed for the last of these, which puzzled me a little, since Thalwil didn't appear on my much-trusted Kümmerly and Frey *Alpenländer Strassenkarte*. Where Thalwil should have been, Horgen was instead. I couldn't conceive that the conscientious draftspeople at Kümmerly and Frey could have made an error of this magnitude in their own country, but it was equally unthinkable that the conservative burghers of this corner of Switzerland would have elected at some time during the last eighteen years to change the name of one of their towns; so I put it down to an act of God and turned my attention instead to spreading out the map on my knees in its full crinkly glory, to the undisguised irritation of the old lady next to me, who hoomphed her bosom and made exasperated noises every time a corner of paper waggled in her direction.

What is it about maps? I could look at them all day, intently studying the names of towns and villages I have never heard of and will never visit, tracing the course of obscure rivers, checking elevations, consulting the marginal notes to see what a little circle with a flag on it signifies (a Burg or Schloss) and what's the difference between a pictogram of an airplane with a circle around it and one without (one is a Flughafen, the other a Flugplatz), issuing small profound "hmmmms" and nodding my head gravely without having the faintest idea why.

I noticed now that I might alternatively have gone from Brig to Geneva on a more southerly route, by way of Aosta, Mont Blanc, and Chamonix. It would almost certainly have been much more scenically exciting. What a fool I was to have missed the chance to see Aosta and Mont Blanc. How could I have come this far and failed to travel through the heart of the Alps? What a mighty idiot I was. "Hmmmm," I said, nodding gravely and folding up the map.

We chuntered pleasantly through a landscape of small farms and steep wooded hills, along a shallow river, stopping frequently at isolated villages where half a dozen people would climb aboard with empty shopping baskets. When the train was full, it would call at a busy little market town like Langnau or Zug, and all the passengers would pour off, leaving me all alone, and then the slow, steady refilling process would begin again. It was not a bad way to spend a day.

I left the train at Sargans, just short of Liechtenstein. The railway runs through Liechtenstein, but, in line with the national policy of being ridiculous in every possible way, trains don't stop there. Instead, you must get off at Sargans or Buchs and transfer to a yellow post bus to go to Vaduz, the diminutive Liechtenstein capital.

The bus was conveniently waiting at the station. I purchased a ticket and took a seat midway along, the only passenger not clutching bagloads of shopping, and I sat high on the seat, eager to see the little country. It is only about seven miles from Sargans to Vaduz, but the journey takes an hour or so because the bus goes all over the place, darting down every side road and making cautious, circuitous detours around back lanes, as if trying to sneak into Vaduz. I watched carefully out the window, but never did know at what point we entered Liechtenstein—indeed wasn't certain that we were there at all until I saw the city limit sign for Vaduz.

Everything about Liechtenstein is ridiculous. For a start it is ridiculously small—barely 1/250th the size of Switzerland, which is itself ridiculously small. Liechtenstein is the last remaining fragment of the Holy Roman Empire, and so obscure that its ruling family didn't bother to come and see it for 150 years. It has two political parties, popularly known as the Reds and the Blacks, which have so few ideological differences that they share a motto: "Faith in God, Prince, and Fatherland." Liechtenstein's last military engagement was in 1866, when it sent eighty men to fight against the Italians. Nobody was killed. In fact—you're going to like this—they came back with 81 men, because they had made a friend on the way. Two years later, realizing that the Liechtensteiners could beat no one, the crown prince disbanded the army.

Liechtenstein is the world's largest producer of sausage casings and false teeth. It is a notorious tax haven, the only country in the world with more registered companies than people (though most of these companies exist only as pieces of paper in someone's desk). It was the last country in Europe to give women suffrage (in 1984). Its single prison is so small that prisoners' meals are sent over from a nearby restaurant. To acquire citizenship, a referendum must be held in the applicant's village and, if that passes, the prime minister and his cabinet must then vote on it. But this never happens, and hundreds of families who have lived in Liechtenstein for generations are still treated as foreigners.

Vaduz is not terribly picturesque, but its setting is memorable. The town nestles at the very foot of Mount Alpspitz, 6,700 feet high. On an outcrop directly above the town is the gloomy and fortresslike royal Schloss, looking uncannily like the Wicked Witch's castle in *The Wizard of Oz*. Every time I looked up at it I half-expected to see those winged monkeys flying in and out. Curiously, despite centuries as a backwater, Vaduz retains almost no sense of antiquity. The whole town looks as if it were built twenty years ago in a hurry—not exactly ugly, but certainly undistinguished.

It was a Saturday and the main road through the town was backed up with big Mercedeses from Switzerland and Germany. The rich must come on the weekends to visit their money. There were only four hotels in the central area. Two were full and one was closed, but I managed to get a room at the fourth, the Engel. It was friendly but expensive for what it offered: a lumpy bed, a reading light with a forty-watt bulb, no TV, and a radio so old that it would not have surprised me to hear Edward R. Murrow broadcasting details of the battle of Monte Cassino. Instead, all I could get was polka music, mercifully interrupted at frequent intervals by a German-speaking disk jockey who had evidently overdosed on sleeping pills (or possibly on polka music), judging by the snappiness of his delivery. He . . . talked . . . like . . . this, like someone trapped in a terrible dream, which I suppose might not be far from the case.

The sole virtue of the room was that it had a balcony with a view over the main church and town square (really just a strip of lawn with a parking lot) and beyond that a handsome prospect of mountains. By leaning out perilously over the street and craning my neck, I could just see the Schloss high above me. It is still the home of the crown prince, one of the richest men in Europe and possessor of the second finest private collection of paintings in the world, outdone only by the queen of England. He has the only Leonardo in private hands and the largest collection of Rubenses, but a fat lot of good that does the eager visitor because the castle is completely off limits, and plans to build a modest national gallery to house a few of the paintings have yet to get off the ground. Parliament has been debating the matter for almost twenty years, but the thought of parting with the necessary funds has proved too painful so far and evidently no one would dare to ask the royal family (worth an estimated $1.3 billion) to dip into their treasure chest and pass down some bauble to get the ball rolling.

I went out for a walk and to check out the possibilities for dinner, which were not abundant. The business district was only a couple of blocks square and the shops were so pedestrian and small-town—a newsstand, a drugstore, a gift shop selling the sort of gifts that you dread receiving at Christmas from your in-laws—that it was impossible to linger. Restaurants were thin on the ground and either very expensive or discouragingly empty. Vaduz is so small that if you walk for fifteen minutes in any direction you are deep in the country. It occurred to me that there is no reason to go to Liechtenstein except to say that you have been there. If it were simply part of Switzerland (which, in fact, it is in all but name and postage stamps—and even then it uses the Swiss postal service), no one would ever dream of visiting it.

I wandered down a pleasant but anonymous residential street where the picture windows of every living room offered a ghostly glow of television, and then I found myself on a straight, unpaved, and unlighted road through flat, freshly tilled fields. The view back to Vaduz was lovely. Darkness had fallen like a theater curtain and a pale moon hung in the sky. The Schloss, bathed in yellow flood-lights, stood commandingly above the town, looking impregnable and drafty.

The road ended in a T-junction to nowhere, so I turned back for another look around the town. I settled for dinner in the dining room of the Vaduzerhof Hotel. Two hours earlier I had been solemnly assured that the hotel was closed, but the dining room was certainly open, if not exactly overwhelmed with customers, and people also seemed to be coming in through the front door, taking keys off hooks in the hallway and going upstairs to bedrooms. Perhaps the people at the hotel just didn't like the look of me, or maybe they correctly suspected that I was a travel writer and would reveal to the world the secret that the food at the Vaduzerhof Hotel at number 3 Stadtlestrasse in Vaduz is Not Very Good. Who can say?

I N T H E morning I presented myself in the dining room of the Engel for breakfast. It was the usual continental breakfast of bread, cold cuts, and cheese, which I didn't really want, but it was included in the room charge and with what they were charging me I felt bound to empty a couple of minitubs of butter and waste some cheese, if nothing else. The waiter brought me coffee and asked if I wanted orange juice.

"Yes, please," I said.

It was the strangest orange juice I'd ever seen. It was a peachy color and had red stringy bits suspended in it like ganglia. They looked unnervingly like those red squiggles you sometimes find in the yolks of eggs. It didn't even taste like orange juice, and after two polite sips I pushed it to one side and concentrated on my coffee and cutting a slice of ham into small, unreusable pieces.

Twenty minutes later I presented myself at the check-out desk and the pleasant lady there handed me my bill to review while she did brusque things with my credit card in a flattening machine. I was surprised to see that there was a charge of four francs for orange juice. Four francs is a lot of money.

"Excuse me, but I've been charged four francs for orange juice."

"Did you not have orange juice?"

"Yes, but the waiter never said I'd be charged for it. I thought it was part of the breakfast."

"Oh, no, our orange juice is very special. Fresh-squeezed. It is—" She said some German word, which I assumed translated as "full of stringy red bits," then added—"and as it is *razzer* special we charge four francs for it."

"Fine, splendid, but I really feel you should have told me."

"But, sir, you ordered it and you drank it."

"I didn't drink it—it tasted like duck's urine—and besides I thought it was free."

We were at an impasse. I don't usually make a scene in these circumstances—I just come back at night and throw a brick through the window—but this time I was determined to take a stand and declined to sign the bill until the four-franc charge was removed. I was even prepared to be arrested over it, though for one unsettling moment I had a picture of me being brought dinner in jail and, taking a linen cloth off the tray, finding a glass of peach-colored orange juice and a single slice of ham cut into tiny pieces.

Eventually, she relented, with more grace than I probably deserved, but it was clear from the rigid all-is-forgiven smile she gave me as she handed me back my card that there will never be a room for me at the Hotel Engel in Vaduz, and with the Vaduzerhof also evidently barred to me for life, it was obvious that I had spent my last night in Liechtenstein.

AS IT was a Sunday, there was no sign of any buses running, so I had no choice but to walk to Buchs, half a dozen miles to the north, but I didn't mind. It was a flawless spring morning. Church bells rang out all across the valley, as if a war had just ended. I followed the road to the nearby village of Schaan, successfully gambled that a side lane would lead me to the Rhine, and there found a gravel footpath waiting to conduct me the last half mile to the bridge to Switzerland. I had never crossed a border by foot before and felt rather pleased with myself. There was no border post of any kind, just a plaque in the center of the bridge showing the formal dividing line between Liechtenstein and Switzerland. No one was around, so I stepped back and forth over the line three or four times just for the novelty of it.

Buchs, on the opposite bank of the river, wasn't so much sleepy as comatose. I had two hours to kill before my train, so I had a good look around the town. This took four minutes, including rest stops. Everything was *geschlossen*.

I went to the station and bought a ticket to Innsbruck, then went and looked for the station buffet. It was shut, but a newsstand was open and I had a look at it. I was ready for something to read—Ziegler's relentless body count of fourteenth-century European peasants was beginning to lose its sparkle—but the only English-language publication on offer was the weekend edition of *USA Today*, a publication that always puts me in mind of a newspaper we used to get in grade school called *My Weekly Reader*. I am amazed enough that they can find buyers for *USA Today* in the U.S.A., but the possibility that anyone would ever present himself at the station kiosk in Buchs, Switzerland, and ask for it seemed to me to set a serious challenge to the laws of probability. I thought about stealing a look at the paper, just to check the major league baseball standings, but the kiosk lady was watching me with a bulldog look that suggested this could be a punishable offense in Switzerland.

Instead, I found the way to my platform, unburdened myself of the rucksack, and took a seat on a bench. I allowed my eyelids to droop, and passed the time by composing Swiss riddles:

Q: What is the best way to make a Swiss roll?
A: Take him to a mountaintop and give him a push.

Q: How do you make a Swiss person laugh?
A: Hold a gun to his head and say, "Laugh."

Q: What do you call a great lover in Switzerland?
A: An immigrant.

Q: What do you call a gathering of boring people in Switzerland?
A: Zürich.

Tiring of this, I switched, for no explainable reason, to multiple-choice Adolf Hitler-Eva Braun jokes, but I had completed only one—

Q.: What were Adolf Hitler's last words to Eva Braun?
A.: Did you remember to cancel the milk?
A.: Bang! Okay, it's your turn.
A.: All right, all right, I'll see to it that they name a range of small electrical appliances after you.

—when the train pulled in. With more than a little relief, I boarded it, pleased to be heading for yet another new country.

~~~~~~~~~~~~~~~~~~~~~~~~~~~~~~~~~

AUSTRIA

~~~~~~~~~~~~~~~~~~~~~~~~~~~~~~~~~

I WALKED through the station at Innsbruck with an almost eerie sense of familiarity, a sensation halfway between déjà vu and actual memory. I hadn't been to Innsbruck for eighteen years, and hadn't thought about it more than once or twice in that time, but now it was as if no more than a day or two had passed and the years in between had never happened. The station appeared not to have changed at all. The buffet was where I remembered it and still serving goulash with dumplings, a meal that I ate four times in three days because it was the cheapest and most substantial food in town. The dumplings were the size of cannon balls and just as filling. Approximately as tasty as well.

I took a room in a small hotel in the center, the Goldene Krone, and spent the dying hours of the afternoon walking through slanting sunshine that bathed the town in golden light. Innsbruck really is an ideal little city, with solid baroque buildings and a roofscape of bulbous towers. It is carefully preserved without having the managed feel of an open-air museum, and its setting is as near to perfection as could be imagined. At the end of every street you are confronted by a towering backdrop of mountains, muscular and snow-peaked beneath intensely clear skies.

I walked the paved footpath along the river Inn, swift and shallow and clear as polished glass, passed through a small park called the Hofgarten, and drifted out into the residential avenues beyond: long, straight, shaded streets lined with solid three-story houses whose roofs disappeared in the treetops. Many of them—too many surely for such a small city—contained doctors' surgeries and had shiny brass plates on the walls or gates announcing DR. G. MUNSTER/

ZAHNARZT or DR. ROBERT SCHLUGEL/PLASTISCHE CHIRURGIE—the sort of offices where you would be ordered, whatever the complaint, to undress, climb onto the table, and put your feet in the stirrups. Bright trams, empty but for the driver, trundled heavily past from time to time, but all the rest was silence.

One of my first vivid impressions of Europe was a Walt Disney movie I saw as a boy. I believe it was called *The Trouble with Angels.* It was a hopelessly sentimental fictionalized account of how a group of cherry-cheeked boys with impish instincts and voices like angels made their way into the Vienna Boys' Choir. I enjoyed the film hugely, being hopelessly sentimental myself, but what made a lasting indent on me was the European-ness of the movie background— the cobbled streets, the toytown cars, the corner shops with a tinkling bell above the door, the modest, lived-in homeyness of each boy's familial flat. It all seemed so engaging and agreeably old-fashioned compared with the sleek and modern world I knew, and it left me with the unshakable impression that Austria was somehow more European than the rest of Europe. And so it seemed here in Innsbruck. For the first time in a long while, certainly for the first time on this trip, I felt a palpable sense of wonder to find myself here, on these streets, in this body, at this time. I was in Europe now. It was an oddly profound notion.

I **FOUND** my way back to the hotel along the city's main street, Marie-Theresienstrasse. It is a handsome thoroughfare and well worth an amble so long as you don't let your gaze pause for one second on any of the scores of shop windows displaying dirndls and *lederhosen*, beer mugs with pewter lids, peaked caps with a feather in the brim, long-stemmed pipes, and hand-carved religious curios. I don't suppose any small area of the world has as much to answer for in the way of kitschy keepsakes as the Tyrol, and the sight of so much of it brings a depressing reminder that you are among a nation of people who like this sort of thing.

This is the down side of Austria. The same impulse that leads people to preserve the past in their cities leads them also to preserve it in their hearts. No one clings to former glories as the Austrians do, and since these former "glories" include one of the most distasteful interludes in history, this is not their most attractive feature.

Austrians are notoriously red-necked. Katz and I, while hitchhiking through Austria, had made friends with two Germans of a similar age, Thomas and Gerhard, who were making their way by thumb from Berlin to India with a view to finding spiritual enlightenment and good drugs. We camped together in a high Alpine pass, somewhere along the road between Salzburg and Klagenfurt, and in the evening we walked into the nearest village, where we found awaiting us a perfect inn, full of black paneled wood and a log fire with a sleeping dog before it and ruddy-faced yeoman customers swinging steins of beer. We ate sausages with dabs of mustard and drank many beers. It was all most convivial.

I remember sitting there late in the evening, glowing with drink and thinking what a fine place this was and what good, welcoming people the Austrians were—they were smiling warmly at us and occasionally raising glasses to us in a toast—when the Germans leaned forward and told us in low voices that we were in danger. The Austrians, it seemed, were mocking us. Unaware that two of our party could understand every word they said, they were talking freely—every one of them: the men, the women, the landlord, the landlord's wife, the whole damn village—about taking us out back and, as Gerhard translated, "of giving us a haircut and running us through wiz zer pitchforks."

A roar of laughter passed across the room. Gerhard showed a flicker of smile. "Zey say zat perhaps zey should also make us to eat of zer horse dung."

"Oh, swell," said Katz. "As if I haven't eaten enough shit on this trip already."

My head swiveled like a periscope. Those cheery smiles had become demonic leers. A man opposite toasted me again and gave me a wink that said: "Hope you like horse shit, kid."

I turned to Gerhard. "Should we call the police?"

"I sink zat man over zere *is* zer police."

"Oh, swell," Katz said again.

"I sink maybe we should just go to zer door as *quietly* as we can and zen run like hell."

We arose, leaving behind unfinished beers, strolled casually to the door, nodding to our would-be assailant as we passed, and ran like crazy. We could hear a fresh roar of laughter lift the inn roof off its moorings, but no one followed us and the threat of being forced to eat horse shit remains—thank you, God, thank you, thank you— forever in the realms of the imagined.

As we lay in our sleeping bags in a dewy meadow beneath a thousand stars, with the jagged mountains outlined against a fractionally less black sky and the smell of mown hay hanging on the night air, I remarked to no one in particular that I had never seen such a beautiful place as this.

"Zat's zer whole trouble wiz Austria," said Thomas with sudden passion in one of the few times I actually heard him speak. "It's such er lovely country, but it's full of fucking Austrians."

THE NEXT day I traveled to Salzburg. I found it hard to warm to, which surprised me because I had fond, if somewhat hazy, memories of the place. It was full of tourists and, worse still, full of shops selling things that only a tourist could want: Tyrolean crap and Alpine crap and, above all, Mozart crap—chocolates, marzipan, busts, playing cards, ashtrays, liqueurs. Building and road works seemed to be in progress everywhere, filling the town with dust and noise. I seemed to be forever walking on planks over temporary ditches.

The streets of the old town, crammed into a compact space between the Salzach River and the perpendicular mountain walls of the Mönchsberg, are undeniably quaint and attractive, but so overbearingly precious as to bring on frequent bouts of dry heaving. Along Getreidegasse, the site of Mozart's birthplace, every shop had one of those hanging pretzel signs above the door, including, God help us, the local McDonald's (the sign had a golden arches M worked into its filigree), as if we were supposed to think that they have been dispensing hamburgers there since the Middle Ages. I sank to my knees and beat my poor old head on the cobbled pavement.

I'm all for McDonald's in European cities, I truly am, but we should never forget that any company that chooses a halfwitted clown named Ronald McDonald as its official public face cannot be relied on to exercise the best judgment in matters of corporate presentation.

The people of McDonald's need guidance. They need to be told that Europe is not Disneyland. They need to be instructed to take suitable premises on a side street and given, without option, a shop design that is recognizable, appropriate to its function and yet reasonably subdued. It should look like a normal European bistro, with perhaps little red curtains and lamps on the tables and nothing to tell you from the outside that this is a McDonald's except for a discreet golden arches decal on each window and a steady stream of people with outsized butts going in and out the doors. While we're at it, they should also be told that they will no longer be allowed to provide each customer with his own weight in Styrofoam boxes and wastepaper. And finally they have to promise to shoot Ronald. When these conditions are met, McDonald's should be allowed to operate in Europe, but not until.

The main square in Salzburg, the Mozartplatz, was quite astonishingly ugly for a city that prides itself on beauty. It was a big expanse of asphalt, as charming as a supermarket parking lot, one extraordinarily begrimed statue of the great man, and a few half-broken benches, around every one of which was crowded a noisy cluster of thirteen-year-old Italians in whom the hormonal imbalances of adolescence were clearly having a deleterious effect. It was awful, awful.

What was most surprising was that I remembered Salzburg as being a beautiful place. It was in Salzburg that Katz and I met Gerhard and Thomas, in a bar around the corner from the Mozartplatz, and it was such a thrill to have someone to dilute Katz's company that I think my enthusiasm may have colored my memory of the city. In any case, I could find nothing now in the old town but wretched souvenir shops and restaurants and bars whose trade was overwhelmingly nonlocal and thus offered about as much charm and local color as a Pizza Hut on Carnaby Street.

When I crossed the river to the more modern right bank, I liked Salzburg much better. A long, quiet street of big houses stood overlooking the Salzach, and the views across to the old town were captivating: the ancient roofs, the three domed spires of the cathedral, and the vast, immensely heavy-looking Hohensalzburg fortress sinking into the low mountaintop at its back. The shopping streets of the modern town were to my mind much more interesting and appealing and certainly more real than their historic counterparts across the river. I had a coffee in a Konditorei on Linzergasse, where every entering customer got a hearty "Grüss Gott!" from every member of the staff. It was like *Cheers* when Norm comes in, only they did it for everybody, including me, which I thought was wonderful. Later, I had a good dinner, a couple of beers, and a long evening walk along the river and felt that Salzburg wasn't such a bad place at all. But it wasn't the Salzburg that most people come to see.

VIENNA IS a little under three hundred kilometers east of Salzburg, but it took all morning and half the afternoon to get there. There is this curiously durable myth that European trains are wonderfully swift and smooth and a dream to travel on. The trains in Europe are in fact often tediously slow, and for the most part the railways persist in the antiquated system of dividing the carriages into compartments. I used to think this was rather jolly and friendly, but you soon discover that it is like spending seven hours in a waiting room waiting for a doctor who never arrives. You are forced into an awkward intimacy with strangers, which I always find unsettling. If you do anything at all—take something from your pocket, stifle a yawn, rummage in your rucksack—everyone looks over to see what you're up to. There is no scope for privacy and of course there is nothing like being trapped in a train compartment on a long journey to bring all those unassuagable little frailties of the human body crowding to the front of your mind—the withheld fart, the three and a half square yards of boxer shorts that have somehow become concertinaed between your buttocks, the Kellogg's corn flake that is unaccountably lodged deep in your left nostril. It was the corn flake that I ached to get at. The itch was all-consuming. I longed to thrust a finger so far up my nose that it would look as if I were scratching the top of my head from the inside, but of course I was as powerless to deal with it as a man with no arms.

You even have to watch your thoughts. For no reason I can explain, except perhaps that I was inordinately preoccupied with bodily matters, I began to think of a copy editor I used to work with on the business section of *The Times*. I shall call him Edward, since that was his name. Edward was crazy, which in those palmy pre–Rupert Murdoch days was no impediment to employment, or even promotion to high office, on the paper, and he had a number of striking peculiarities, but the one I particularly remember was that late at night, after the New York markets had shut and there was nothing much to do, he would straighten out half a dozen paper clips and probe his ears with them. And I don't mean delicate little scratchings. He would jam those paper clips home and then twirl them between two fingers, as if tuning in a radio station. It looked excruciating, but Edward seemed to derive immense satisfaction from it. Sometimes his eyes would roll up into his head and he would make ecstatic gurgling noises. I suppose he thought no one was watching, but we all sat there fascinated. Once, during a particularly intensive session, when the paper clip went deeper and deeper and looked as if it might be stuck, John Price, the slot man, called out: "Would it help, Edward, if one of us pulled from the other side?"

I thought of Edward as we went *tracketa-tracketa* across the endless Austrian countryside, and I laughed out loud—a sudden, lunatic guffaw that startled me as much as my three companions. I covered my mouth with my hand, but more laughter—embarrassed, helpless— came leaking out. The other passengers looked at me as if I had just been sick down my shirt. It was only by staring out the window and concentrating very hard for twenty minutes that I was able to compose myself and return once again to the more serious torments of the corn flake in my nostril.

AT VIENNA'S huge central station I paid to have a room found for me, then walked to the city center along the long and ugly Mariahilferstrasse, wondering if I had been misled about the glories of Vienna. For a mile and half, from the station to the Ringstrasse, the street was lined with seedy-looking discount stores—the kind that sell goods straight out of their cardboard boxes—and customers to match. It was awful, but then near the Hofburg Palace I passed into the charmed circle of the Ringstrasse, and it was like the sun breaking out from behind clouds. Everything was lovely and golden.

My hotel, the Wandl, was not particularly charming or friendly, but it was reasonably cheap and quiet, and it had the estimable bonus of being in almost the precise geographical center of the city, just behind the baroque Schottenkirche and only half a block from Graben, one of the two spacious pedestrian shopping streets that dominate the heart of Vienna. The other is Kärtnerstrasse, which joins Graben at a right angle by the cathedral square. Between them, they provide Vienna with the finest pedestrian thoroughfare in Europe. Strøget in Copenhagen may be a hair longer, others may have slightly more interesting buildings, and a few may be fractionally more elegant, but none is all of these things. I knew within minutes that I was going to like Vienna.

I went first to the cathedral, St. Stephen's. It is very grand and Gothic outside, but inside I found it oddly lifeless—the sort of place that gives you a cold shiver—and rather neglected as well. The brass was dull and unpolished, the pews were worn, the marble seemed heavy and dead, as if all the natural luminescence had been drained from it. It was a relief to step back outside.

I went to a nearby Konditorei for coffee and a 15,000-calorie slice of cake and planned my assault on the city. I had with me the *Observer Guide to Vienna*, which included this piece of advice: "In Vienna, it is best to tackle the museums one at a time." Well, *thank* you, I thought. All these years I've been going to museums two at a time and I couldn't figure out why I kept getting depressed.

I decided to start at the top with the Kunsthistorische Museum. It was fabulous—vast, grand, full of great paintings. They employ a commendable system there. In every room there is a rack of cards giving the histories of the paintings in that room in a choice of four languages. You wander around with a card, looking at the paintings and reading the notes, and then replace it in the rack before passing on to the next room where you collect another card. I thought it was a great idea.

The only problem with the Kunstmuseum is that it is so enormous. Its lofty halls just run on and on, and before a third of the way through it, I was suffering museum fatigue. In these circumstances, especially when I have paid a fortune to get in and feel that there are still a couple of hours standing between me and my money's worth, I find myself involuntarily supplying captions to the pictures: Salome, on being presented the head of John the Baptist on a salver saying: "No, I ordered a double cheeseburger," or an exasperated Saint Sebastian whining, "I'm warning you guys, the next person who shoots an arrow is going to be reported." But this time I did something that astonished even me. I left, deciding that I would come back for a second sweep later in the week, despite the cost.

Instead, for a change of pace, I went to the tobacco museum, not far away behind the Messepalast. It was expensive, too. Most things in Vienna are. The entrance charge was twenty schillings, two thirds as much as at the Kunstmuseum, but it was hardly two thirds as good. In two not very large rooms I was treated to a couple of dozen display cases packed with old pipes (including a few grotesquely anti-Semitic ones), cigars, matches, cigarettes, and cigarette boxes. Around the larger of the two rooms was an elevated gallery of paintings with little artistic merit and nothing in common with the museum theme except that one or more of the people portrayed was smoking. Not recommended.

Nor, I have to say, is the Albertina Museum. This was even more expensive—forty-five schillings. For that kind of money, I would expect to be allowed to take one of the drawings away with me. But I paid without a whimper because I had read that the Albertina had one of the world's great collections of graphic art, which I just happen to like a lot, but in fact there was hardly anything on show. It was a huge building, but the public gallery was confined to eight small rooms at the back, all with creaking floors and students sketching and unmemorable drawings by mostly obscure artists.

The postcard stand outside was full of drawings "from the Albertina collection" by artists like Rubens and Dürer, but I had seen none of these. The woman running the stall didn't speak English, and when I held up a Dürer postcard and asked her where the original was, she just kept saying, with that irritability for which the Viennese are noted, "Ja, ja, das ist ein *postcard*," as if I had said, "Pardon me, is this a postcard or is it a snackfood?" and refused to try to grasp my question until finally I had no choice but to slap her to the ground and leave.

Apart from the postcard seller, however, I didn't find the Viennese especially rude and pushy, which rather disappointed me because I had heard many times that they are the most disagreeable people in Europe. In *The Double Eagle*, Stephen Brook's excellent account of Vienna, Budapest, and Prague, he notes that he met many foreign residents of the city who reported being stopped on the streets by strangers and rebuked for crossing against the lights or letting their children walk with their coats unbuttoned.

Brook also promised that at the famous Café Landtmann, on the Ringstrasse next to the Burgtheater, "the waiters and cloakroom attendants treat you like shit," and in this he was certainly closer to my experience. I didn't feel *precisely* like shit, but the waiters certainly did have that studied air of superiority that you find among a certain class of European servant. When I was younger, this always cowed me, but now I just think, "Well, if you're so hot how come I'm sitting down and you're not?" Let's be honest, if your career consists of nothing more demanding than conveying trays of food back and forth between a kitchen and dining room all day, there's not really much of anyone you are superior to, is there, except perhaps disk jockeys and lawyers.

On the whole, the cafés were the biggest disappointment in Vienna. I've reached the time of life where my idea of a fabulous time is to sit around for half a day with a cup of coffee and a newspaper, so a city teeming with coffeehouses seemed made for me. I had expected them to be more special, full of smoky charm and eccentric characters, but they were just restaurants really. The coffee was okay, but not sensational, and the service was generally slow and always unfriendly. They provide you with newspapers, but so what? I can provide newspapers.

Even the Café Central, where Trotsky used to hang out, sitting for long hours every day doing nothing, was a disappointment. It had some atmosphere—vaulted ceilings, marble tables, a pianist—but coffee was thirty-four schillings a throw and the service was indifferent. Still, I do like the story about the two Viennese who were sitting in the Central with coffees, discussing politics. One of them,

just back from Moscow, predicted a revolution in Russia before
long. "Oh, yeah?" said the other doubtfully and flicked his head in
the direction of the ever-idle Trotsky. "And who's going to lead
it—him?"

The one friendly café I found was the Hawelka, around the corner
from my hotel. It was an extraordinary place, musty, disheveled,
and so dark that I had to feel my way to a table. Everywhere newspapers lay on racks resembling carpet beaters. An old boy, who was
dressed more like a housepainter than a waiter, brought me a cup of
coffee without asking if I wanted one and, upon realizing that I was
an American, began gathering up copies of USA Today.

"Oh, no, please," I said as he presented me with half a dozen, "put
these on the fire and bring me some newspapers." But I don't think
his hearing was good, and he scuttled around the room collecting
even more and piling them on the table. "No, no," I protested,
"these are for lining drawers." But he kept bringing them until I had
a stack two feet high. He even opened one up and fixed it in front of
me, so I drank my coffee and spent half an hour reading features
about Vanna White, Sylvester Stallone, and other great thinkers of
our age.

VIENNA IS certainly the grandest city I have ever seen. All
along the Ringstrasse colossal buildings proclaim an imperial past—
the Parliament, the Palace of Justice, the Natural History Museum,
the Kunsthistorisches Museum, the Opera House, the Burgtheater,
and above all the Hofburg Palace, with its 2,600 rooms. They all
look much the same—mighty piles of granite and sandstone with
warlike statuary crowded along the roofs and pediments. A Martian
coming to earth would unhesitatingly land at Vienna, thinking it the
capital of the planet.

The one thing you soon learn to adjust to in Vienna is that the
Danube is entirely incidental to the city. The river is so far from the
downtown that it doesn't even appear on most tourist maps. I tried
walking to it one afternoon and never made it, only getting as far as
the Prater, the vast and famous park, which is bordered by the
Danube on its far side. But the Prater is so immense that after a half
hour it seemed pointless to continue walking on aching feet just to

confirm with my own eyes what I have read a hundred times: that the Danube isn't blue at all. Instead, I plodded lengthwise through the park along the long, straight avenue called Hauptallee, passing busy playing fields, swings, a sports stadium, cafés and restaurants, and eventually the amusement park with its Ferris wheel—the one made famous by Orson Welles and Joseph Cotten in *The Third Man.*

A sign by the Ferris wheel, or Riesenrad as it is called, gave a history of the wheel in German. It was built in 1896–97 by an Englishman named Walter Basset. I assume old Walter had some help because it's a pretty good size. It cost twenty-five schillings to go up, but it wasn't operating. The rest of the park, however, was doing brisk business, though I am hard-pressed to explain why, since it seemed to be rather a dump.

LATE ONE afternoon I went to the Sigmund Freud museum, in his old apartment on Berggasse, a mile or so to the north of the downtown. Berggasse nowadays is a plain and dreary street, though the Freuds lived in some style. Their apartment had sixteen rooms, but of these only four are open to the public and contain almost no furniture, original or otherwise, and only a few trifling personal effects of Freud's: a hat and walking stick, his medical bag, and a steamer trunk. Still, this doesn't stop the trust that runs the museum from charging you thirty schillings to come in and look around.

The four rooms are almost entirely bare but for the walls, which are lined with four hundred photographs and photocopies of letters and other documents relating to Freud's life—though some of these, it must be said, are almost ludicrously peripheral: a picture of Michelangelo's "Moses," which Freud had admired on a trip to Italy, and a photograph of Sarah Bernhardt, included not because Freud treated her or slept with her or even met her, but because he once saw her perform. Almost all the personal effects Freud collected during a half century of living in this apartment—his library, his 2,500 pieces of classical statuary, his furniture, his famous consulting couch—are now in a much superior museum in London because, of course, Freud was driven from Vienna by the Nazis two years before he died.

The wonder to me is that it took him so long to leave. By well before the turn of the century, Freud was one of the most celebrated figures in world medicine, and yet, only because he was a Jew, he wasn't made a professor at the University of Vienna until 1902, when he was nearly fifty.

Before the war there were 200,000 Jews in Vienna. Now there are hardly any. As Jane Kramer notes in her book *Europeans,* most Austrians today have never met an Austrian Jew, and yet Austria remains the most ferociously anti-Semitic country in Europe. According to Kramer, polls repeatedly show that about 70 percent of Austrians do not like Jews, a little over 20 percent actively loathe them, and not quite a tenth find Jews so repulsive that they are "physically revolted in a Jew's presence." I would have thought this scarcely credible except that I saw another poll in the *London Observer,* revealing that almost 40 percent of Austrians thought the Jews were at least partly responsible for what happened to them during the war and 48 percent believed that the country's eight thousand remaining Jews—who, I should point out, account for just a little over 0.001 percent of the entire population—still enjoy too much economic power and political influence.

The Germans, however unseemly their past, have made some moving attempts at atonement—viz., Willy Brandt weeping on his knees in the Warsaw ghetto and Richard von Weizsacker apologizing to the world for the sins of his country on the fiftieth anniversary of the start of the war. What do the Austrians do? They elect a former Wehrmacht officer as president.

I thought about this as I was walking from the Freud museum back to my hotel along Karl Luegerstrasse. At a set of traffic lights, a black limousine, led by a single motorcycle policeman, pulled up. In the backseat, reading some papers, was—I swear to God—the famous Dr. Kurt Waldheim, the aforementioned Wehrmacht officer and current president of Austria.

A lot of people aren't sure of the difference between the offices of chancellor and president in Austria, but it's quite simple. The chancellor decides national policy and runs the country, while the president rounds up the Jews. I'm only joking, of course! I wouldn't suggest for a moment that President Waldheim would have anything to do with the brutal treatment of innocent people—and not these days certainly. Moreover, I fully accept Dr. Waldheim's explanation that when he saw forty thousand Jews being loaded onto cattle trucks at Salonika, he genuinely believed they were being sent to the seaside for a holiday.

For the sake of fairness, I should point out that Waldheim insists he never even knew that the Jews of Salonika were being shipped off to Auschwitz. And let's be fair again—they accounted for no more than *one third of the city's entire population* (italics theirs), and it is of course entirely plausible that a high-ranking Nazi officer in the district could have been quite unaware of what was happening within his area of command.

Let's give the man a break. I mean to say, when the Sturm-abteilung, or storm troopers, burned down forty-two of Vienna's forty-three synagogues during Kristallnacht, Waldheim did wait a whole week before joining the unit. And after the Anschluss, he waited *two whole weeks* before joining the Nazi Student Union. Christ, the man was practically a resistance hero. I don't know what all the fuss is about.

Austrians should be proud of him and proud of themselves for having the courage to stand up to world opinion and elect a man of his caliber, overlooking the fact that he is a pathological liar, that he has been officially accused of war crimes, that he has a past so mired in mistruths that no one but he knows what he has done. It takes a special kind of people to stand behind a man like that.

What a wonderful country.

YUGOSLAVIA

I FLEW to Split, halfway down the Adriatic coast of Yugoslavia. Katz and I had hitchhiked there from Austria. It took four days of standing on baking roadsides on the edge of a series of nowheres watching carloads of German tourists sweep past, so there was a certain pleasure even now in covering the same ground in hours. I had no choice. I was running out of time. I had to be in Bulgaria in six days or my visa would lapse.

I caught a bus into town from the airport, and was standing at the harborside in that state of mild indecisiveness that comes with the sudden arrival in a strange country, when a woman of late middle years approached and said quietly, as if offering something illicit, "Zimmer? Room? You want?"

"Yes, please," I said, suddenly remembering that this was how Katz and I had found a room in Split. "How much?"

"Ten t'ousan dinar," she said.

Five dollars. This sounded like my kind of a deal. I considered the possibility that she might have four grown sons at home waiting to throttle me and take my money—I have long assumed that this is how I will die: trussed up and dumped into the sea after following a stranger offering an unbeatable bargain—but she looked honest enough. Besides, she had to trust that I wasn't an ax murderer. "Sure," I said. "Let's go."

We took a bus to her neighborhood, twenty minutes away up a long hill, and stepped off on a nondescript residential street somewhere at the back of the town. The lady led me down a complicated series of steps and sunny alleyways, full of scrawny cats. It was the sort of route you would follow if you were trying to give someone the slip. It wouldn't have altogether surprised me if she had asked me to put on a blindfold. Eventually, we crossed a plank over a narrow ditch, made our way across a grassless yard, and entered a four-story building that looked only half-finished. A cement mixer was standing by the stairwell. I was beginning to have my doubts. This was just the place for an ambush.

"Come," she said and I followed her up the stairs to the top floor and into her apartment. It was small and plainly furnished, but spotless and airy. Two men in their twenties, both vaguely thuggish-looking, dressed in T-shirts were sitting at the table in the kitchen/living room. "Uh-oh," I thought, casually sliding my hand into my pocket and fingering my Swiss army knife, but knowing that even in ideal circumstances it takes me twenty minutes to identify a blade and prize it out. If these guys came at me, I would end up defending myself with a toothpick and tweezers.

In fact, they turned out to be nice fellows. They were her sons and knew a little English because they worked as waiters in town. One of them, in fact, was just off for work and would give me a lift if I wanted. I gratefully accepted, on account of the distance and my considerable uncertainty as to where I was. He donned a red waiter's jacket and walked me to a dusty blue Skoda parked on a nearby street, where he fired up the engine and took off at a speed that had the back of the car fishtailing and me holding the armrest with both hands. It was like being in one of those movie chase scenes where the cars scatter trash cans and demolish vegetable carts. "I'm a little bit late," he explained as he chased a flock of elderly pedestrians off a zebra crossing and turned on two wheels onto a busy avenue without pausing to see if any cars were coming. There were, but they generously made way for him by veering sideways into buildings. He dropped me by the marketplace and was gone before I could barely get out a thank-you.

Split is a wonderful place, with a pretty harbor overlooking the Adriatic and a cluster of green islands lurking attractively a mile or two offshore. Somewhere out there was Vis, where Katz and I had spent an almost wonderful week. We were sitting at an outdoor café one morning, trying to anesthetize hangovers with coffee, when two Swedish girls came up to us and said brightly: "Good morning! How are you today? Come with us. We're going on the bus to a beach on the other side of the island."

Unquestioningly, we got up and followed. If you had seen these girls, you would have, too. They were gorgeous: healthy, tanned, deliciously fresh-smelling, soft all over, with good teeth and bodies shaped by a loving God. I whispered to Katz as we walked along behind, massaging our eyeballs on the perfect hemispheres of their backsides: "Do we know them?"

"I dunno. I think maybe we talked to them last night at that bar by the casino."

"We didn't go to the bar by the casino."

"Yes we did."

"We *did*?"

"Yeah."

"*Really?*" I could remember nothing of the night before other than a series of Bip Pivo beers passing before me, as if on a bottling line. I shrugged it off, youthfully unaware that I was in a single summer disabling clusters of brain cells at a pace that would leave me, just seventeen years later, routinely standing in places like a pantry or toolshed, gazing at the contents and trying to remember what the hell it was that I had wanted.

We went on a bouncing bus to the far side of the island, to a fishing village called Komiza, had a long swim in a warm sea and a couple of beers at a beachside taverna, caught a bouncing bus back to Vis town, had some more beers, ordered dinner, had some more beers, told stories, compared lives, fell in love.

Well, I did anyway. Her name was Marta. She was eighteen, dark, and came from Uppsala, and she seemed to me the fairest creature I had ever run eyes over—though it must be said that by this stage of the trip even Katz, in certain lights, was beginning to look not half bad. I thought she was lovely, and the miracle was that she appeared to find a certain charm in me. She and the other girl, Trudi, grew swiftly drunk and loquacious and spent half the time talking in Swedish, but it didn't matter. I sat with my chin in my hands, just gazing at this Swedish fantasy, hopelessly besotted, stirring to my senses from time to time just long enough to suck back drool and take a sip of beer. Occasionally, she would lay a hand on my bare forearm, sending my hormones into delirious turmoil, and once she glanced over and absently stroked my cheek with the back of her hand. I would have sold my mother as a galley slave and plunged a dagger into my thigh for her.

Late in the evening, when Katz and Trudi had gone off to pee, Marta turned to me, abruptly pulled my head to hers, and swabbed my throat with her tongue. It felt as if a fish were flopping around in my mouth. She released me, wearing a strange, dreamy expression and breathed: "I'm fool of lust."

I couldn't find words to communicate my appreciation. Then the most awful thing happened. An abrupt, startled look seized her, as if she had been struck by a sniper's bullet. He eyes snapped shut and she slid bonelessly from her chair.

I gaped for a long moment and cried: "Don't do this to me, God!" But she was gone, as dead to the world as if she had been hit sidelong by a Mack truck. I looked at the sky. "How could You do this to me? I'm a *Catholic*."

Trudi reappeared, tutted in a sudden maternal fashion, and said, "Well, well, well, we'd better get this one to bed." I offered to carry Marta to their hotel for her, thinking that at the very least I might manage to lay my tingling mitts on her splendid buttocks—only for a moment, you understand, just a little something to sustain me till the end of the century—but Trudi, doubtless sensing my intent, wouldn't hear of it. She was as strong as a steam locomotive, and before I could blink she had hoisted Marta over her shoulder and had disappeared down the street, leaving behind a fading good night.

I watched them go, then stared moodily into my beer. Katz arrived and saw from my face that there would be no naked twining in the moonlight surf this night. "What am I supposed to do now?" he said, sinking into his chair. "She was coming on to me outside the men's room. I've got a boner like Babe Ruth's bat. What am I supposed to do?"

"You'll just have to take matters into your own hands," I said, but he failed to see any humor in the situation, as indeed on reflection did I, and we spent the rest of the evening drinking in silence.

We never saw the Swedish girls again. We had no idea which was their hotel, but Vis town was not a big place and we were certain that we would run into them. For three days we went everywhere, peered in restaurant windows, walked up and down the beaches, but we never saw them. After a time I half began to wonder if it wasn't all a product of an overheated imagination. Maybe Marta had never even said, "I'm fool of lust." Maybe she had said, "I'm fit to bust." I didn't know. But as it became clearer and clearer that she was gone forever, it didn't really seem to matter.

I WANDERED along the quayside looking at the sailboats, then ventured into the sun-warmed lanes and courtyards that form the heart of Split. Once this area, roughly a quarter of a mile square, was the palace of Diocletian. But after the fall of the Roman Empire, squatters moved in and started building houses inside the crumbling palace walls. Over the centuries a little community grew up. What were once corridors became streets. Courtyards and atriums evolved into public squares. Now the lanes—some so narrow you have to turn sideways to pass through them—are mostly lined with houses and shops, and yet there is a constant, disarming sense of being *inside* a palace. Incorporated into many of the façades are parts of the original structure—stairways that go nowhere, columns supporting nothing, niches that once clearly held Roman busts. The effect is that the houses look as if they grew magically out of the ruins. It is entrancing and there is no place else in Europe quite like it.

I walked around for a couple of hours, then had an early dinner on a square bounded on three sides by old buildings with outdoor restaurants and on the fourth by the quay. It was a fine summery evening, with the kind of still air on which aromas hang—on this evening, a curious but not displeasing mixture of vanilla, grilled meat, and dead fish. Swifts circled and darted overhead and the masts of yachts rocked lazily on the water. It was such a pleasant spot and dusk was settling in so nicely that I sat for some time drinking Bips and watching the nightly promenade.

They do this in Yugoslavia. Every person in town dresses up in his best clothes and goes for an evening stroll along the main street—families, hunched groups of furtive-looking teenaged boys, giggling clumps of dolled-up, overfragranced teenaged girls, young couples with heavy-footed toddlers, old men and their wives. It had the same chatty, congenial air of the gatherings around the square in Capri, except that here they kept moving, marching up and down the long quayside in their hundreds. The parade seemed to go on for much of the night.

As I drank my fourth, or possibly fifth, beer, I suddenly felt drowsy—drowsy enough to lay my head on my arms and sleep. I looked at the label on the beer bottle and discovered with a start that the alcoholic content was 12 percent. It was as strong as wine and I had drunk a bucket of it. No wonder I felt weary. I called the waiter and paid the bill.

Solitary drinking is a strange and dangerous thing. You can drink all night and not feel the remotest sense of intoxication, but upon rising, you discover that while your head feels clear enough, your legs have suddenly decided to go in for a little moonwalking or some other involuntary embarrassment. I moved erratically across the square, dragging one reluctant leg behind me, as if under the strain of a gunshot wound, and realized I was too far gone to walk anywhere.

I found a cab at the quayside, climbed in the front passenger seat, waking the driver, and realized I had no idea where I was going. I didn't know the name of the street, the name of the woman to whom I had entrusted my personal effects, the part of town in which she lived. I just knew it was up a hill. Suddenly Split seemed to be full of hills.

"Do you speak English?" I asked the driver.

"Nay," he said.

"Okay, let's not panic. I want to go sort of that direction. Do you follow me?"

"Nay."

"Over there—just drive that way." We went all over the place. His meter spun like the altimeter on a crashing airplane. Occasionally, I would spot a corner that looked familiar, grab his arm, and cry, "Left here! Left here!" only to find ourselves coming up a minute later against the gates of a prison or something. "No, I think we may have gone wrong here," I would say, not wanting to let his spirits down. "It was a good try though." Eventually, when it became apparent that he was convinced that I was insane as well as drunk and was considering pushing me out, we blundered onto the correct street. At least I thought it was correct. I gave him a pile of dinars and stumbled out. It was correct—I recognized a corner shop—but I still had to find my way along the steps and alleys. Everything looked different at night and I was drunk and weary. I wandered blindly through the alleys, occasionally stepping on a cat, and peered through the darkness for a four-story building with a plank of wood outside.

Finally, I found it. The plank was thinner and wobblier than I remembered. Shuffling along it, I was about halfway across when it turned sideways and my footing went. I fell through black space for an instant—it seemed longer and was really rather pleasant—unaware that my feet were on either side of the plank and that I was about to break my fall with my reproductive organs.

Well, it was a surprise, let me say. I teetered for a moment, gasping, then fell heavily sidelong into the ditch. I lay on my back for a long minute, waiting for my lungs to reflate, wondering in an oddly detached way if the dull, unspeakable ache in my midsection indicated permanent damage and the embarrassing burden of a catheter bag, until it occurred to me that there might be rats in the ditch and that they might find me of interest. Abruptly I rose, scrabbled my way to the top against the loose dirt, slipped back, scrabbled again, and tumbled out. I hobbled into the building and up to the fourth floor, where I tapped on the door to the lady's flat. A minute later a woman opened the door to find an American man, disheveled, covered in dirt, swaying slightly and clutching his scrotum with both hands, standing on her threshold. We had never seen each other before. It was the wrong flat.

I tried to think of words to explain the situation, but could not, and wandered wordlessly off down the hall, giving an ambiguous wave as I went. I found the right flat and knocked, and after a minute knocked again. Eventually, I heard shuffling inside and the door was opened by my lady acquaintance. She was wearing a nightdress and a frightening array of hair curlers, and she said something cross to me about, I guess, the lateness of the hour. I tried to explain things, but she looked at me as if I had brought shame into her home, and I gave up. She showed me to my room, her slippers flopping ahead of me down the hall. Her sons were also in there, fast asleep. My bed was an upper bunk. Suddenly, five dollars seemed like a lot of money. She shut the door and plodded off.

Still dressed, I crossed the room in the dark and hoisted myself onto the upper bunk, stepping inadvertently on the stomach of one of the sleeping brothers, "Oomph," he went, like a deflated punching bag, but he seemed not to wake. I lay on the bed and took ten minutes to push my nuts back into place. That done, I tried to sleep but without much success.

In the morning the brothers were gone. I went into the kitchen with my rucksack. The flat was silent but for an insistently ticking clock and a periodic *bloop bloop* of a dripping tap, which somehow made the silence more intense. I didn't know if my landlady was out or still in bed. I brushed my teeth quietly in the sink and made myself fractionally more presentable with the application of a little cold water and a tea towel. Then I took out a five-dollar bill and put it on the table, then took out another and put it on the table, too. And then I left.

I walked into town and to the bus station. I had intended taking the bus to Belgrade, as Katz and I had done, but discovered that there was no longer a direct daytime route to Belgrade. I would have to travel to Sarajevo, halfway along, and hope that I could make a connection there. I bought a ticket for the ten o'clock bus and, with two hours to kill, went off to find some coffee. Midway along the quay, directly across the street from two of the city's grandest hotels, I noticed a gloopy sound and a smell as of a slurry wagon. Peering over the quay edge, I saw that a small outfall pipe was disgorging raw sewage straight into the harbor. You could see everything—turds, wriggling condoms, pieces of toilet paper—it was awful, and only feet from the main street, mere yards from the cafés and hotels. I decided not to have coffee at my usual spot, and instead found a café well inside the old town where the view wasn't so good but the chances of cholera were presumably slighter.

THE BUS was crowded—buses in Yugoslavia always are—but I found a seat three quarters of the way back and gripped the seat bar ahead of me with both hands. When Katz and I had crossed

Yugoslavia, it had been nothing if not exciting. The roads through the mountains were perilous beyond words, much too narrow for a bus, full of impossible bends and sheer falls from unimaginable heights. Our driver was an escaped lunatic who had somehow talked his way into a job with the bus company. Young and handsome, wearing his cap at a rakish angle, he drove as if cheerfully possessed, passing on blind bends, driving at breakneck speed, honking at everything, slowing for nothing. He sang hearty tunes and carried on lively conversations with the passengers—often turning around in his seat to address them directly—while simultaneously sweeping us along the edge of ragged roads on the brink of sheer-sided cliffs. I remember pressing my face to the window many times and being able to see no road beneath us—just a straight drop and the sort of views you get from an airplane. There was never more than an inch of shoulder standing between us and wingless flight.

Katz and I were sitting at the front, and the driver, taking a sudden liking to us, decided to amuse us with some visual jokes—pretending to nod off for a few moments, then jerking back to consciousness just in time to avoid an oncoming truck or acting as if the brakes had failed as we hurtled down a more or less perpendicular incline at a speed usually experienced only by astronauts, causing Katz and me to try to sit on each other's laps.

In the afternoon, after many hours of such bouncing excitement, the bus crested the mountains and began a steep descent into a broad valley of the most inexpressible lushness and beauty. I had never seen such a charmed and dreamy landscape. At every town and village people would emerge from houses as if our arrival were a kind of miracle and trot along with the bus, sometimes passing little bags of cherries through the windows to their friends and the driver and even to Katz and me.

We arrived in Belgrade in the early evening, found by some good fortune a cheap and attractive hotel high on a hill, and dined on a rooftop terrace as we watched the sun sink over the Danube and the lights of the city twinkle on. We drank many beers and ate the last of our cherries.

It had been a nearly perfect day and I itched to repeat it. In a strange way, I was looking forward to the dangers of the mountain road—it was such an exhilarating combination of terror and excitement, like having a heart attack and enjoying it. The bus labored through the streets of Split and up into the steep, cement-colored mountains at its back. I was disappointed to discover that the roads had been improved in my long absence—in many places they had been widened, and crash barriers had been installed on the more dangerous bends—and that the driver was not obviously psychotic. He drove with both hands and kept his eyes on the road.

Clearly, any drama would come from the landscape, though of this there was plenty. Most people are unaware of the rich beauty of Yugoslavia's interior. It is as green as England and as stunningly scenic as Austria, but almost wholly untouristed. Within an hour or two of leaving the hot coastline, with its teeming resorts and cereal-box hotels, you find yourself descending from the empty mountains into this lush, lost world of orchards and fields, lakes and woodlands, tidy farmhouses and snug villages—a corner of Europe lost to time. In the fields people cut and gather hay by hand, with scythes and wooden pitchforks, and cross their fields behind horse-drawn plows. In the villages elderly women are almost all dressed in black with scarves around their heads. It is like a picture out of the distant past.

Seven slow, hot hours after leaving Split, we rolled into Sarajevo, capital of the republic of Bosnia-Hercegovina. I was truly in another world now. There were minarets everywhere, and the writing on shops and street signs was in Cyrillic. Sarajevo is surrounded by steep hills—the 1984 Winter Olympics were held there—and bisected by a narrow, swift, very straight river, the Miljacka. The street along one side of the river, connecting the new part of town near the bus station with the old town a mile or so away, was the scene of Sarajevo's most famous incident, the assassination in June 1914 of Archduke Franz Ferdinand, the heir to the Austro-Hungarian throne, the event that set off the First World War.

I got a room in the Hotel Europa, a dark and faded establishment still clinging to a hint of former grandness. There was no television in the room and only about fourteen watts of illumination with all the lights on, but the bed looked comfortable enough and the bath, I noted with a sigh of gratitude, issued steaming water. I had a long soak and, much refreshed, went out to see the town.

Sarajevo was a wonderful surprise, with lots of small parks and leafy squares. In the center of town is one of Europe's largest bazaars, a series of alleyways lined with tiny shops selling hand-worked brass and copperware. Because there are no tourists, there are none of those irksome people tugging at your sleeve and thrusting goods in your face as you find in the more famous bazaars of Istanbul and Tangier. Here no one paid any attention to me at all.

I took a steep walk up into the hills, where old, frequently tumbledown houses were packed together in a dense and picturesque jumble along roughly cobbled streets that were sometimes all but vertical. It was a strenuous climb—even locals could be seen pausing for breath, a hand against a wall—but the views from the higher points were exotic, with the setting sun crowning a skyline of minarets, and the muezzins' tortured calls to prayer echoing over the rooftops.

I returned to town in time to join the nightly promenade along the main street—the only time, it appeared, when Yugoslavs get cheerful. I examined restaurant menus along the way and settled on the dining room of the Hotel Central, which had much the same faded grandeur of the Europa, like a stately home inhabited by an impoverished aristocrat. I was the only customer. Yugoslavia was going through a period of economic upheaval. Inflation was in hundreds of percent and the dinar was being devalued daily, sometimes two or three times daily, to the almost embarrassing benefit of the tourist and the detriment of the locals. A generous dinner of soup, steak, vegetables, salad, bread, beer, and coffee cost just eight dollars, and yet I was evidently the only person in town who could afford it.

The service, as elsewhere in Yugoslavia, was indifferent—not so much hostile as just past caring. The waiter dribbled my soup across the carpet and tablecloth and disappeared for long periods between courses, leaving me to stare at empty bowls and plates, but I couldn't entirely blame him. The difficulty with being a visitor in a place where you can live like a prince is that your wealth makes a menial of everyone you deal with. In Split, I had noticed some Germans tipping a waiter as if it were play money, almost teasing him with it, and I trusted that he had had the sense to add some spittle to their meal. I just hoped that this wasn't what was keeping my waiter.

*　　*　　*

IN THE morning I returned to the station and tried to find out about a bus to Belgrade, but the girl behind the information window was having such a delightful conversation on the phone that she was clearly not going to answer any inquiries. I waited for many minutes, and even said a few words to her through the hole in the glass, but she just looked at me blankly and carried on talking, curling the phone cord around her finger. Eventually, I trudged off and found the proper bus by asking around among the drivers.

The trip to Belgrade took eight hours, and the bus was even hotter, slower, duller, and more crowded than the one the day before. I sat beside a man whose concern for personal hygiene was rather less than obsessive, and spent much of the day wishing I knew the Serbo-Croat for "Pardon me but your feet are a trifle malodorous. I wonder if you would be good enough to stick them out the window." Gradually, to escape the smell, I fell into the mindless oblivion that seemed more and more to sustain me on these periods of getting from place to place, and patiently awaited the appearance of Belgrade through the front window.

I stepped off the bus feeling cheated. The trip to Belgrade had taken two days and had offered none of the reckless speed and adventure I had been hankering after. I found a room in an old-fashioned hotel called the Excelsior, expensive but comfortable, and immediately embarked on the usual business of acquainting myself with the city. I spent two days wandering around and discovered I remembered almost nothing about Belgrade. For old times' sake, I tried to locate the hotel where Katz and I had stayed, thinking I might dine on the rooftop terrace if it was still there, but I soon realized the quest was hopeless. I didn't remember enough about it to know where to begin to look in such a sprawling city.

Still, I was rather taken with Belgrade. It is the quintessential Mittel-European city—long avenues of stolid, gloomy five- and six-story buildings, interspersed with parks and monumental institutions with copper domes. There was an indefinable sense of the dead hand of central planning everywhere, but alongside it a refreshing shortage of Western enterprises—McDonald's, Benettons, and the like.

There was not a great deal to do in Belgrade. I strolled through the main shopping streets to a central city park called Kalemegdan, built around an old fortress and neatly arrayed with trees and benches and statues of Yugoslavian, and particularly Serbian, heroes. Most of the benches were taken up with men hunched intently over chessboards, each pair with a congregation of onlookers freely offering advice to both players. At the park's edge was a high terrace with an unopposed view of the city and of the spot where the Sava and the Danube flow together to make one truly monumental river.

In the afternoon I walked some distance out to Hajd Park, a wooded and rolling estate where Tito had his executive compound and where he is buried now. A long, paved path led up to his mausoleum. I was the only visitor and there wasn't much to see. Tito was not, as I had hoped, preserved in a glass case. He was safely hidden beneath a marble slab covered with scores of fresh wreaths and flowers. A lone soldier, looking desperately young and bored and uncomfortable, stood at attention beside the tomb. He was clearly supposed to stare straight ahead, but I could see his eyes following me around the room, and I had the terrible feeling that my visit was the high point of his day. "Mine too," I mumbled.

I went outside and felt the sudden weight of not knowing what to do with myself. Before me lay a panoramic view of a city I had no keen urge to explore. I spent most of the afternoon sitting in a park by a playground watching young parents pushing children on swings. I kept telling myself to get up and go do something, but my legs wouldn't respond, and anyway all I wanted to do was sit and watch children play. I was, I realized at length, homesick. Oh dear.

I AWOKE the next day in a better frame of mind. Today I would fulfill a little dream. I was going to take a first-class sleeper from one European capital to another. This mode of transport had long seemed to me the very pinnacle of luxury, and I breakfasted in the dining room of the Excelsior with the serene composure of a man who knows his time has come. My plan was to buy the ticket directly after breakfast and spend the day going around the museums before heading to the station in the evening to take my place among the dispossessed duchesses, Hercule Poirot look-alikes, and other exotic characters I presumed still traveled by first-class sleeping carriage in this part of the world.

The concierge told me not to buy my ticket at the station—"It is hysterical there," he said, shaking his head sadly—but to go to the main office of Sputnik, the state-run travel agency, where I could make a reservation in an atmosphere of relative tranquility.

The Sputnik office was orderly but unfriendly and full of sluggish lines of people. I had to stand in one line to find out which line to stand in. Then I had to stand in another to reserve a sleeping compartment, but these, I was told with withering disdain by a nasty-looking piece of work masquerading as a middle-aged woman, were booked solid for weeks and no amount of money could secure one for me now. Well, there goes another dream whooshing down the sluice pan of life, I thought bleakly. The woman directed me to a third line where I *might* get a seat ticket if I were lucky, but she gave a wave of her hand that told me that this was unlikely. She was right.

Without even a seat on the train, I returned to the first line to see if there were any other lines I could usefully stand in. The girl in the first line, who happened to be the only nice person in the place, told me that I should stand in the airline line because flights across Yugoslavia were nearly as cheap as the train. I went and stood in the airline line, which was exceptionally long and slow-moving, and discovered when my turn came that it wasn't the airline line at all—ha, ha, ha—that the airline line was one more line to the left. So I went and stood in the airline line and eventually discovered that there were no airline seats available either, not that day or the next.

A sense of helpless frustration was overcoming me, with weepy panic nipping at its heels. I had been here for nearly two hours. I explained to the girl as patiently as I could that I *had* to be in Sofia the next day on account of my visa. She gave me a look that said, "Well, why on earth do you expect me to give a shit?" but she said she would put my name on the standby list for the evening flight and told me to come back at four.

I went to the bus station, hoping by some miracle that there would be a bus to Sofia. The station was chaos—throngs of people bunched around every ticket window or sitting on piles of suitcases, waiting listlessly or erupting into little localized riots whenever a bus arrived. The babble of a dozen tongues filled the air. All the signs were in Cyrillic. I examined the timetables on the wall, but had no notion what Sofia would look like in Cyrillic. Suddenly, the idea of being innocent and free in a foreign land didn't seem exotic and appealing. I couldn't even tell which was the information window. I was as helpless as an infant.

It took most of the afternoon to discover that there were no buses directly to Sofia. My best hope was to take a bus to Nis then another on to Dimitrovgrad, on the Bulgarian border, and hope that I could find some kind of transport the last forty miles to Sofia. It would take three days at least, but I was so eager by now to get out of Yugoslavia and into any other country that I bought a ticket to Nis for twelve dollars, pocketed it, and trudged back up the long hill to the Sputnik office.

I arrived two seconds after the stroke of four. A new girl was seated at the airlines reservations computer. I told her the situation and she looked through the standby list for my name. After a moment she informed me that my name was not on the list. I looked at her with the expression of a man who has lost his job and had his car stolen and now has learned that his wife has run off with his best pal. I said: "What?"

She said it didn't matter because there were still plenty of seats left on the evening flight.

I said: "What?"

She looked at me with manifest indifference.

A ticket to Sofia would cost $112. Did I want one?

Did I want a ticket? Is the pope Catholic? Is Betty Ford a clinic? "Yes," I said. She did some tinkering with the computer and at length issued me a ticket. A wave of relief washed over me. I would be in Sofia for dinner—or at least for a late snack. I was getting out of Belgrade. Hooray!

I went outside and hailed a taxi. "Take me to the airport!" I said to the driver, falling into the back as he shot away from the curb. Pulling myself upright, I discovered he was young and cheerful and wore his cap at rakish angle. He drove like a lunatic. It was great.

~~~~~~

SOFIA

~~~~~~

I WAS looking forward to Bulgaria. It had been easily the most interesting, if not the most comfortable, of all the places Katz and I had visited.

I remembered Sofia being a city of broad boulevards so empty of traffic that people walked down the middle of them, stepping aside only to make room for the occasional black Zill limousine carrying party functionaries to some dark, Orwellian ministry. I have never been in a more timeless city. It could have been any time in the last forty or fifty years. There were simply no clues to suggest what decade it was; the shape of the few cars on the road, the clothes people wore, the looks of the shops and buildings were all curiously uninformed by fashion.

Sofia had a dark and enormous department store called TSUM, at least as big as Selfridge's in London, spread over five floors and containing not a single product that looked as if it had been produced more recently than 1938—chunky Bakelite radios, big stubby black fountain pens, steam-powered washing machines, that sort of thing. I remember standing in the television and radio department in a crowd of people watching a historical drama in which two actors, wearing beards that were hooked over their ears, sat talking in a study, the walls of which were clearly painted on canvas. The television set had—no exaggeration—a four-inch circular black-and-white screen, and *this* was attracting a crowd.

I spent almost a whole day in TSUM wandering in amazement, not just because the products were so wondrously old-fashioned but because whole families were visiting the store as if it were some marvelous museum of science and technology. I hoped things hadn't changed.

We arrived at Sofia's airport a little after nine. The foreign exchange office was closed and, as you cannot get Bulgarian money outside of the country, I was effectively penniless. I woke a sleeping cab driver and asked him if he would take me into the city for dollars. This is illegal, and I had visions of him reporting me to two guys in trench coats, but he was only too pleased to get his hands on hard currency and took me the fifteen kilometers into the city for ten dollars. The cab, an ancient Moskvich, was propelled by a series of smoky blue explosions from the exhaust. It would move ten feet, pause, and then be pushed another ten feet by a fresh explosion. We were almost the only car on the streets.

He dropped me at the Sheraton on Lenin Square, quite the grandest hotel I had stayed at on this trip, but I had been told that it was the *only* place to stay in Sofia. Until a couple of years earlier it had been the Hotel Balkan, but then Sheraton took it over and the company did a consummate job of renovating it. The place was all shiny marble and plush sofas. I was impressed.

The girl at the check-in desk explained the hard-currency system in operation at the hotel, which was confusing. Some of the hotel's several restaurants, bars, and shops accepted only hard currency, and some accepted only Bulgarian leva, and some accepted both. I didn't really take any of this in.

Going straight out for a walk, eager to see the town, I was delighted to note that I remembered so much of it. There across the square was the big statue of Lenin. Facing it was TSUM, as vast as I remembered it and still clearly in business, and around the corner was the Place 9 Septemvri, a boulevard paved in golden bricks and dominated by the massive headquarters of the Communist party, soon to be sacked by a mob and nearly burned down. I walked down the boulevard and plunged off into the dark and narrow streets of the downtown.

Sofia must be one of the darkest cities in the world. Only the occasional lightning flashes of a tram at the far end of a street revealed the full outlines of the buildings. For the rest, there were just weak pools of light beneath an occasional well-spaced lamppost and a little seepage of illumination from the few bars and restaurants that were still open and doing, without exception, a desultory business. Almost every shop window was dark. Nonetheless, the streets were crowded with people, many of them evidently having just concluded a night out and were standing in the road trying to flag down the few cabs that flew past.

I made a lazy circuit of the downtown and emerged once again in front of TSUM. The goods in the darkened windows looked distinctly more up to date than they had on my previous visit, but at least the store was still in operation. This, I decided, would be my first port of call in the morning.

IN THE event, TSUM wasn't open when I hit the sunny streets next day, so instead I walked up a long, straight avenue called Vitosha where most of the other main shops seemed to be. None of them were open yet either, but already long lines were forming at most doors. I had read that things were desperate in Bulgaria—that people began lining up for milk at 4:30 in the morning, that the price of some staples had gone up 800 percent in a year, that the country had $10.8 billion of debt and so little money that there were only funds enough in the central bank to cover seven minutes' worth of imports—but nothing had prepared me for the sight of several hundred people queuing around the block just to buy a loaf of bread or a few ounces of scraggy meat.

When they opened, most shops posted some beefy sourpuss in the doorway who would let customers in one at a time. The shelves were always bare. Things were sold straight out of a crate on the floor by the till, and presumably when the crate was empty the door was locked and the rest of the people in line were sent away. I watched as one woman came out of a baker's shop with a small loaf of bread and immediately joined another long line at a butcher's next door. Bulgarians must have to do this every day with everything they buy. What a life.

It had been nothing like this in 1973. Then the shops had been full of goods, but no one appeared to have money to buy them. Now everyone was clutching fistfuls of money, but there was nothing to spend it on.

I went into a shop called 1001 СТОКИ. There was no orderly

line, just an almost incredible crush of people around the door. I didn't enter of my own volition, but got swept in. Inside there was a mob around a single glass display case, waving money and jockeying for attention. All the other cases in the shop were empty, though there were salespeople still posted behind them. I slid through the crowd to see what it was everyone was so eager to buy. It was just a pathetic assortment of odds and ends—some plastic salt and pepper sets, twenty long-handled brushes with no identifiable function, some small glass ashtrays, and an assortment of tinfoil plates and pie dishes such as you get free in the West when you buy something to heat in the oven.

Clearly, people weren't shopping so much as scavenging for purchasable goods. Again and again, as I ventured up Vitosha, I would peer into the impenetrable gloom of shop windows and discover after a moment that I had attracted two or three people looking over my shoulder to see what I had spotted. But there was nothing to spot. One electrical shop I passed had three Russian hi-fi systems, two stereo and one mono (when was the last time you saw a mono hi-fi?), but they all had knobs missing and didn't look as if they would last five minutes.

Another shop sold nothing but two kinds of cans—yellow cans and green cans, stacked by the hundreds in neat pyramids on every shelf. It was the only well-stocked shop I saw all day. I have no idea what was in the cans—the labels gave no hint—but I can only assume that it must have been pretty dire or they would have sold out long ago. It was the most depressing morning I have spent in a long time.

I went to TSUM fearing the worst and found it. Whole departments were stripped bare, including my beloved TV section. The premier department store in the country couldn't offer its customers a single television, radio, or other electrical item. In some departments three salespeople stood by a till with nothing to sell but perhaps a single small stack of tea towels, but elsewhere there would be a lone desperate salesgirl trying to deal with throngs of people because a shipment of something desirable had just come in. At one counter on the third floor, a big cardboard box full of socks had just arrived—hundreds and hundreds of socks, all an identical mustard-brown color, all in thin cotton in the same size, and all in bundles of a dozen—and people were buying double armloads of them. I suppose you buy what you can and think about what you are going to do with it afterward—give some to your father-in-law for Christmas, trade some for a hunk of meat, reward a neighbor for queuing up for you.

The saddest area was the toy department—one shelf full of identical, ineffably cruddy teddy bears made out of synthetic wool, two dozen identical plastic toy trucks with bowed wheels and peeling, crooked labels, and fourteen metal tricycles all painted the same shade of blue and every one of them scraped or bashed in some way.

On the top two floors were whole departments full of boxes of unidentifiable odds and ends. If you have ever taken apart some mechanical contraption—a doorbell or a washing machine motor—and had it all spring loose on you and 150 mysterious pieces have gone bouncing in every direction, well, that's what they sell upstairs at TSUM—springs and cogs and small oddments of shaped metal that look as if they must fit together in some way. Scores of people were gravely picking through the boxes.

The busiest department was on the ground floor in what I suppose could be called the notions department. It resembled a crowd scene in a Godzilla movie after the news has got out that the monster is on his way to town. All that seemed to be for sale was buttons, wristwatch straps, and ribbons, but then I saw that what everyone was lining up for was a freshly arrived consignment of alarm clocks. They were just simple, cheap-looking stainless-steel and plastic clocks, but the shoppers were clearly ready to kill to get one. This department was run by two of the most disagreeable-looking women I ever hope to see. I watched them with a kind of dumb fascination. A shy-looking young man, whom I took to be North Vietnamese, finally reached the till and they ignored him. He held out a wad of money with an entreating look, and they just dealt with the people behind him. Finally, one of the salesladies pushed his money away and told him to clear off. The man looked as if he could cry; I almost felt as if I could, too. I don't know why they were so nasty to him. He put the money in his pocket and melted into the crowd.

Imagine living like that. Imagine coming home from work and your partner saying: "Honey, guess what? I had the most wonderful day shopping. I found a loaf of bread, six inches of ribbon, a useful-looking metal thingy, and a doughnut."

"*Really?* A doughnut?"

"Well, actually, I was lying about the doughnut."

The odd thing was that people looked amazingly stylish. I don't know how they managed it with so little to buy. In the old days, the clothes everyone wore looked as if they had been designed by the manager of a Russian tractor factory. People constantly came up to Katz and me offering to buy our jeans. One young guy was so dementedly desperate for a pair of Levi's that he actually started taking his pants off on the street and urged us to do likewise so that we could effect a trade. Katz and I tried to explain that we didn't want his trousers—they were made out of, like, *hemp*—and asked him if he had anything else, a younger sister or some Cyrillic porno, but he appeared to have nothing worth swapping, and we left him standing desolate on a street corner, his heart broken and his fly gaping. Now, however, everyone was as smartly dressed as anywhere else in Europe—actually more so, since they took such obvious care and pride in their wardrobe. The women were simply gorgeous, all with black hair, chocolate eyes, and the most wonderful white teeth. Sofia has, without any doubt, the most beautiful women in Europe.

I spent the better part of a week just walking around. Sofia is full of monuments with crushingly socialist names—the Stadium of the People's Army, the Memorial of the Anti-Fascist Campaigners, the National Palace of Culture—but most of them are contained within some quite lovely parks with long avenues of chestnut trees, benches, swings, sometimes even a boating lake, and often attractive views of the green, hazy mountains that stand at the city's back.

I saw the sights. I went to the old royal palace on Place 9 Septemvri, now the home of the National Gallery of Painting and Sculpture, where I suddenly understood why I was unable to name a single Bulgarian artist. Afterward I crossed the street to have a look at the tomb of Georgi Dmitrov, the national hero—or at least he was until the fall of the Iron Curtain. Now the Bulgarians appeared not to be so certain. There were some minor graffiti on his mausoleum—unthinkable even a couple of months earlier, I would wager—and you could no longer go in and look at his body, preserved under glass in the fashion beloved of Communists. I remembered that when Katz and I went to see it in 1973, he leaned close to the case, sniffed in an obvious manner, and said to me in a slightly too loud voice, "Something smell a bit off to you?," which nearly got us arrested. Dmitrov was treated like a god. Now with communism crumbling, people didn't even want to see him anymore.

I also visited the National History Museum and the Alexander Nevsky Church and the National Archaeological Museum and one or two other diversions, but mostly I just went for long walks and waited for evening to come.

Evening was kind to Sofia. When the shops were shut, the lines vanished, and people took to strolling the streets, looking much happier. Sometimes there were small political gatherings outside Dmitrov's tomb, and it was obvious that people were enjoying the unaccustomed luxury of being able to talk freely. One evening, out-side the old royal palace, somebody set up along a wall an arrange-ment of photographs of the exiled royals, King Simeon and his family. Crowds pressed to see the pictures. I thought this odd at first, but imagine what it would be like in Britain if the royal family had been banished forty years ago (there's a thought for you) and people had been denied any official information about them. Now suddenly the Bulgarians could see what had become of their equiv-alents of Princess Margaret and the Duke of Edinburgh and all the others. I had a look myself, rather hoping to discover that King Simeon was now managing a Dairy Queen in Sweetwater, Texas, but in fact he appeared to be living a life of elegance and comfort in Paris, so I declined the invitation to sign a petition calling for his reinstatement.

Every evening, I went looking for the Club Babaloo, a nightclub where Katz and I hung out every night of our stay. That wasn't its real name; we called it that because it looked so much like Desi Arnaz's Club Babaloo on *I Love Lucy*. The club looked like some-thing straight out of the early 1950s, and it was *the* hot spot in Sofia. People went there for anniversaries.

Every night Katz and I sat in a balcony overlooking the dance floor, drinking Polish beer and watching a rock 'n' roll band (I use the word in its Bulgarian sense) whose enthusiasm almost made up for its near-total lack of talent. The band played songs that had not been heard in the rest of the world for twenty years—"Fernando's Hideaway," "Love Letters in the Sand," "Green Door"—and young people were dancing to them as if they were the latest thing, which in Bulgaria they may have been. The best part was that Katz and I were treated like celebrities—American tourists were that rare in Sofia then. (They still are, come to that.) People joined us at our table, bought us drinks. Girls asked us to dance with them. We got so drunk every night that we missed a dozen opportunities, but it was wonderful nonetheless.

I so much wanted to find the Babaloo again that I looked all over the city and even strolled out to the train station, a long and unrewarding walk, thinking that if I retraced the route Katz and I had taken into the city, I might kindle my memory, but no such luck. And then on a Friday evening, as I was going past the restaurant of the Grand Hotel for about the twentieth time that week, I was brought up so short by the sound of tinny guitars and scratchy amplifiers that I actually smacked my nose against the glass in turning to look. It was the Club Babaloo! I had walked past it again and again, but without the awful music I hadn't even noticed it. Now suddenly I recognized every inch of it. There was the balcony. There was our table. Even the waitresses looked vaguely familiar, if a tad older. Happy memories came flooding back.

I went straight in to order a Polish beer, but a guy at the door in an oversized black suit wouldn't let me enter. He wasn't being nasty, but he just wouldn't let me in. I didn't understand why. You get used to not understanding why in Bulgaria after a while, so I continued with my walk. About twenty minutes later, after my nightly circuit of the dark hulk of the Nevsky Church, I ambled back past the Grand and realized why I had been denied entrance. The club was closing. It was 9:30 on a Friday night and this was the liveliest place in town. Bulgaria, I reflected as I walked back to the hotel, isn't a country, it's a near-death experience.

I WAS lucky to be able to retreat whenever I wanted to the luxurious sanctum of the Sheraton, where I could get cold beers and decent food and watch CNN on the TV in my room. I cravenly took all my meals there. I tried hard to find a local restaurant that looked halfway decent and could not. Sofia has the most unlively bars and restaurants—plain, poorly lighted, with maybe just a factory calendar on the wall and every surface covered in Formica. I did stop once at a place out near the Juzen Park, but the menu was in Cyrillic and I couldn't decipher a thing. I looked around to see what other people were eating, thinking I might point to something on someone else's table, but they were eating food that didn't even look like food—gruel and watery vegetables—and I fled back to the hotel, where the menu was in English and offered anything from hamburgers to duck à l'orange.

However, I paid for my comfort with a twice-daily dose of guilt. Each time I dined in the Sheraton, I was glumly aware that I was eating better than nine million Bulgarians. I found this economic apartheid repugnant, if irresistible. If a Bulgarian was by some miracle of thrift and enterprise sufficiently well-heeled, he could go to two of the Sheraton restaurants, the Wiener Café and the Melnik Grill, but their entrances were on a side street. You couldn't get to them through the hotel. You had to go out the front door and walk around the corner. Common people couldn't come into the hotel proper, as I could. Hundreds must walk by it every working day and wonder what it's like inside. Well, it's wonderful—to a Bulgarian it would seem to offer a life of richness and comfort almost beyond conception: a posh bar where you could get cocktails with ice cubes, restaurants serving foods that haven't been seen elsewhere in the country for years, a shop selling chocolates and brandy and cigarettes and other luxuries so unattainable that the average Bulgarian would be foolish even to dream of them.

It amazed me that I didn't get beaten up every time I emerged from the hotel—*I'd* want to beat me up—but no one showed me anything but kindness and friendship. People would come up to me constantly to ask if I wanted to change money, but I didn't, I couldn't. It was illegal and besides I didn't want any more Bulgarian money than I already had; there was nothing to buy with it. Why should I stand in line for two hours to buy a pack of cigarettes with leva when I could get better cigarettes for less money in ten seconds in my own hotel? "I'm really sorry," I kept saying, and they seemed to understand.

I began to get obsessed with trying to spend some money, but there was nothing to spend it on, nothing. One of the parks, I discovered one Sunday morning, was full of artists selling their own work, and I thought: "Great! I'll buy a picture." But they were all terrible. Most of them were technically accomplished, but the subjects were awful—vivid sunsets with orange and pink clouds, and surreal, Salvador Dali–like paintings of melted objects. It was as if the artists were so far out of touch with the world that they didn't know what to paint.

The farther you roam in Sofia the better everything gets. I took to going for daylong walks out into the hilly districts on the southeast side of the city, an area of forests, parks, neighborhoods of rather grand apartment buildings, winding tranquil streets, some nice homes. As I was walking back into the city center, over a footbridge across the Slivnica River and down some anonymous residential street, it struck me that this really was quite a beautiful city. More than that, it was the most European-looking of all the cities I had been to. There were no modern shopping centers, no big gas stations, no McDonald'ses or Pizza Huts, no revolving signs for Coca-Cola. No city I had visited had more thoroughly resisted the blandishments of American culture. It was completely, comprehensively European. This was, I realized with a sense of profound unease, the Europe I had dreamed of as a child.

IT'S HARD to know what will become of Bulgaria. A couple of weeks after my visit, the people, in a moment of madness, freely voted for a Communist regime, the only country in Eastern Europe to retain voluntarily the old form of government.

This was 1990, the year the communism died in Europe, and it seemed strange to me that in all the words that were written about the fall of the Iron Curtain, nobody anywhere lamented that it was the end of a noble experiment. I know that communism never worked, and I would have disliked living under it myself, but nonetheless it seemed there was a kind of sadness in the thought that the only economic system that appeared to work was one based on self-interest and greed.

My guess is that communism in Bulgaria won't last. It can't last. No people will retain a government that can't feed them or let them provide toys for their children. I'm certain that if I come back to Sofia in five years it will be full of Pizza Huts and Laura Ashleys, and the streets will be clogged with BMWs, and all the people will be much happier. I can't blame them a bit, but I'm glad I saw it before it changed.

ISTANBUL

KATZ AND I went from Sofia to Istanbul on the Orient Express. I had thought it would be full of romance—I rather imagined some turbaned servant coming around with cups of sweet coffee and complimentary hot towels—but in fact it was awful in every way: hot, fetid, airless, threadbare, crowded, old, slow. By 1973, the Orient Express was just a name on a rusty piece of metal on the side of any old train between Belgrade and Istanbul. A couple of years later the train was discontinued altogether.

We had a compartment to ourselves as we left Sofia, but about two stops later the door slid brusquely open and an extended family of rustics, looking like a walking testimonial to the inadvisability of chronic inbreeding, barged in, laden with cardboard suitcases and string bags of evil-smelling food. They plunked themselves down, forcing Katz and me into opposite corners, and immediately began delving in the food bags, passing around handkerchiefs of little fish, hunks of dry bread, runny boiled eggs, and dripping slabs of curdled cheese whose pungent aroma put me in mind of the time we returned from summer vacation to discover that my mother had inadvertently locked the cat in the broom cupboard for the three hottest weeks of the year. They ate with smacking lips, wiping their stubby fingers on their shirts, before sinking one by one into spluttering comas. By some quirk of Balkan digestion, they expanded as they slept, squeezing us further and further into our corners until we were pressed against the wall like lumps of modeling clay. We had twenty-two hours of this to get through.

By this point on our trip, Katz and I had spent nearly four months together and were thoroughly sick of each other. We had long days in which we either bickered endlessly or didn't speak. On this day, as I recall, we hadn't been speaking, but late in the night, as the train trundled sluggishly across the scrubby void that is western Turkey, Katz disturbed me from a light but delirious slumber by tapping me on the shoulder and asking accusingly: "Is that dog shit on the bottom of your shoe?"

I sat up a fraction. "What?"

"Is that dog shit on the bottom of your shoe?"

"I don't know, the lab report's not back yet," I replied drily.

"I'm serious. Is it?"

"How should I know?"

Katz leaned far enough forward to give it a good look and a cautious sniff. "It *is* dog shit," he announced with an odd tone of satisfaction.

"Well, keep quiet about it or everybody'll want some."

"Go and clean it off, will ya? It's making me nauseous."

And here the bickering started, in intense little whispers.

"You go and clean it off."

"It's your shoes."

"Well, I kind of like it. Besides it kills the smell of this guy next to me."

"Well, it's making me nauseous."

"Well, I don't care."

"Well, I think you're a fuckhead."

"Oh, you do, do you?"

"Yes, as a matter of fact. You've been a fuckhead since Austria."

"Well, you've been a fuckhead since birth."

"*Me?*" A wounded look. "That's rich. You were a fuckhead in the *womb,* Bryson. You've got three kinds of chromosomes: X, Y, and fuckhead."

And so it went. Istanbul clearly was not destined to be a success for us. Katz hated it and he hated me. I mostly hated Katz, but I didn't much care for Istanbul either. It was, like the train that took us there, hot, fetid, crowded, and threadbare. The streets were full of urchins who snatched anything you didn't cling to with both hands, and the food was simply dreadful—foot-odor cheeses and mysterious lumps of goo. One night Katz nearly got us killed when he inquired of a waiter: "Tell me, do you have the cows shit straight onto the plate or do you scoop it on afterwards?"

One of the sustaining pleasures for Katz in the later stages of the trip was talking candidly in this way to people who could not understand him, making smiling inquiries of a policeman concerning the celebrated tininess of his penis or telling a surly waiter: "Can we have the check, Boris? We've got to run because your wife's promised to have sex with us."

But in this instance it turned out that the waiter had worked in a little place off the Tottenham Court Road in London for thirteen years and he understood Katz's question only too well. He directed us to the door with the aid of a meat cleaver, making wholly justified remarks about the nobility of Turkish cuisine and the insolence of young tourists.

With this final pleasure denied him on the grounds of prudence and a sincere threat from me that I would kill him myself if an English-speaking Turk didn't do it first, Katz spent the remainder of our time in Istanbul in a moody silence, except for growling at touts in the Grand Bazaar to fuck off and leave him alone, but this I excused on the basis of justified provocation. We had reached the end of the road in every sense. It was a long week.

I wondered now, as I rode a taxi in from the airport through the hot, teeming streets of Istanbul, whether my attitude would be more receptive this time.

Things did not start well. I had made a reservation at the Sheraton through the company's internal reservation system in Sofia, but the hotel turned out to be in a modern, featureless neighborhood, some distance from the exotic throngs of the Golden Horn and old town. My room was clean and passably swank, but the air conditioning was sluggish, the television didn't work, and when I went to the bathroom to wash my hands and face, the pipes juddered and banged like something from a poltergeist movie and then, with a series of ominous gasps, issued a steady brown soup. I let the water run for ten minutes, but it never cleared or even thinned. For this I was paying $150 a night.

I sat on the toilet, watching the water run, thinking what an odd thing tourism is. You fly off to a strange land, eagerly abandoning all the comforts of home, and then expend vast quantities of time and money in a largely futile effort to recapture the comforts that you wouldn't have lost if you hadn't left home in the first place.

Sighing, I smeared a little of the brown water around my face, then went out to see Istanbul. I took a cab down the long hill to the waterfront, paid the driver, and, with a startled cry, was sucked into the random mass of motion along the old town's winding streets.

What a place. Istanbul isn't a city; it is a collective delirium. I had never seen such activity—people rushing, pushing carts, carrying trays of food or coffee, hefting huge and ungainly loads (I saw one man with a ten-foot-long sofa on his back moving through the crowds as easily as if he were carrying a deck of cards), people every five feet selling something: lottery tickets, wristwatches, cigarettes, replica perfumes. Every few paces someone comes up to you wanting to shine your shoes, sell you postcards or guidebooks, take your photograph, weigh you, lead you to his brother's carpet shop, or otherwise induce you to part with some trifling sum of money. Nowhere else on earth can there be a city where the visitor's every sense is so relentlessly tugged and shaken. It is an experience that is at once confusing, mildly unnerving, and strangely exciting.

The Galata bridge swarmed with pedestrians, beggars, vendors, and load bearers. Along its length, amateur fishermen were pulling the most poisoned-looking fish I ever hope to see from the oily stew below. At the end of the bridge two men crossed the street to Sirkeci Station, the main railroad terminus, threading their way through the stationary traffic, leading brown bears on leashes. No one gave them a second glance.

The one unbearable thing in Istanbul is the Turkish pop music. It is inescapable. It assaults you at full volume from every restaurant doorway, from every lemonade stand, from every passing cab. To say that it is reminiscent of the sounds made by a man who has his head trapped in, oh, say, some industrial machinery is merely to hint at its singular and frantic tunelessness. They say it grows on you. So do tumors.

I wandered around for half an afternoon, impressed by the tumult, amazed that so much enterprise and commercial activity could result in such meager prosperity, for Istanbul is a strikingly poor city. I walked at length up a steep hill to Sultanahmet Square. Peeling post-card salesmen from my sleeve, I strolled into that great byzantine pile of stone, the Ayasofiya. It is a vast and wondrously beautiful build-ing, nearly as airy and awesome as St. Peter's, but it was the relief at finding myself in cool shadow, away from the noise and heat and endless madness of the Istanbul streets, that endeared it to me for-ever. I wandered for an hour through its echoing depths, almost the only person there, and had a wonderful time.

Afterward, I reemerged into the blinding sunshine and crossed the square in the company of a chattering gaggle of postcard salesmen, photographers, peanut vendors, nightclub representatives, street bar-bers, shoeshine boys, and a couple of guys who apparently just liked to be with me, and had a look at the Blue Mosque, which was also very fine. Because it is a functioning house of worship, you have to leave your shoes at the door and enter in your stocking feet, which is kind of a nuisance because it can take hours to find your shoes among the hundreds of other pairs when you come out, though the system does at least give you the opportunity to trade up to some-thing better if your own shoes are past their best.

I had intended to go to Topkapi, but it was closed. I headed instead for what I thought was the national archeological museum, but I somehow missed it and found myself presently at the entrance to a large and miraculously tranquil park called Gilhane, full of leafy shade, twittering birds, and happily ambling families. At the bottom of a gently sloping central avenue, the park ended in a sudden and arresting view of the Bosphorus, glittery and blue. I took a seat at an open-air taverna there, in a refreshing wisp of breeze, ordered a Coke, and sank into the scenery: the deep blue sky, the shining water, the white houses spilling across the burlap hills of Üsküdar, two miles across the strait. Ferries plied doggedly across the Bos-phorus below me and on out to the distant Princes' Islands, adrift in a bluish haze. Gulls reeled and swooped in their wake. It was beau-tiful beyond words, the perfect place to stop.

I had come to the end of my own road. That was Asia over there; this was as far as I could go in Europe. It was time to end this long indulgence and go home. My long-suffering wife was pregnant with her semiannual baby. The grass, she had reported by telephone, was waist-high. One of the field walls had fallen down. The sheep were in the meadow. The cows were in the corn. There was much for me to do.

And I was, I admit, ready to go. I missed my family and the comfortable familiarities of home life. I was tired of the daily drudgery of keeping myself fed and bedded, tired of trains and buses, tired of existing in a world of strangers, tired of being forever perplexed and lost, tired above all of my own dull company. How many times in recent days had I sat trapped on buses or trains listening to my idly prattling mind and wished that I could just get up and walk out on myself?

At the same time, I had a quite irrational urge to keep going. There is something about the momentum of travel that makes you want to just keep moving, to never stop. That was Asia over there, after all—right there in my view. The thought of it seemed incredible. I could be there in minutes. I still had money left. An untouched continent lay before me.

But I didn't go. Instead, I ordered another Coke and watched the ferries. In other circumstances, I think I might have gone. But that of course is neither here nor there.

INDEX

A NOTE

ABOUT THE AUTHOR

BILL BRYSON is a journalist who grew up in Iowa. He has worked for *The Times* (London) and *The Independent* and has written articles for *The New York Times, Granta, Esquire, GQ,* and *National Geographic*. His previous books include *A Dictionary of Troublesome Words, The Lost Continent,* and *The Mother Tongue.* He lives in Yorkshire, England.

ICELAND
FAEROE ISLANDS
Atlantic
Ocean
Glasgow
Liverpool
Yorkshire
ENGLAND
London
BELG.
Ardennes
LUX.
Paris
FRANCE
Zurich
Geneva
Lyon
Genoa
Marseille
PORTUGAL
Lisbon
Madrid
SPAIN
Barcelona
Gibraltar
Tangier
MOROCCO
ALGERIA